The Maximum Consensus Problem

Recent Algorithmic Advances

Synthesis Lectures on Computer Vision

Editors

Gérard Medioni, *University of Southern California*
Sven Dickinson, *University of Toronto*

Synthesis Lectures on Computer Vision is edited by Gérard Medioni of the University of Southern California and Sven Dickinson of the University of Toronto. The series publishes 50- to 150 page publications on topics pertaining to computer vision and pattern recognition. The scope will largely follow the purview of premier computer science conferences, such as ICCV, CVPR, and ECCV. Potential topics include, but not are limited to:

- Applications and Case Studies for Computer Vision

- Color, Illumination, and Texture

- Computational Photography and Video

- Early and Biologically-inspired Vision

- Face and Gesture Analysis

- Illumination and Reflectance Modeling

- Image-Based Modeling

- Image and Video Retrieval

- Medical Image Analysis

- Motion and Tracking

- Object Detection, Recognition, and Categorization

- Segmentation and Grouping

- Sensors

- Shape-from-X

- Stereo and Structure from Motion

- Shape Representation and Matching

- Statistical Methods and Learning
- Performance Evaluation
- Video Analysis and Event Recognition

The Maximum Consensus Problem: Recent Algorithmic Advances
Tat-Jun Chin and David Suter
2017

Extreme Value Theory-Based Methods for Visual Recognition
Walter J. Scheirer
2017

Data Association for Multi-Object Visual Tracking
Margrit Betke and Zheng Wu
2016

Ellipse Fitting for Computer Vision: Implementation and Applications
Kenichi Kanatani, Yasuyuki Sugaya, and Yasushi Kanazawa
2016

Computational Methods for Integrating Vision and Language
Kobus Barnard
2016

Background Subtraction: Theory and Practice
Ahmed Elgammal
2014

Vision-Based Interaction
Matthew Turk and Gang Hua
2013

Camera Networks: The Acquisition and Analysis of Videos over Wide Areas
Amit K. Roy-Chowdhury and Bi Song
2012

Deformable Surface 3D Reconstruction from Monocular Images
Mathieu Salzmann and Pascal Fua
2010

Boosting-Based Face Detection and Adaptation
Cha Zhang and Zhengyou Zhang
2010

Image-Based Modeling of Plants and Trees
Sing Bing Kang and Long Quan
2009

The Maximum Consensus Problem: Recent Algorithmic Advances

Tat-Jun Chin and David Suter

ISBN: 978-3-031-00690-6   paperback
ISBN: 978-3-031-01818-3   ebook

DOI 10.1007/978-3-031-01818-3

A Publication in the Springer series

SYNTHESIS LECTURES ON COMPUTER VISION

Lecture #11
Series Editors: Gérard Medioni, *University of Southern California*
                Sven Dickinson, *University of Toronto*
Series ISSN
Print 2153-1056   Electronic 2153-1064

The Maximum Consensus Problem

Recent Algorithmic Advances

Tat-Jun Chin and David Suter
The University of Adelaide

SYNTHESIS LECTURES ON COMPUTER VISION #11

ABSTRACT

Outlier-contaminated data is a fact of life in computer vision. For computer vision applications to perform reliably and accurately in practical settings, the processing of the input data must be conducted in a robust manner. In this context, the maximum consensus robust criterion plays a critical role by allowing the quantity of interest to be estimated from noisy and outlier-prone visual measurements. The *maximum consensus problem* refers to the problem of optimizing the quantity of interest according to the maximum consensus criterion. This book provides an overview of the algorithms for performing this optimization. The emphasis is on the basic operation or "inner workings" of the algorithms, and on their mathematical characteristics in terms of optimality and efficiency. The applicability of the techniques to common computer vision tasks is also highlighted. By collecting existing techniques in a single article, this book aims to trigger further developments in this theoretically interesting and practically important area.

For updates, errata, demo programs, and other information, please visit:

http://cs.adelaide.edu.au/~tjchin/maxcon/

We welcome contributions to the errata list.

KEYWORDS

robust fitting, maximum consensus, algorithms, optimization

Always try the problem that matters most to you.

Andrew Wiles

Contents

Preface

The book is organized into four chapters. The first chapter is primarily concerned with defining the maximum consensus problem as an optimization problem, and what is meant by the term "solution." An outline of the computational hardness of the problem is also given. This sets up the kinds of algorithms and efficiencies that one can realistically expect, with respect to theoretical complexity limitations.

The second chapter describes approximate algorithms for maximum consensus. These include the popular randomized sample-and-test heuristics, as well as more recent algorithms that employ some form of convex optimization as a subroutine. A large part of Chapter 2 is devoted to Chebyshev approximation (ℓ_∞ minimization) and linear program (LP)-type problems. Though they seem tangential to robust fitting or maximum consensus at the onset, these topics provide a consistent mathematical framework to talk about maximum consensus estimation for a useful class of nonlinear models.

The third chapter describes exact algorithms for maximum consensus. The fundamental intractability of maximum consensus means that all exact algorithms conduct some form of search. Thus, in a nutshell, Chapter 3 is about how to conduct the search efficiently (as least more efficiently than brute-force search). To this end, the underlying geometric structure of the model plays a crucial role, and it is thus given attention in the chapter.

The fourth chapter is about a relatively new idea in maximum consensus optimization—preprocessing, or data reduction. Different from a simple culling of input data, the preprocessing must preserve the optimal solution in the original input data. This implies retaining the maximum consensus set and removing only true outliers. How to efficiently identify true outliers and remove them is the main topic in this chapter.

The intention of this book is *not* to propose the "best-performing method"—such an endeavor should be carried out via comprehensive benchmarking, taking into account the requirements of the specific application (available time budget, desired repeatability of estimates, minimum solution quality, etc.) and the expected variability in the data. The main aim of this book is to explore the underlying concepts of the various algorithms and to establish properties related to efficiency and optimality. In some sections, however, sample results and brief comparisons are provided to illustrate the operation of the method.

Tat-Jun Chin and David Suter
February 2017

Acknowledgments

Throughout the authors' careers, they have been fortunate enough to work with many talented and dedicated individuals, including former and current students, postdocs under (and sometimes not under) our supervision, fellow academic staff in our immediate vicinity and more broadly in the community, as well as the researchers and R&D engineers from industry and nonacademic research organizations. These collaborations have had direct and indirect impact on making this book a reality.

We are indebted specifically to Álvaro Parra Bustos, Jin Yu, Huu Minh Le, Pulak Purkait, Trung Thanh Pham, Quoc Huy Tran, Hoi Sim Wong, and Yang Heng Kee, who co-contributed to the development of several of the algorithms and/or their predecessors, to some of the sample results, and to a number of the illustrative diagrams. We would also like to thank Alireza Khosravian, who proofread parts of the book. Special mention is given to Anders Eriksson, Wojciech Chojnacki, and Frank Neumann, who have been careful listeners and sanity testers of some of our initial ideas—it is increasingly rare to find brilliant researchers who are also generous enough with their time to think about "other people's problems."

Certainly the ideas in this book do not exist in a vacuum, as we have leveraged the hard work of a large number of researchers in computer vision and beyond. We can only express our appreciation by citing their excellent work (as far as the local context permits) in our book. We apologize in advance if we left out important works, and we would love to hear about them via email or the next time we cross paths at the conferences.

We thank the editors and editorial staff for their encouragement, kind understanding, and timely reminders to complete the book. We also record our appreciation of the reviewers who provided useful comments to improve the book.

Lastly, we thank the Australian Research Council (ARC), whose funding has been instrumental in enabling the necessary basic research.

Tat-Jun Chin and David Suter
February 2017

The Maximum Consensus Problem

On two occasions I have been asked, "Pray, Mr. Babbage, if you put into the machine wrong figures, will the right answers come out?" I am not able rightly to apprehend the kind of confusion of ideas that could provoke such a question.

Charles Babbage

1.1   INTRODUCTION

Computer vision algorithms rely on the ability to reconcile ideal mathematical models with imperfect measurements. More specifically, there is a frequent need to estimate the parameters of a prescribed model using visual data that is noisy and contaminated by outliers. The existence of outliers precludes the usage of least squares (LS) estimation because it is easily biased by outliers. Rather, one must apply a class of estimation techniques called *robust fitting*. Owing to the inevitable existence of noise and outliers in real-life data, robust fitting plays a central role in computer vision [Meer, 2004, Stewart, 1999, Zhang, 1997].

Outliers exist in visual data for several reasons. First, data acquisition devices (imaging sensors, depth sensors, laser scanners, etc.) are inherently imperfect in that they cannot completely avoid making incorrect or spurious measurements. Second, the sensors seldom directly measure the quantity of interest; thus, some form of preprocessing on the recorded data is usually required to extract quantities that are more suited to estimation. This preprocessing step frequently introduces errors or outliers.

Figure 1.1 illustrates the task of estimating the trajectory of a satellite in an image recorded via telescope. The extreme velocity of the satellite relative to the image exposure time causes the satellite to be imaged as a linear streak. Estimating the satellite trajectory can thus be accomplished by finding a line (the model of interest) in the image. To obtain a data format that is more amenable to further processing, the image is converted into a set of discrete points on the plane by intensity thresholding, the removal of large "blobs," and centroiding (replacing each connected component with its centroid). After preprocessing, however, apart from the points lying close to the target line (i.e., the inliers), there also remain many points that are unrelated to the structure of interest (i.e., the outliers). Such a condition necessitates the usage of robust fitting techniques to find the line.

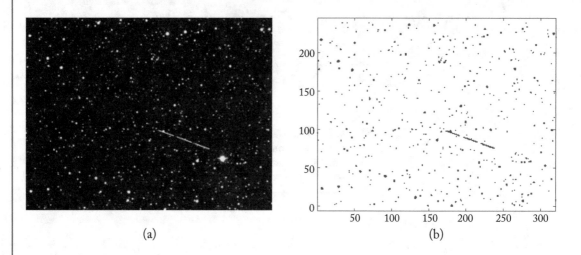

(a)   (b)

Figure 1.1: Estimating satellite trajectory by finding linear streaks. (a) Input image containing an orbiting satellite obtained via telescope (courtesy of Defense Science Technology Group, Australia's primary defense science research organization). (b) A set of points obtained by intensity thresholding, removal of large blobs, and centroiding. Observe that there exist a significant number of outliers, or points not lying on the target line.

Another example is illustrated in Figure 1.2, where the task is to estimate a warping function (the model of interest) that aligns two partially overlapping images. An automatic feature detection and matching algorithm [Mikolajczyk et al., 2005, Mikolajczyk and Schmid, 2005] is first used to establish putative point correspondences across the images (i.e., the preprocessing step). Such automatic techniques invariably produce erroneous feature matches that behave as outliers to the correct warping function. A robust fitting technique must thus be used to estimate the warping function based on the set of outlier contaminated feature correspondences.

Numerous computer vision capabilities depend on robust fitting. Line fitting alone enables many applications: satellite detection, tracing subatomic particles, lane marker detection in smart vehicles—to name a few. The extension of line fitting to the fitting of various geometric "shapes" (circle, ellipse, polygon, etc.) is useful for object recognition in images. Robust feature-based image alignment plays an important role in automated cartography, panoramic stitching, medical image analysis, computational photography, and video stabilization. Robust fitting techniques have also been applied extensively in tasks that support three-dimensional (3D) vision, for example the estimation of epipolar geometry, structure-from-motion, 3D object recognition, motion analysis, and robot localization and navigation.

Figure 1.2: To estimate a warping function that aligns two images, an algorithm such as an automatic feature detection and matching algorithm is first used to extract putative feature correspondences. Such automatic methods invariably produce mistakes, for example, observe that parts of one of the trees were wrongfully matched. These incorrect correspondences represent outliers to the correct warping function.

Since the early days of computer vision, researchers have been aware of the need for robust fitting techniques to deal with outliers in visual data [Rosenfeld, 1969]. This has motivated the invention of robust fitting techniques that were inspired by computer vision applications [Duda and Hart, 1972, Fischler and Bolles, 1981, Stewart, 1999], or the adaptation of methods from the statistical community [Huber, 1981, Rousseeuw, 1984] to computer vision [Bab-Hadiashar and Suter, 1996, Deriche et al., 1994, Torr, 1997].

One of the most successful robust fitting paradigms in computer vision is *maximum consensus* [Fischler and Bolles, 1981]. We motivate using line fitting: let $\mathcal{D} = \{(p_i, q_i)\}_{i=1}^{N}$ be a set of points on the plane. A line can be mathematically defined with the equation

$$q = mp + c, \tag{1.1}$$

where (p, q) is a point on the line with slope m and intercept c; any two real numbers (m, c) thus represent a line. Given a candidate line (m, c), the error or *residual* at the i-th point (p_i, q_i) with respect to that line can be obtained as

$$|mp_i + c - q_i|. \tag{1.2}$$

Geometrically, the residual is the vertical distance[1] (distance along the q-axis) from point (p_i, q_i) to the line (m, c). The conventional LS approach estimates the line parameters that minimize the

---

[1]Defining the residual instead as the orthogonal distance of the point to the line, or more generally, affine hyperplane, may make more "geometrical sense" [Kanatani, 1996]. For simplicity in motivating the maximum consensus problem and the algorithms, we adopt the vertical distance for linear fitting in this book. In any case, as we branch into more sophisticated models, geometrically meaningful distances are used.

sum of squared residuals

$$\sum_{i=1}^{N} (mp_i + c - q_i)^2,\tag{1.3}$$

which subscribes to the maximum likelihood principle. This entails assuming that the residuals are independent and identically distributed (i.i.d.) Gaussian. However, LS is *not robust*, meaning that a single outlier can arbitrarily bias the estimated line. Fundamentally, if outliers exist in the data, then the residuals with respect to (w.r.t.) the correct line are not i.i.d. Gaussian.

To estimate the line in a manner that is tolerant toward outliers, an inherently robust objective function or *criterion* must be employed. Define the *consensus* of a line (m, c) as

$$\Psi(m, c) = \sum_{i=1}^{N} \mathbb{I}\left(|mp_i + c - q_i| \leq \epsilon\right),\tag{1.4}$$

where $\mathbb{I}(\cdot)$ is the indicator function that returns 1 if its input condition $\cdot$ is true and 0 otherwise, and ϵ is a user-defined constant called the *inlier threshold*. Intuitively, $\Psi(m, c)$ counts the number of points with distance less then ϵ from line (m, c). The maximum consensus approach seeks the line with the *highest consensus*. To appreciate why this is a sensible thing to do, Figure 1.3 shows two candidate lines and their respective consensus (for $\epsilon = 5$ pixels) based on the data in Figure 1.1. Evidently the line with the higher consensus represents a better fit to the data.

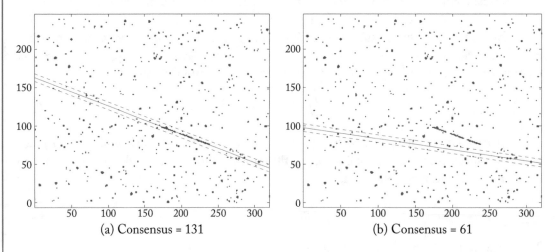

(a) Consensus = 131   (b) Consensus = 61

Figure 1.3: Lines with respectively 131 and 61 consensus with $\epsilon = 5$ pixels. The dashed lines indicate the boundary of the inlier threshold ϵ.

The tolerance of the maximum consensus estimate toward outliers derives from the fact that the function Ψ disallows data that lie beyond distance ϵ from influencing the result. This differs from standard LS estimation, where the weights of outlying data can be unbounded, thus the existence of a single outlier can bias the estimate tremendously.

1.1.1   PROBLEM DEFINITION

We first generalize line fitting to linear model fitting, then generalize later to nonlinear models. Line fitting is a special case of fitting linear models

$$b = \mathbf{a}^T \mathbf{x}, \tag{1.5}$$

where $\mathbf{x} \in \mathbb{R}^d$ is a vector of d variables, and $(\mathbf{a}, b)$ is a point in $(d + 1)$-dimensional space. The aim is to estimate $\mathbf{x}$ robustly from a set of noisy and outlier-contaminated measurements $\mathcal{D} = \{(\mathbf{a}_i, b_i)\}_{i=1}^N$. Given a candidate $\mathbf{x}$, the residual at the i-th point is

$$\left| \mathbf{a}_i^T \mathbf{x} - b_i \right|, \tag{1.6}$$

and the consensus of $\mathbf{x}$ is defined as

$$\Psi(\mathbf{x}) = \sum_{i=1}^N \mathbb{I} \left(\left| \mathbf{a}_i^T \mathbf{x} - b_i \right| \le \epsilon \right). \tag{1.7}$$

The *maximum consensus problem* is thus defined as

$$\underset{\mathbf{x} \in \mathbb{R}^d}{\text{maximize}} \quad \Psi(\mathbf{x}). \tag{1.8}$$

The special case of line fitting is realized by setting $\mathbf{x} = [m, c]^T$, $\mathbf{a}_i = [p_i, 1]^T$, and $b_i = q_i$.

Often in computer vision, conducting robust fitting by maximum consensus is synonymous with *outlier identification* or *outlier removal*. Typically, the subset of the data that is not consistent with the maximum consensus estimate (i.e., those with residual greater than ϵ w.r.t. the estimate) are discarded as outliers. This reflects the emphasis of certain applications on rejecting erroneous data, rather than on the parameter vector $\mathbf{x}$. Indeed, a common practice is to further conduct LS estimation on the set of remaining inliers in the hope of yielding a more statistically valid estimate.

Although the robust fitting of linear models is fundamentally important to many scientific disciplines, including computer vision, we often need to deal with more complex problems. To generalize (1.8), let ω be a set of parameters from domain Ω (not necessarily Euclidean) that defines the model of interest, and $r_i : \Omega \mapsto \mathbb{R}^+$ be a nonnegative function that computes the residual of the i-th datum. The consensus of ω is

$$\Psi(\omega) = \sum_{i=1}^N \mathbb{I} \left(r_i(\omega) \le \epsilon \right), \tag{1.9}$$

and the general maximum consensus problem is defined as

$$\underset{\omega \in \Omega}{\text{maximize}} \quad \Psi(\omega). \tag{1.10}$$

The following examples illustrate common robust fitting problems in computer vision.

Example 1.1   (Affine registration)   Invoking the image alignment problem (Figure 1.2), our goal is to estimate a warping function $f : \mathbb{R}^2 \mapsto \mathbb{R}^2$ that aligns two images I and I' from outlier-contaminated point correspondences $\mathcal{D} = \{(\mathbf{p}_i, \mathbf{p}'_i)\}_{i=1}^N$. We may choose to model f as affine transformation

$$f(\mathbf{p} \mid \mathbf{\Lambda}) = \mathbf{\Lambda}\tilde{\mathbf{p}}, \tag{1.11}$$

where $\tilde{\mathbf{p}} = [\mathbf{p}^T, 1]^T$ is $\mathbf{p}$ in homogeneous coordinates, and $\mathbf{\Lambda} \in \mathbb{R}^{2 \times 3}$ is a matrix that defines the affine transformation. Given $\mathbf{\Lambda}$, the residual at the i-th "datum" $(\mathbf{p}_i, \mathbf{p}'_i)$ can be defined as the *transfer error*

$$r_i(\mathbf{\Lambda}) = \left\| f(\mathbf{p}_i \mid \mathbf{\Lambda}) - \mathbf{p}'_i \right\|_2, \tag{1.12}$$

which is simply the Euclidean distance between the warped version of point $\mathbf{p}_i$ and the observed point $\mathbf{p}'_i$. Identifying $\mathbf{\Lambda}$ as ω and defining Ω as the set of all real matrices of size 2×3, we have thus formulated an instance of (1.10) for robust affine registration.

Example 1.2   (Homography fitting)   We may also choose to model the warping function f for image alignment as a planar perspective warp or a *homography*

$$f(\mathbf{p} \mid \mathbf{H}) = \frac{\mathbf{H}^{(1:2)}\tilde{\mathbf{p}}}{\mathbf{H}^{(3)}\tilde{\mathbf{p}}}, \tag{1.13}$$

where $\mathbf{H}$ is a 3×3 homogeneous matrix that defines the homography, $\mathbf{H}^{(1:2)}$ is the first-two rows of $\mathbf{H}$, and $\mathbf{H}^{(3)}$ is the third row of $\mathbf{H}$. Given $\mathbf{H}$, the i-th residual can be defined using the transfer error again as

$$r_i(\mathbf{H}) = \left\| f(\mathbf{p}_i \mid \mathbf{H}) - \mathbf{p}'_i \right\|_2. \tag{1.14}$$

Identifying $\mathbf{H}$ as ω and defining Ω as the set of all homogeneous 3×3 matrix, we have thus formulated robust homography fitting as an instance of (1.10).

Example 1.3 (Triangulation) The 3×4 camera matrix $\mathbf{P}$ underlying an image encodes the pose and internal parameters of the camera that captured the image. A point $\mathbf{x} \in \mathbb{R}^3$ in the scene is projected onto the image according to the function

$$f(\mathbf{P} \mid \mathbf{x}) = \frac{\mathbf{P}^{(1:2)}\tilde{\mathbf{x}}}{\mathbf{P}^{(3)}\tilde{\mathbf{x}}}. \tag{1.15}$$

In the problem of triangulation, we are given N image observations $\mathcal{D} = \{\mathbf{p}_i\}_{i=1}^N$ of the same scene point $\mathbf{x}$, and we wish to estimate $\mathbf{x}$. Let $\mathbf{P}_i$ be the camera matrix of the i-th image. Since a subset of the observations $\mathcal{D}$ may be erroneous (e.g., owing to mistakes in feature association), $\mathbf{x}$ must be estimated robustly. Given $\mathbf{x}$, the residual in the i-th view can be taken as the *reprojection error*

$$r_i(\mathbf{x}) = \| f(\mathbf{P}_i \mid \mathbf{x}) - \mathbf{p}_i \|_2, \tag{1.16}$$

which is the Euclidean distance between the projected and observed points.

In this example, the parameter ω is the 3D point $\mathbf{x}$. Additional constraints must be placed on $\mathbf{x}$ such that only points that lie in front of all the cameras are allowed. This can be done by forcing the denominators $\mathbf{P}_i^{(3)}\tilde{\mathbf{x}}$ for all i to be strictly positive. Hence, $\Omega = \{\mathbf{x} \in \mathbb{R}^3 \mid \mathbf{P}_i^{(3)}\tilde{\mathbf{x}} > 0, i = 1, \ldots, N\}$.

Example 1.4 (Point set registration) Given N corresponding points $\mathcal{D} = \{(\mathbf{p}_i, \mathbf{p}_i')\}_{i=1}^N$ from two 3D point sets, we wish to estimate the rigid transformation

$$f(\mathbf{p} \mid \mathbf{R}, \mathbf{t}) = \mathbf{R}\mathbf{p} + \mathbf{t} \tag{1.17}$$

that aligns the point sets. Here, $\mathbf{R}$ is a 3×3 rotation matrix, and $\mathbf{t}$ is a translation vector. Since a subset of the correspondences $\mathcal{D}$ may be incorrect (i.e., the outliers), the rigid transform must be estimated robustly. Given candidate parameters $(\mathbf{R}, \mathbf{t})$, the residual at the i-th datum $(\mathbf{p}_i, \mathbf{p}_i')$ can be defined as

$$r_i(\mathbf{R}, \mathbf{t}) = \| \mathbf{R}\mathbf{p}_i + \mathbf{t} - \mathbf{p}_i' \|_2, \tag{1.18}$$

which is simply the Euclidean distance between the rigidly transformed version of $\mathbf{p}_i$ and the matching point $\mathbf{p}_i'$. In this example, $\omega = (\mathbf{R}, \mathbf{t})$, and Ω is the space of all rigid transformations, also known as the special Euclidean group $SE(3)$.

A Note on the Inlier Threshold

An input value critical to the correctness of the maximum consensus estimate is the inlier threshold ϵ. By "correct estimate," we mean an output parameter vector $\mathbf{x}$ or ω that "fits" the true structure in the data. Intuitively, for the output estimate to be correct, ϵ should be equal to the maximum deviation expected of the inliers from the true structure. Ideally, the inlier threshold, or more generally the *inlier scale*, should be estimated in a data-driven manner. However, automatically determining the inlier scale on top of conducting robust fitting is a significantly more challenging problem. Most of the approaches for this broader problem are based on random sampling heuristics [Chen and Meer, 2003, Chin et al., 2009, Stewart, 1995, Subbarao and Meer, 2006, Wang and Suter, 2004].

In many computer vision problems, often an appropriate ϵ can be "guesstimated" from the application context. For satellite trajectory estimation (Figure 1.1), for example, owing to the distances involved between observer and target, we would expect that the pixels arising from the satelite would lie no more than a few pixels from the trajectory. Similarly, for the image alignment problem (Figure 1.2), practitioners usually have a good idea of the localization uncertainty (e.g., a few pixels) of commonly used feature detectors, on the basis of empirical studies such as Schmid et al. [2000] and Mikolajczyk et al. [2005].

Therefore, many works in the vision literature assume that the inlier threshold is known in advance, or can be obtained reasonably easily by trial and error. Since the focus of this book is on algorithms for consensus maximization, throughout the book we take ϵ to be fixed at a suitable constant for the respective examples.

Finally, it is also worth noting that in the approaches that can estimate inlier scale, quite often other forms of "hyperparameter" (a constant) must be *a priori* determined (e.g., the bandwidth for the mean shift kernel [Chen and Meer, 2003, Wang and Suter, 2004], the minimum population size of the structure [Chin et al., 2009]). These hyperparameters have a direct effect on the estimated inlier scale and model parameters, hence the associated algorithms are not totally "user-independent" as such.

1.1.2   WHAT IS THIS BOOK ABOUT?

This book focuses on *algorithms* for maximum consensus. Specifically, the book surveys and describes known algorithms for the maximum consensus problem, drawing from extensive previous research in various applications contexts by multiple researchers. Emphasis is placed on describing the fundamental concepts and characteristics of the algorithms (optimality, convergence, etc.). The main aim is to collect these techniques in a single text, for archiving purposes and to facilitate conceptual differentiation. The authors hope to inspire future work in this interesting and active research area.

In the course of explaining the algorithms, we present some results and brief comparisons of several of the algorithms (or combinations thereof) to demonstrate their operation and to show that they work. **It is not the purpose of this book to identify the "best method"**—such a task should be conducted only via comprehensive benchmarking, which considers the specific require-ments of the target application and the range of data difficulty. We recommend the introduced references to readers who are interested in such results.

In the rest of the book, we base our exposition mainly on the linear regression version of maximum consensus (1.8). This is primarily to focus on the algorithmic aspects, since the generic formulation (1.10) includes an extensive breadth of problem types, each potentially requiring a separate treatment. However, whenever possible, we also show how a particular algorithm can be customized or extended for nonlinear models. Note that since the emphasis of this book is on the computational aspects, we do not dwell on the statistical motivations and properties behind the maximum consensus estimator. Interested readers are referred to current texts on robust statistics.

Why Study the Maximum Consensus Problem?
The importance of maximum consensus robust fitting to computer vision calls for the development of effective algorithms to solve the problem. Arguably the most popular algorithm currently is *random sample consensus (RANSAC)* [Fischler and Bolles, 1981], which operates by randomly sampling subsets of the data to generate candidate fits of the model. The premise is that if a sufficient number of subsets are sampled, we will find one that contains only inliers from the target structure, and that subset of data will give a good fit.

The widespread usage of RANSAC and its variants [Choi et al., 2009, Matas, 2011, Ragu-ram et al., 2013] may give the impression that the problem is "solved." However, there are serious weaknesses in this class of methods. First, because RANSAC is a randomized heuristic, there is never absolute certainty that the result obtained via RANSAC is a satisfactory approximation, let alone an optimal solution. Frequently in practical applications, when an unsatisfactory estimate is obtained, it is difficult to tell whether it was because there were no good solutions to be found, or simply because one was unlucky. Second the RANSAC-type algorithms tend to be computa-tionally costly, given input data with a high proportion of outliers, simply because the probability of randomly hitting a clean subset decreases exponentially with the number of outliers, thus more sampling iterations are required.

Owing to the importance of maximum consensus in robust fitting tasks in computer vision, developing better techniques for solving maximum consensus is a very active research area. A particular aim is to construct algorithms that are "theoretically justified" (i.e., algorithms that can provide some form of convergence, optimality guarantees, or bounds on approximation error). Ideally, the algorithms should also be practical on the large-scale problem instances commonly encountered in real-life applications.

Generally speaking, however, maximum consensus is an intractable problem (Section 1.3 examines the computational hardness of the problem). However, theoretical hardness results are based on worst-case inputs, whereas what computer vision practitioners really need are techniques that work efficiently enough for most real-life cases. To this end, there may be useful structures or regularity in common instances that can be exploited to develop theoretically justified algorithms that are also efficient in practice. This is an intellectually challenging endeavor that requires deep insights and creativity, and is likely to remain an active research topic in computer vision in the future.

1.1.3   ROAD MAP

In the rest of this chapter, the connections between maximum consensus and other popular robust fitting approaches are drawn, and the computational hardness of maximum consensus is examined. The rest of the book is organized as follows.

- Chapter 2 is devoted to surveying important approximate algorithms for maximum consensus, including random sampling methods such as RANSAC and its variants, and methods that employ some form of convex optimization (ℓ_1, ℓ_∞) as a subroutine.

- Chapter 3 surveys exact algorithms for maximum consensus, including plane sweep, mixed integer programming, branch-and-bound (BnB), subset search, and tree search.

- In Chapter 4, we introduce preprocessing techniques that are able to efficiently reduce the size of the problem instance in a way that preserves the optimality of the solution. This represents a novel paradigm for solving maximum consensus.

1.2   RELATION TO OTHER ROBUST FITTING METHODS

In this section, we draw connections between maximum consensus and several other well-established robust fitting techniques: Hough transform (HT), M-estimator, and least median squares (LMedS). Again, since we focus on algorithms, we highlight the shared computational structure between maximum consensus and the other methods.

1.2.1   HOUGH TRANSFORM

One of the earliest robust fitting techniques to receive systematic study in computer vision is the HT [Hough, 1962]. The core idea is to discretize the parameter space into a set of bins, and accumulate the support given by each datum to the bins. For line fitting, Duda and Hart [1972] proposed to conduct HT using the rho-theta parametrization of the line: specifically, a line $q = mp + c$ is represented as

$$r = p \cos \theta + q \sin \theta. \tag{1.19}$$

Intuitively, r is the distance from the origin to the closest point on the line, and θ is the angle between the p-axis and the line connecting the origin to that closest point. The parameter space $(\theta, r) \in [0, \pi] \times \mathbb{R}_+$ is often called the *Hough space*. The basic version of HT then discretizes the Hough space based on a pre-specified boundary and binning resolution.

   Under the rho-theta parametrization, a point (p, q) is converted to the sinusoid (1.19) in the Hough space. Intuitively, the sinusoid contains the rho-theta parameters of all the straight lines that pass though point (p, q) in the original space. See Figure 1.4 for an illustration of this procedure. For each input point (p_i, q_i), we increment the votes in the bins that intersect with the sinusoid defined using (p_i, q_i). A representative parameter vector (θ, r) for the bin with the highest number of votes is then returned as the solution.

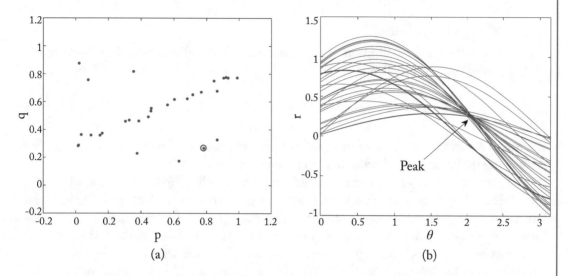

Figure 1.4: Illustration of rho-theta parametrization of lines in HT. The set of input points on the left is converted to the sinusoids in the Hough space on the right (the sinusoid of a sample point is drawn in red). Notice that many sinusoids intersect roughly at the same point. These sinusoids correspond to the input points that lie on the same line. HT finds the peak by discretizing and accumulating votes in the Hough space.

The technique has since been extended to general curves and shapes [Ballard, 1981], thus promoting HT as a generic robust fitting approach. The major difficulties, however, lie in specifying how to discretize the parameter space (binning resolution, etc.) and find genuine peaks in the generated histogram. Often, these settings require significant tuning, especially for high-dimensional models. In practice, therefore, HT is applied to fit mainly simple 2D geometric models such as lines and circles.

The Randomized Hough Transform (RHT) by Xu et al. [1990] attempts to alleviate the shortcomings above. In the context of line fitting, instead of allowing each point (p_i, q_i) to vote in the Hough space, RHT randomly samples pairs of points. For each pair of sampled points, the parameters of the line that intersects the two points are calculated (recall that two points are sufficient to determine a line). Either the parameters of a newly sampled line are combined with a previously discovered line and with the votes increased, or a new bin is created for the new line; thus, the RHT avoids maintaining a full uniform grid of the parameter space. The number of samples to generate is determined heuristically.

Evidently, although RHT and RANSAC are based on different objective functions (RHT seeks the bin with the highest support whereas RANSAC aims to maximize consensus), the basic computational structures are very similar. Thus, one expects that RHT also suffers from several of the problems of RANSAC mentioned previously.

1.2.2   M-ESTIMATOR

The M-estimator is a generalization of the maximum likelihood estimator. The M-estimate is obtained by solving the problem

$$\underset{\mathbf{x} \in \mathbb{R}^d}{\text{minimize}} \quad \sum_{i=1}^{N} \rho \left(|\mathbf{a}_i^T \mathbf{x} - b_i| \right), \tag{1.20}$$

where $\rho(r)$ is a symmetric, positive-definite function with a unique minimum at $r = 0$. Intuitively, ρ computes the amount of influence of each residual toward the estimate.

Setting $\rho(r) = r^2/2$ yields the standard LS (maximum likelihood) estimator, which is not robust since ρ increases quadratically and is unbounded. Setting $\rho(r) = |r|$ yields the least absolute deviations (LAD) estimator (see Section 2.3); although the ρ function in this case increases linearly with r, it still does not completely discount the effect of outlying data. The class of *redescending* M-estimators has a high degree of robustness; they can have breakdown points of up to 0.5 (i.e., they can tolerate up to 50% outliers before returning arbitrarily large estimate values). An example is Tukey's biweight function

$$\rho(r) = \begin{cases} \frac{\epsilon^2}{6}(1 - [1 - (\frac{r}{\epsilon})^2]^3) & \text{if } |r| \le \epsilon \\ \frac{\epsilon^2}{6} & \text{otherwise,} \end{cases} \tag{1.21}$$

where ϵ is analogous to the inlier threshold in maximum consensus. Observe that the function is increasing until $|r| > \epsilon$, after which it remains constant; see Figure 1.5. Also, since the ρ in (1.21) is nonconvex, the sum of N of them is also nonconvex.

The standard technique to solve (1.20) is iteratively reweighted least squares (IRLS) [Björck, 1996, Chapter 4]. Given an initial estimate $\mathbf{x}^{(0)}$ at $t = 0$, the method iterates between assigning weights $w_i^{(t)}$ to the data based on the current estimate $\mathbf{x}^{(t)}$, and updating the estimate by solving a weighted LS problem:

$$\mathbf{x}^{(t+1)} := \underset{\mathbf{x}}{\text{argmin}} \sum_{i=1}^{n} w_i^{(t)} \left(\mathbf{a}_i^T \mathbf{x} - b_i \right)^2, \qquad w_i^{(t)} := \frac{\rho'(|\mathbf{a}_i^T \mathbf{x}^{(t)} - b_i|)}{|\mathbf{a}_i^T \mathbf{x}^{(t)} - b_i|}, \tag{1.22}$$

where ρ' is the first derivative of ρ. The two steps are sequentially performed until convergence. IRLS guarantees that a local minimum will be achieved.

Maximum consensus (1.8) can also be expressed in the form (1.20) if

$$\rho(r) = \begin{cases} 0 & \text{if } |r| \le \epsilon \\ 1 & \text{otherwise;} \end{cases} \tag{1.23}$$

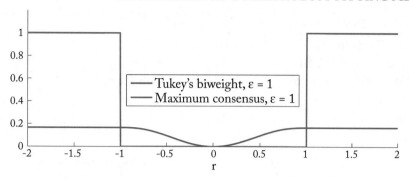

Figure 1.5: Tukey's biweight (1.21) and ρ function (1.23) equivalent to maximum consensus.

see Figure 1.5. However, this does not imply that maximum consensus is an M-estimator, since ρ does not satisfy all the requisite properties (e.g., it does not have a unique minimum. See Aftab and Hartley [2015] for other required conditions). Observe that non-trivial weights $w_i^{(t)}$ cannot be obtained based on the ρ in (1.23), since ρ' is not defined everywhere, and where it is defined, ρ' equals 0. Indeed, the objective function of maximum consensus is piecewise constant, thus complicating gradient-based iterative optimization in general; Section 1.3.1 further explores this issue. For now, the immediate consequence of interest is that IRLS cannot be used to solve maximum consensus.

Note also that in general, an optimum of the M-estimator with Tukey's biweight (or a similar redescending ρ function) is not an optimum of the maximum consensus problem. Thus, a standard M-estimator cannot be used as a proxy to solve maximum consensus.

1.2.3 LEAST MEDIAN SQUARES

Another well-known robust technique is LMedS, originally proposed by Rousseeuw [1984], which is defined[2] as

$$\underset{\mathbf{x} \in \mathbb{R}^d}{\text{minimize}} \underset{i=1,\ldots,N}{\text{median}} \left| \mathbf{a}_i^T \mathbf{x} - b_i \right|. \tag{1.24}$$

LMedS has an analytically proven breakdown point of 0.5. Intuitively, the robustness of LMedS derives from the fact that it effectively considers only half of the data. Owing to the non-differentiability of the median operator, LMedS cannot be solved analytically, such as by using IRLS. The original algorithm for LMedS, called program for robust regression (PROGRESS) [Rousseeuw and Leroy, 1987, Chapter 5], is a randomized sample-and-test algorithm similar to RANSAC.

---

[2]Although the original definition of LMedS involves squaring the residual, to simplify analysis and algorithm development, we do not take the square. Note that the ordering of the residuals is the same in both versions. Many authors also use the nonsquared version of LMedS [Edelsbrunner and Souvaine, 1990, Erickson, 1999].

Algorithm 1.1 An algorithm for maximum consensus.

Require: Data $\mathcal{D} = \{(\mathbf{a}_i, b_i)\}_{i=1}^N$, inlier threshold ϵ.
 1: **for** $t = N, N-1, \ldots, 1$ **do**
 2:     $(\delta_t, \mathbf{x}_t) \leftarrow$ Value and minimizer of LkOS (1.25) with $k = t$.
 3:     **if** $\delta_t \leq \epsilon$ **then**
 4:         **return** $\mathbf{x}_t$.
 5:     **end if**
 6: **end for**

A generalization of the LMedS estimator is the least k-th order statistic (LkOS) estimator [Lee et al., 1998], which is defined as

$$\underset{\mathbf{x} \in \mathbb{R}^d}{\text{minimize}} \ v_k\left(|\mathbf{a}_1^T\mathbf{x} - b_1|, |\mathbf{a}_2^T\mathbf{x} - b_2|, \ldots, |\mathbf{a}_N^T\mathbf{x} - b_N|\right), \qquad (1.25)$$

where function v_k returns the k-th smallest value among its given input values. The LkOS estimator has been shown to have a breakdown point of

$$\min\left(k/N, \ 1 - k/N\right). \qquad (1.26)$$

Lee et al. [1998] proposed a method that can adaptively choose the best k for the given data, although the main optimization machinery is still random sampling.

Here, we point out a dual relationship between maximum consensus and LkOS. Specifically, it is possible to solve maximum consensus using LkOS as a subroutine, and vice versa.

For a given data $\mathcal{D} = \{(\mathbf{a}_i, b_i)\}_{i=1}^N$ and k, let δ_k be the globally minimized cost of (1.25), and $\mathbf{x}_k$ be the corresponding minimizer. If $\delta_k \leq \epsilon$, then we know that there exist at least k data that are consistent up to ϵ with an $\mathbf{x}$. On the other hand, if $\delta_k > \epsilon$, then it is not possible to find a subset of $\mathcal{D}$ of size k that agree with an $\mathbf{x}$ up to threshold ϵ. This suggests a hypothetical algorithm, outlined in Algorithm 1.1, for maximum consensus.

Conversely, to solve LkOS using maximum consensus, we can couch LkOS as finding the smallest ϵ, such that the maximized consensus is at least k. Let $\mathbf{x}_\epsilon$ be the maximizer of (1.8) with threshold ϵ. Algorithm 1.2 shows a hypothetical algorithm for LkOS, where the technique of bisection is used to search for the optimal ϵ.

Observe that the main loop of the above two algorithms are very simple. The overall efficiency of the algorithms depends on the "feasibility tests" conducted at each iteration, respectively based on solving LkOS and maximum consensus. This implies that if one problem can be solved efficiently, so too can the other. It is no coincidence, therefore, that no efficient algorithms are known for both problems. Section 1.3 further explores the issue of computational hardness of maximum consensus.

Note that there have been many "efficient" algorithms proposed for LkOS [Edelsbrunner and Souvaine, 1990, Matoušek, 1995, Mount et al., 2000, Olson, 1997, Souvaine and Steele,

---

Algorithm 1.2 An algorithm for least k-th order statistic (LkOS).

Require: Data $\mathcal{D} = \{(\mathbf{a}_i, b_i)\}_{i=1}^N$, order k, initial bracket $[\epsilon_l, \epsilon_h]$ for ϵ, and precision γ.

  1: **while** $\epsilon_h - \epsilon_l > \gamma$ **do**

  2:    $\epsilon \leftarrow 0.5(\epsilon_l + \epsilon_h)$.

  3:    $\mathbf{x}_\epsilon \leftarrow$ Maximizer of (1.8) with inlier threshold ϵ.

  4:    If $\Psi(\mathbf{x}_\epsilon) < k$ then $\epsilon_l \leftarrow \epsilon$, else $\epsilon_h \leftarrow \epsilon$.

  5: **end while**

  6: **return** $\mathbf{x}_\epsilon$.

1987, Steele and Steiger, 1986, Stromberg, 1993]. However, these algorithms are primarily specialized for line fitting, where $\mathbf{x}$ is a 2D vector. Section 3.2 describes the modification of one of the techniques for maximum consensus. However, extending these algorithms to higher-dimensional problems involves nontrivial increases in time complexity. Thus, they are practical mainly for the low-dimensional cases.

1.3   PROBLEM DIFFICULTY

How hard is maximum consensus? Section 1.2 provides some clues to the difficulty of the problem. In this section, a brief discussion on the combinatorial nature and theoretical hardness of maximum consensus is provided. First, the notions of "solving" and "approximating" the maximum consensus problem are more clearly established.

1.3.1   EXACT VS. APPROXIMATE SOLUTIONS

Consider a simple robust 1D "point-fitting" problem, where $\mathcal{D} = \{p_i\}_{i=1}^N$ are N points on the real line, and the estimate of interest is another point $x \in \mathbb{R}$ that lies at the "center" of $\mathcal{D}$. If outliers exist in the data (i.e., there are points that do not belong to any center, or there are multiple centers in $\mathcal{D}$), the measure of centrality must be robust. Under the maximum consensus paradigm, we implicitly accept that points belonging to a center are no more than ϵ away from the center. This defines the consensus function as

$$\Psi(x) = \sum_{i=1}^N \mathbb{I}(|x - p_i| \le \epsilon). \tag{1.27}$$

Figure 1.6 plots $\Psi(x)$ for a sample instance of robust point fitting, where we can clearly observe the piecewise constant nature of the objective function.

As another illustration of the maximum consensus objective, Figure 1.7 depicts the contour plot of $\Psi(\mathbf{x})$ for a line-fitting problem, where $\mathbf{x} \in \mathbb{R}^2$. Though significantly more complex than the one in Figure 1.6, it can be discerned that the objective function is piecewise constant, where each piece corresponds to a 2D region in the plot with the same color.

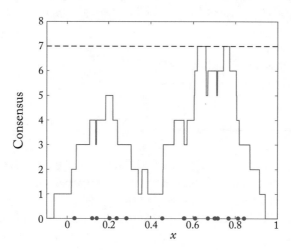

Figure 1.6: Consensus function $\Psi(x)$ for a sample instance of robust point fitting, where $\epsilon = 0.1$. The input points $\mathcal{D}$ are plotted as blue dots on the x-axis. The maximum value of the function is indicated by the dashed line.

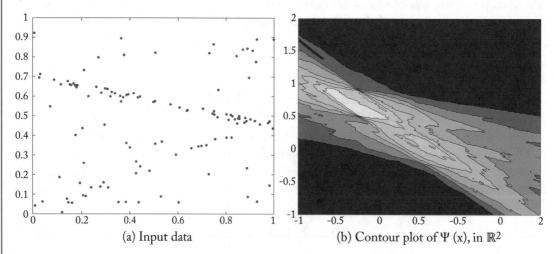

(a) Input data

(b) Contour plot of $\Psi(x)$, in $\mathbb{R}^2$

Figure 1.7: Panel (b) shows the colored contour plot of consensus function $\Psi(\mathbf{x})$, $\mathbf{x} \in \mathbb{R}^2$, for the sample instance of line fitting in panel (a), where $\epsilon = 0.2$. Regions of the same color in panel (a) indicate locations in $\mathbb{R}^2$ with the same consensus.

Now, we define an *exact* or *global* solution to the maximum consensus problem as a parameter vector $\mathbf{x}^*$ such that $\Psi(\mathbf{x}^*) \geq \Psi(\mathbf{x})$ for all other $\mathbf{x} \in \mathbb{R}^d$. In Figure 1.6, x^* are the positions on the x-axis where the $\Psi(x)$ curve touches the dashed line, whereas in Figure 1.7, $\mathbf{x}^*$ are the yellow colored regions in the plot. As can be inferred from both examples, in general $\mathbf{x}^*$ is not unique. The non-uniqueness of $\mathbf{x}^*$ is due not only to $\Psi(\mathbf{x})$ potentially having multiple peaks, but also to the fact that a "peak" is actually often a plateau in the objective function where $\mathbf{x}$ has the same maximum consensus.

We then define an *approximate* solution as a parameter vector $\hat{\mathbf{x}}$ such that $\Psi(\hat{\mathbf{x}}) \leq \Psi(\mathbf{x}^*)$. Of course, any $\mathbf{x} \in \mathbb{R}^d$ is an approximate solution, and we primarily use the hat symbol to emphasize $\hat{\mathbf{x}}$ as an output of a particular algorithm.

Recall that a *local* solution of an unconstrained optimization problem

$$\text{maximize}_{\mathbf{x} \in \mathbb{R}^d} \ f(\mathbf{x}) \tag{1.28}$$

is a point $\hat{\mathbf{x}}$ such that there is a neighborhood $\mathcal{N}$ of $\hat{\mathbf{x}}$ where $f(\hat{\mathbf{x}}) \geq f(\mathbf{x})$ for all $\mathbf{x} \in \mathcal{N}$ (a neighborhood of $\hat{\mathbf{x}}$ is simply an open subset of $\mathbb{R}^d$ that contains $\hat{\mathbf{x}}$) [Nocedal and Wright, 2006, Chapter 2]. Many nonlinear optimization algorithms are locally optimal in that they strive for local solutions, which are considered theoretically desirable.

For maximum consensus, however, any $\mathbf{x}$ is a local solution by the above definition, since $\Psi(\mathbf{x})$ is piecewise constant. Thus, local optimality is not meaningful in our context. Indeed, the lack of gradient information for $\Psi(\mathbf{x})$ complicates the usage of gradient-based nonlinear optimization schemes for consensus maximization (cf. IRLS in Section 1.2.2). In this book, we thus do not mention locally optimal algorithms for maximum consensus, though Chapter 2 includes a method that conducts deterministic local refinement.

1.3.2   COMPUTATIONAL HARDNESS

In this section, the intractability, or more specifically the *NP*-hardness, of maximum consensus is established. Roughly, an optimization problem is *NP*-hard if there are no algorithms that can solve it in polynomial time, unless the unlikely hypothesis of $P = NP$ is true. To prove *NP*-hardness of an optimization problem, the decision version of the problem is considered. The decision version of maximum consensus is as follows.

Problem 1.5   (Maximum consensus)   Given N points $\mathcal{D} = \{(\mathbf{a}_i, b_i)\}_{i=1}^N$ in $\mathbb{R}^{d+1}$, inlier threshold ϵ, and a positive integer ψ, is there an $\mathbf{x} \in \mathbb{R}^d$ such that $\Psi(\mathbf{x}) \geq \psi$?

Like most decision problems, Problem 1.5 accepts a "yes/no" answer. One can readily see that if Problem 1.5 is tractable (i.e., can be answered in polynomial time), then so is the optimization version [e.g., simply solve Problem 1.5 for $\psi = 1, 2, \ldots, N$, stop when the answer is "no" (cf. Algorithm 1.1)]. From the opposite angle, if the solution $\mathbf{x}^*$ to the optimization problem is available, then Problem 1.5 can be instantly answered by comparing $\Psi(\mathbf{x}^*)$ with ψ. Proving that the decision problem is intractable or *NP*-complete then establishes the *NP*-hardness of the optimization version [Garey and Johnson, 1979].

To prove *NP*-completeness of Problem 1.5, we exploit again the dual relationship between maximum consensus and LkOS. The decision version of LkOS is as follows.

Problem 1.6   (Least k-th order statistic)   Given N points $\mathcal{D} = \{(\mathbf{a}_i, b_i)\}_{i=1}^{N}$ in $\mathbb{R}^{d+1}$, an integer k where $1 \leq k \leq N$, and a real number ϕ, is there an $\mathbf{x} \in \mathbb{R}^d$ such that $v_k \left(|\mathbf{a}_1^T \mathbf{x} - b_1|, |\mathbf{a}_2^T \mathbf{x} - b_2|, \ldots, |\mathbf{a}_N^T \mathbf{x} - b_N| \right) \leq \phi$?

Recall that the function v_k returns the k-th smallest value among its input scalars. Via previous efforts [Bernholt, 2006, Erickson et al., 2006], Problem (1.6) can be shown to be *NP*-complete. We leverage the previous results by demonstrating a simple Turing reduction from Problem (1.6) to Problem (1.5). Given input $(\mathcal{D}, k, \phi)$ to Problem (1.6), simply set $\epsilon = \phi$, $\psi = k$, and input the same points $\mathcal{D}$ to Problem (1.5). If the answer to Problem (1.6) is "yes," then we know that there is an $\mathbf{x}$ such that there are k points with distance not greater than ϕ from $\mathbf{x}$—simply take these k points as the consensus set, and Problem (1.5) will also answer "yes." Conversely, if the answer to Problem (1.6) is "no," then there is no consensus set of size at least k, and Problem (1.5) must also yield "no". This completes the Turing reduction, and proves the *NP*-completeness of Problem (1.5).

In fact, a reverse reduction from Problem (1.5) to Problem (1.6) can be constructed, thus establishing that maximum consensus and LkOS are equivalently hard.

The total size of the input to Problem 1.5 is proportional to $N \times d$. The *NP*-hardness result basically states that the runtime to solve maximum consensus may grow exponentially with either N or d. Erickson [1999] in fact suggested that there is a minimum rate of increase in runtime, and that N and d affect this rate differently.

Conjecture 1 *Solving LkOS with N points and d dimensions ($\mathbf{x} \in \mathbb{R}^d$) requires $\Omega(N^d)$ time in the worst case.*

Recall that the big-Ω notation refers to a lower bound function of the asymptotic growth of runtime. Transporting Conjecture 1 to maximum consensus, in the worst case, we can expect runtime increases that are at least a d-th order polynomial of N, and exponentially in d. In fact, as we see in Chapter 3, some of the algorithms do approach the $\Omega(N^d)$ lower bound. By Conjecture 1, however, algorithms that are faster than $\mathcal{O}(N^d)$ are unlikely. The practical ramification is that on specific applications where the dimensionality is low, we can look forward to runtimes that increase polynomially with the number of measurements. However, nontrivial runtime growths are to be expected for moderate d's.

The above analysis of difficulty pertains only to linear models. The maximum consensus fitting of nonlinear models is unlikely to be easier. In fact, previous analyses have established results similar to Conjecture 1 for the closely related *maximum depth* problem [Aronov and Har-Peled, 2008, Ben-David et al., 2002, Johnson and Preparata, 1978].

Although the theory paints a grim picture of what is algorithmically achievable, the fundamental analysis caters to the worst case inputs. As mentioned in Section 1.1.2, the computer vision engineer deals with "typical" cases for specific applications, thus there remain plenty of avenues for research, including constructing theoretically justified approximate algorithms or customizing exact algorithms for specific applications.

1.4   BIBLIOGRAPHICAL REMARKS

In 1981, Fischler and Bolles published their seminal paper on RANSAC, which contains one of the earliest mentions of the concept of consensus in the context of robust fitting in computer vision [Fischler and Bolles, 1981]. Their original application of the RANSAC algorithm was the estimation of camera pose given outlier-prone 3D-2D point correspondences. Around the same time, Rousseeuw proposed LMedS [Rousseeuw, 1984]. Both papers proposed the usage of random sampling to optimize their respective robust criterion. Rousseeuw called his random sampling algorithm PROGRESS (Program for RObust reGRESSion); see Chapter 5 of Rousseeuw and Leroy [1987] for more details.

The naming convention in the robust statistics literature reflects a clear detachment of the robust fitting problem (LMedS, M-estimators) and the means with which to solve the problem (PROGRESS, IRLS). Owing to its roots as an applied or engineering field, often in computer vision, the names of the problem and technique are used interchangeably—even today, by "RANSAC," many computer vision researchers actually mean "robust fitting with the maximum consensus criterion," and they may propose a solution technique that departs significantly from Fischler and Bolle's original algorithm.

As recounted in Section 4.9 of Hartley and Zisserman [2004], some of the earliest applications of RANSAC and LMedS to multiple view geometry were by Torr and Murray [1993] and Zhang et al. [1995]. Since then, there has been an explosion of papers related to robust fitting in computer vision; in particular, numerous variants of the RANSAC algorithm have been proposed; see Choi et al. [2009], Matas [2011] and Raguram et al. [2013] for a recent survey. More recently, there is a shift away from Fischler and Bolle's randomized sample-and-test framework for maximum consensus. The recent tutorial "Robust Optimization Techniques in Computer Vision" by Enqvist, Kahl, and Hartley at the European Conference on Computer Vision (ECCV) 2014 is a clear indication of this trend.

CHAPTER 2

Approximate Algorithms

Far better an approximate answer to the right question, which is often vague, than an exact answer to the wrong question, which can always be made precise.

John Tukey

2.1 INTRODUCTION

With reference to the linear model (1.5), the *consensus set* of a candidate $\mathbf{x}$ is defined as

$$\mathcal{I}(\mathbf{x}) = \left\{ i \in \{1, \dots, N\} \mid \left| \mathbf{a}_i^T \mathbf{x} - b_i \right| \leq \epsilon \right\}, \tag{2.1}$$

i.e., $\mathcal{I}(\mathbf{x})$ indexes the subset of data $\mathcal{D}$ that agrees (up to threshold ϵ) with $\mathbf{x}$. Henceforth, we do not distinguish between the *indices* contained in $\mathcal{I}(\mathbf{x})$, and the *actual data* that is indexed by $\mathcal{I}(\mathbf{x})$. Trivially,

$$\Psi(\mathbf{x}) = |\mathcal{I}(\mathbf{x})|, \tag{2.2}$$

where $| \cdot |$ represents set cardinality. Problem (1.8) can thus be re-expressed as

$$\underset{\mathbf{x} \in \mathbb{R}^d}{\text{maximize}} \quad |\mathcal{I}(\mathbf{x})|, \tag{2.3}$$

which makes explicit the goal of finding the largest possible consensus set $\mathcal{I}(\mathbf{x}^*)$. An approximate algorithm for maximum consensus is an algorithm that cannot guarantee that its solution $\hat{\mathbf{x}}$ is a globally optimal solution $\mathbf{x}^*$; that is,

$$|\mathcal{I}(\hat{\mathbf{x}})| \leq |\mathcal{I}(\mathbf{x}^*)|. \tag{2.4}$$

Note that in general, there may be data in $\mathcal{I}(\hat{\mathbf{x}})$ that are not in $\mathcal{I}(\mathbf{x}^*)$; that is,

$$\mathcal{I}(\hat{\mathbf{x}}) \not\subseteq \mathcal{I}(\mathbf{x}^*). \tag{2.5}$$

The major advantage of approximate algorithms is that they are able to provide solutions relatively quickly, though no guarantees of optimality are available.

In this chapter, we describe approximate algorithms for maximum consensus. We begin with the randomized sample-and-test heuristics, which form the most well-known class of techniques in the vision literature. Such methods rely on randomization and the efficiency of model instantiation on small data subsets to quickly find solutions. The rest of the chapter is devoted to deterministic methods, all of which employ some form of convex optimization as core routines. A moderately large part of the chapter discusses Chebyshev approximation and its generalization to LP-type problems. Apart from enabling an outlier removal heuristic, some of the core concepts of LP-type problems provide foundations for some of the topics in Chapter 3.

2.2   RANDOM SAMPLE CONSENSUS

RANSAC [Fischler and Bolles, 1981] is one of the most widely used techniques for maximum consensus. The method is simple: generate a number of *model hypotheses* by randomly sampling *minimal subsets* of the data $\mathcal{D}$ and fitting the model onto each minimal subset. For each model hypothesis, evaluate its consensus; the hypothesis with the largest consensus is then returned as the result $\hat{\mathbf{x}}$. The core idea is that if a sufficient number of minimal subsets are sampled, there would be at least one that contains all inliers, and the associated hypothesis $\hat{\mathbf{x}}$ would represent a good estimate of the underlying model.

In the context of Problem 1.8, the data takes the form $\mathcal{D} = \{(\mathbf{a}_i, b_i)\}_{i=1}^{N}$. A minimal subset $\mathcal{M}$ is defined as a subset of $\mathcal{D}$ that provides the minimum required number of constraints to fully estimate $\mathbf{x}$. For a d-dimensional $\mathbf{x}$, d measurements are thus sufficient. Without loss of generality, let $\mathcal{M}$ be $\{(\mathbf{a}_i, b_i)\}_{i=1}^{d}$. To estimate $\mathbf{x}$ from $\mathcal{M}$, the LS technique is invoked: the following minimal linear system is first constructed

$$\mathbf{A}_{\mathcal{M}} = \begin{bmatrix} \mathbf{a}_1^T \\ \vdots \\ \mathbf{a}_d^T \end{bmatrix}, \quad \mathbf{b}_{\mathcal{M}} = \begin{bmatrix} b_1 \\ \vdots \\ b_d \end{bmatrix}, \tag{2.6}$$

then take $\mathbf{x} = \mathbf{A}_{\mathcal{M}}^{-1} \mathbf{b}_{\mathcal{M}}$ (for numerical stability, the Singular Value Decomposition or SVD is preferable over a direct matrix inversion [Björck, 1996, Chapter 1]). Since $\mathcal{M}$ contains only d measurements, the LS fitting error on $\mathcal{M}$ is zero.

To determine the number of hypotheses to generate, let η be the proportion of inliers in $\mathcal{D}$. If $\mathcal{M}$ is sampled randomly from $\mathcal{D}$, then the probability that $\mathcal{M}$ contains all inliers is η^d; conversely, the probability that $\mathcal{M}$ contains at least one outlier is $(1 - \eta^d)$. If T minimal subsets $\mathcal{M}$ are sampled, the probability that none of them contains all inliers is thus

$$\left(1 - \eta^d\right)^T. \tag{2.7}$$

To determine T such that, with confidence γ, at least one of the T minimal subsets contain only inliers, equate $1 - \gamma = (1 - \eta^d)^T$ and solve for

$$T = \left\lceil \frac{\log(1 - \gamma)}{\log(1 - \eta^d)} \right\rceil. \tag{2.8}$$

Figure 2.1 illustrates how T changes with the outlier rate $\xi = (1 - \eta)$ and d for a fixed $\gamma = 0.99$. In particular, observe that T grows exponentially with ξ, indicating that the runtime of RANSAC can be considerable for highly contaminated data.

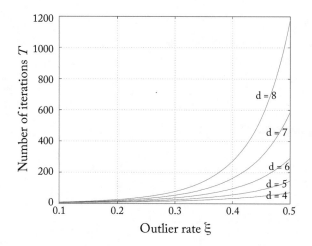

Figure 2.1: Number T of minimal subsets to generate in RANSAC such that, with confidence $\gamma = 0.99$, at least one minimal subset contains all inliers; see (2.8).

Of course, in practical settings, the proportion of inliers η is *a priori* unknown. Hartley and Zisserman [2004] (see Section 4.7.1 in their book) proposed to incrementally update η and T based on the largest consensus set found thus far. This version of RANSAC is summarized in Algorithm 2.3 (page 24). Figure 2.2 shows an application of this algorithm on an instance of the line-fitting problem.

RANSAC is a randomized algorithm; thus, apart from the possibility of giving different results in different runs, it does not provide guarantees of optimality. Though it can provide good estimates in practice, generally it is unknown how large the quantitative difference can be between the obtained results and the optimal result. Therefore when a low-quality estimate is obtained, without further assessing the data, it is impossible to tell if there are no high-quality estimates to be found, or RANSAC simply had a "bad run."

Minimal Subset Fitting for Nonlinear Models

Apart from the obvious change of linear parameters $\mathbf{x}$ to nonlinear parameters ω, the main challenge in extending Algorithm 2.3 to robustly estimate nonlinear models is to devise a minimal subset fitting procedure for the model of interest. In general, a method analogous to LS fitting for the particular model is used as the minimal solver. The exact procedure, however, depends closely on the particular nonlinear model.

Algorithm 2.3 Basic RANSAC algorithm.

Require: Data $\mathcal{D} = \{(\mathbf{a}_i, b_i)\}_{i=1}^N$, inlier threshold ϵ, and confidence level γ.

1: $\hat{\psi} \leftarrow 0, \hat{\mathbf{x}} \leftarrow NULL, t \leftarrow 0, T \leftarrow \infty$.
2: **loop**
3:    $t \leftarrow t + 1$.
4:    $\mathcal{M} \leftarrow$ Sample a minimal subset from $\mathcal{D}$.
5:    $\mathbf{x} \leftarrow$ Minimal estimate from $\mathcal{M}$.
6:    **if** $\Psi(\mathbf{x}) > \hat{\psi}$ **then**
7:       $\hat{\psi} \leftarrow \Psi(\mathbf{x}), \hat{\mathbf{x}} \leftarrow \mathbf{x}$.
8:       $\eta \leftarrow \hat{\psi}/N$.
9:       $T \leftarrow \lceil \log(1 - \gamma)/\log(1 - \eta^d) \rceil$.
10:   **end if**
11:   **if** $t \geq T$ **then**
12:      Break.
13:   **end if**
14: **end loop**
15: **return** $\hat{\mathbf{x}}$.

A widely used approach for minimal subset fitting on nonlinear models is *direct linear transformation (DLT)* [Gander et al., 1994, Zhang, 1997]. The equation defining the nonlinear model is re-expressed as a homogeneous equation that is linear in the parameters. Given a minimal subset $\mathcal{M}$, a minimal system of homogeneous linear equations is constructed and solved using singular value decomposition (SVD).

Example 2.1 (Minimal estimate for homography)   Denoting $\mathbf{p}' = f(\mathbf{p} \mid \mathbf{H})$, the homographic warp (1.13) can be expressed succinctly in homogeneous coordinates as

$$\tilde{\mathbf{p}}' \cong \mathbf{H}\tilde{\mathbf{p}}, \tag{2.9}$$

where "$\cong$" means "equal up to scale." Taking the cross product with $\tilde{\mathbf{p}}'$ on both sides, we obtain

$$\mathbf{0}_{3\times 1} = \tilde{\mathbf{p}}' \times \mathbf{H}\tilde{\mathbf{p}}. \tag{2.10}$$

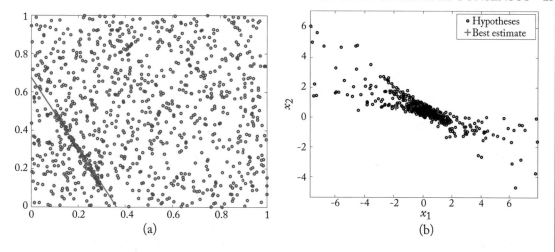

Figure 2.2: (a) An application of Algorithm 2.3 (RANSAC) on a line-fitting problem with $N = 1000$ points and 90% outliers ($\eta = 0.1$). By setting confidence $\gamma = 0.99$, a total of 498 hypotheses were generated in this particular run before terminating in a matter of seconds. (b) A plot of a subset of the hypotheses generated in parameter space $\mathbf{x} = [x_1, x_2]^T \in \mathbb{R}^2$.

Defining $\mathbf{h}$ now as the homogeneous 9-vector obtained by vectorising $\mathbf{H}$ with a column-first raster scan, the equation above can be re-expressed linearly with respect to $\mathbf{h}$ as

$$
\mathbf{0}_{3\times1} = \begin{bmatrix} \mathbf{0}_{1\times3} & -\tilde{\mathbf{p}}^T & y'\tilde{\mathbf{p}}^T \\ \tilde{\mathbf{p}}^T & \mathbf{0}_{1\times3} & -x'\tilde{\mathbf{p}}^T \\ -y'\tilde{\mathbf{p}}^T & x'\tilde{\mathbf{p}}^T & \mathbf{0}_{1\times3} \end{bmatrix} \mathbf{h} \quad \equiv \quad \mathbf{0}_{3\times1} = \mathbf{C}\mathbf{h}, \tag{2.11}
$$

where $\mathbf{p} = [x, y]^T$ and $\mathbf{p}' = [x', y']^T$, and $\mathbf{C} \in \mathbb{R}^{3\times9}$ is a matrix of coefficients. Since only two of the rows of $\mathbf{C}$ are linearly independent, an equivalent condition is

$$
\mathbf{0}_{2\times1} = \mathbf{C}^{(1:2)}\mathbf{h}, \tag{2.12}
$$

where $\mathbf{C}^{(1:2)} \in \mathbb{R}^{2\times9}$ is the first two rows of $\mathbf{C}$.

Since $\mathbf{h}$ is scale-invariant, it has only eight degrees of freedom. From (2.12), a correspondence $(\mathbf{p}, \mathbf{p}')$ provides two equations to constrain $\mathbf{h}$. Thus, a minimum of four correspondences are sufficient to estimate $\mathbf{h}$ uniquely. Given a minimal subset $\mathcal{M} = \{(\mathbf{p}_i, \mathbf{p}_i')\}_{i=1}^4$, we construct the 8×9 design matrix

$$\mathbf{A}_{\mathcal{M}} = \begin{bmatrix} \mathbf{C}_1^{(1:2)} \\ \vdots \\ \mathbf{C}_4^{(1:2)} \end{bmatrix}, \qquad (2.13)$$

where each $\mathbf{C}_i^{(1:2)}$ is the first two rows of matrix $\mathbf{C}_i$ computed according to (2.11) for correspondence $(\mathbf{p}_i, \mathbf{p}_i')$. We aim to find $\mathbf{h}$ such that the sum of squared algebraic errors

$$\sum_{i=1}^{4} \|\mathbf{C}_i^{(1:2)}\mathbf{h}\|_2^2 = \|\mathbf{A}_{\mathcal{M}}\mathbf{h}\|_2^2 \qquad (2.14)$$

is minimized. Discounting the trivial solution $\mathbf{h} = \mathbf{0}$, the optimal value for $\mathbf{h}$ is the kernel (right null space) of $\mathbf{A}_{\mathcal{M}}$. In practice, this is obtained as the least significant right singular vector of $\mathbf{A}_{\mathcal{M}}$. Note that if $\mathbf{A}_{\mathcal{M}}$ is full rank (i.e., rank 8), which is guaranteed if the correspondences $\mathcal{M}$ are in general position, $\mathbf{A}_{\mathcal{M}}$ has nullity 1. ∎

Figure 2.3 illustrates the result of applying Algorithm 2.3 with DLT as the minimal solver to robustly fit a homography on the point correspondences in Figure 1.2. RANSAC with DLT as the minimal solver has been used extensively in computer vision, in particular, in various multiple view geometry problems [Hartley and Zisserman, 2004, Chapter 4]. Not all nonlinear models, however, can be converted as easily as in Example 2.1 into homogeneous linear equations, since the parameter space Ω may have further constraints that complicate linearization. Thus custom-made procedures are sometimes used, such as the five-point method for essential matrix estimation [Nister, 2004], the seven-point method for fundamental matrix estimation (Section 11.1.2 in Hartley and Zisserman [2004]), the quaternion method for rotation estimation [Horn, 1987], and the SVD method for rigid transformation estimation [Arun et al., 1987, Eggert et al., 1997]. A fruitful research direction is the construction of generic minimal solvers [Kukelova et al., 2008, 2012] for highly complex models, such as various projective models under radial distortion.

2.2.1   EXTENSIONS AND IMPROVEMENTS

Owing to the simplicity and versatility of the hypothesize-and-test paradigm, many variants have been proposed for RANSAC. Major developments are as follows.

- Local refinement: One can attempt to refine an approximate solution $\hat{\mathbf{x}}$ in the hope of improving it to become a better solution. This can be achieved by embedding in the main algorithm an "inner RANSAC loop" [Chum et al., 2003, Lebeda et al., 2012], which is invoked whenever $\hat{\mathbf{x}}$ is updated in the main algorithm. Instead of sampling minimal subsets from the overall input data $\mathcal{D}$, the inner RANSAC loop samples larger-than-minimal

Figure 2.3: Applying RANSAC with an inlier threshold of $\epsilon = 3$ pixels for robust homography fitting on the data in Figure 1.2, where there are a total of 70 feature matches. RANSAC found a consensus set with 47 inlying feature matches (plotted in green) in a matter of seconds. Observe that most of the data identified as outliers (plotted in red) do correspond to incorrect matches.

subsets from the consensus set $\mathcal{I}(\hat{\mathbf{x}})$ of $\hat{\mathbf{x}}$. The rationale is that if a higher-quality solution $\hat{\hat{\mathbf{x}}}$ exists near $\hat{\mathbf{x}}$, then $\mathcal{I}(\hat{\mathbf{x}})$ shares many common data with $\mathcal{I}(\hat{\hat{\mathbf{x}}})$, thus sampling from $\mathcal{I}(\hat{\mathbf{x}})$ tends to increase the consensus of $\hat{\mathbf{x}}$.

- Guided sampling: In applications where there is additional information or domain knowledge that can be used to specify inlier priors, the sampling in RANSAC can be biased or guided using the prior confidence values to speed up retrieval of good minimal subsets. In two-view geometry problems, local feature matching scores have been fruitfully exploited to construct such inlier confidence values [Chum and Matas, 2005, Tordoff and Murray, 2005]. In applications where it is valid to assume that the inliers are spatially close, the selection of data can be biased by proximity [Kanazawa and Kawakami, 2004, Myatt et al., 2002].

  Subsequent guided sampling methods estimate the sampling confidence values progressively based on current fitting results [Chen and Lerman, 2009, Chin et al., 2012], thereby obviating the need for additional domain knowledge. Chin et al. [2012] also pointed out that in problems with multiple model instances, using domain knowledge such as local feature matching scores as proxies for inlier confidence values is inappropriate, since inliers from different model instances behave as outliers to each other, and thus should not be selected into the same minimal subsets.

- Depth-first evaluation: A vast majority of the hypotheses generated by random sampling are unpromising, thus preferably one should not use the same effort to evaluate (i.e., calculate the consensus of) all hypotheses. Viewing the number of hypotheses generated as "depth" and the number of data $\mathcal{D}$ for which residual values must be computed as "breadth," a depth-first variant of RANSAC prioritizes depth over breadth. Given a set of hypotheses generated within a fixed time budget, Preemptive RANSAC [Nister, 2003] competitively filters out the bad hypotheses without attempting to calculate consensus values fully using all data. In optimal randomized RANSAC [Chum and Matas, 2008], a randomized technique based on sequential decision making that does not examine all data is used for hypothesis evaluation.

The above list is not exhaustive; consult surveys such as Choi et al. [2009], Matas [2011] and Raguram et al. [2013] for other improvement areas for RANSAC.

2.2.2   DATA SPAN AND QUASIDEGENERACY

A fundamental assumption in calculating the number of hypotheses required (2.8) is that any subset of d inliers can give a good estimate of the target structure. This assumption ignores the fact that, in the minimal case, the spatial extent or span of the data significantly influences the quality of the fitted hypothesis. Specifically, if the d inliers in a minimal subset $\mathcal{M}$ are spatially too close (i.e., has a small span), the corresponding hypothesis can be very distant from the desired estimate. Figure 2.4a illustrates this effect on the line-fitting problem. The practical consequence is that (2.8) is merely a (probabilistic) lower bound of the number of iterations required [Meer, 2004, Tran et al., 2014].

Related to the effect of data span is the problem of data degeneracy, whereby the inliers in $\mathcal{D}$ are numerically insufficient to estimate the model of interest. The issue of quasidegeneracy occurs when a large majority of the inliers lie on a dominant substructure, such that, under random sampling, most of the all-inlier minimal subsets retrieved will have insufficient span. Figure 2.4b illustrates this condition. In practical applications, quasidegeneracy happens, for example, in epipolar geometry estimation when the 3D scene contains a dominant planar structure [Chum et al., 2005, Frahm and Pollefeys, 2006]. Extra care must be taken when applying RANSAC on quasidegenerate data—either the number of iterations must be significantly raised [Scherer-Negenborn and Schaefer, 2010], or an additional step must be invoked to attempt to rectify degenerate model hypotheses.

It has been remarked that estimating a model from minimal subsets amplifies the inlier noise [Meer, 2004]. Tran et al. [2014] systematically analyzed the concept of data span in minimal subset fitting. Consider data $\mathcal{D} = \{(\mathbf{a}_i, b_i)\}_{i=1}^{N}$ that contains only inliers. The LS method estimates $\mathbf{x}$ by minimizing the sum of squared errors

$$\hat{\mathbf{x}} = \underset{\mathbf{x} \in \mathbb{R}^d}{\operatorname{argmin}} \sum_{i=1}^{N} \left(\mathbf{a}_i^T \mathbf{x} - b_i\right)^2. \tag{2.15}$$

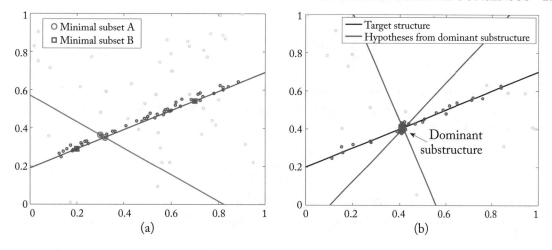

Figure 2.4: Illustrating the effects of data span and data degeneracy toward hypothesis generation from minimal subsets. (a) Not all minimal subsets that are composed purely of inliers give good estimates of the model. In particular, a minimal subset with a small span (e.g., minimal subset A in the figure) can lead to a model hypothesis that is arbitrarily far from the target estimate. (b) A quaside-generate line-fitting problem instance, where most of the inliers lie on a dominant substructure. If the minimal subsets are sampled randomly, most of the all-inlier minimal subsets will be retrieved from the dominant substructure.

Collecting the data according to

$$\mathbf{A} = \begin{bmatrix} \mathbf{a}_1^T \\ \vdots \\ \mathbf{a}_N^T \end{bmatrix}, \quad \mathbf{b} = \begin{bmatrix} b_1 \\ \vdots \\ b_N \end{bmatrix}, \tag{2.16}$$

Problem (2.15) can be expressed in matrix form as

$$\hat{\mathbf{x}} = \underset{\mathbf{x} \in \mathbb{R}^d}{\operatorname{argmin}} \left\| \mathbf{b} - \hat{\mathbf{b}} \right\|_2^2 \quad \text{s.t.} \quad \mathbf{A}\mathbf{x} = \hat{\mathbf{b}}, \tag{2.17}$$

where $\hat{\mathbf{b}}$ is the corrected version of $\mathbf{b}$. The LS solution can be obtained in closed form as

$$\hat{\mathbf{x}} = \left(\mathbf{A}^T \mathbf{A}\right)^{-1} \mathbf{A}^T \mathbf{b}. \tag{2.18}$$

A geometrical interpretation of the solution of LS is that $\mathbf{A}\hat{\mathbf{x}}$ is the orthogonal projection of $\mathbf{b}$ onto the column span of $\mathbf{A}$.

It turns out that the LS estimate $\hat{\mathbf{x}}$ can be written as a linear combination of minimal subset estimates [Jacobi, 1841]. To derive this, apply Cramer's rule on (2.18) to write the j-th value of

$\hat{\mathbf{x}}$ as

$$\hat{x}_j = \frac{|(\mathbf{A}^T\mathbf{A})_j|}{|\mathbf{A}^T\mathbf{A}|} = \frac{|\mathbf{A}^T\mathbf{A}_j|}{|\mathbf{A}^T\mathbf{A}|}, \tag{2.19}$$

where $|\cdot|$ calculates the determinant of a matrix. We define $(\mathbf{A}^T\mathbf{A})_j$ as $\mathbf{A}^T\mathbf{A}$ with its j-th column replaced by $\mathbf{A}^T\mathbf{b}$, and $\mathbf{A}_j$ as $\mathbf{A}$ with its j-th column replaced by $\mathbf{b}$. Via the Binet-Cauchy formula, we can expand (2.19) as

$$\hat{x}_j = \frac{\sum_\lambda |\mathbf{A}(\lambda)||\mathbf{A}_j(\lambda)|}{\sum_\lambda |\mathbf{A}(\lambda)||\mathbf{A}(\lambda)|}, \tag{2.20}$$

where λ indicates a combination of d integers from the set $\{1,\ldots,N\}$, and $\mathbf{A}(\lambda)$ and $\mathbf{A}_j(\lambda)$ are square matrices formed by the d rows of $\mathbf{A}$ and $\mathbf{A}_j$ indexed by λ. The summations in (2.20) are taken over all $\binom{N}{d}$ possibilities of λ.

Picking the rows of $\mathbf{A}$ and $\mathbf{b}$ according to a λ amounts to choosing a minimal subset, since d cases are sufficient to uniquely determine $\mathbf{x}$. The minimal estimate from λ is

$$\hat{\mathbf{x}}^{(\lambda)} = \mathbf{A}(\lambda)^{-1}\mathbf{b}(\lambda), \tag{2.21}$$

where $\mathbf{b}(\lambda)$ is the vector formed by the d rows of $\mathbf{b}$ indexed by λ. Via Cramer's rule again, the j-th value of $\hat{\mathbf{x}}^{(\lambda)}$ is

$$\hat{x}_j^{(\lambda)} = \frac{|\mathbf{A}_j(\lambda)|}{|\mathbf{A}(\lambda)|}. \tag{2.22}$$

By substituting $|\mathbf{A}_j(\lambda)| = |\mathbf{A}(\lambda)|\,\hat{x}_j^{(\lambda)}$ in (2.20) we obtain

$$\hat{x}_j = \frac{\sum_\lambda |\mathbf{A}(\lambda)||\mathbf{A}(\lambda)|\hat{x}_j^{(\lambda)}}{\sum_\lambda |\mathbf{A}(\lambda)||\mathbf{A}(\lambda)|}, \tag{2.23}$$

or in vectorial form for the full parameter vector

$$\hat{\mathbf{x}} = \sum_\lambda w_\lambda \hat{\mathbf{x}}^{(\lambda)}, \quad w_\lambda = \frac{|\mathbf{A}(\lambda)|^2}{\sum_\lambda |\mathbf{A}(\lambda)|^2} \tag{2.24}$$

where $0 \le w_\lambda \le 1$ and $\sum_\lambda w_\lambda = 1$. As claimed, the LS estimate can be expressed as a (weighted) linear combination of minimal subset estimates.

Identity (2.24) provides an algebraic characterization to the notion of "span" in minimal subset fitting. To illustrate, consider line fitting again where we have

$$\mathbf{A} = \begin{bmatrix} p_1 & 1 \\ \vdots & \vdots \\ p_N & 1 \end{bmatrix}, \quad \mathbf{b} = \begin{bmatrix} q_1 \\ \vdots \\ q_N \end{bmatrix}. \tag{2.25}$$

The weight of $\hat{\mathbf{x}}^{(\lambda)}$ corresponding to a minimal subset $\lambda = \{s_1, s_2\}$ is proportional to

$$|\mathbf{A}(\lambda)|^2 = \left|\begin{bmatrix} p_{s_1} & 1 \\ p_{s_2} & 1 \end{bmatrix}\right|^2 = (p_{s_1} - p_{s_2})^2, \tag{2.26}$$

i.e., widely separated points provide better line estimates. More generally, $|\mathbf{A}(\lambda)|$ is the hypervolume of the parallelotope whose vertices are the rows of $\mathbf{A}(\lambda)$, a quantity that is closely related to the relative span of the data indexed by λ.

Tran et al. [2014] showed how a similar minimal subset expansion can be constructed for DLT (algebraic least squares). This is relevant for RANSAC with nonlinear models, where DLT is the primary minimal subset fitting technique. Tran et al. [2014] also proposed a minimal subset sampling algorithm that consciously targets minimal subsets with large spans; refer to their paper for more details.

2.3 ℓ_1 MINIMIZATION

We begin our exploration of deterministic approximate algorithms for maximum consensus. The objective of maximizing consensus can be equivalently restated as minimizing the number of outliers. With respect to the linear model (1.5), this can be formulated as

$$\begin{aligned} \underset{\mathbf{x} \in \mathbb{R}^d, \mathbf{s} \in \mathbb{R}^N}{\text{minimize}} \quad & \|\mathbf{s}\|_0 \\ \text{subject to} \quad & \left|\mathbf{a}_i^T \mathbf{x} - b_i\right| \le \epsilon + s_i, \\ & s_i \ge 0, \\ & i = 1, \dots, N, \end{aligned} \tag{2.27}$$

where $\mathbf{s} = [s_1, \dots, s_N]^T$ is a vector of nonnegative slack variables. The symbol $\|\cdot\|_0$ represents the ℓ_0 norm, where $\|\mathbf{s}\|_0$ is the number of elements in $\mathbf{s}$ that are non-zero.

Of course, converting consensus maximization to outlier count minimization does not make the solution any easier. Problem (2.27) can be drastically simplified, however, by replacing the ℓ_0 norm with the ℓ_1 norm

$$\begin{aligned} \underset{\mathbf{x} \in \mathbb{R}^d, \mathbf{s} \in \mathbb{R}^N}{\text{minimize}} \quad & \|\mathbf{s}\|_1 \\ \text{subject to} \quad & \left|\mathbf{a}_i^T \mathbf{x} - b_i\right| \le \epsilon + s_i, \\ & s_i \ge 0, \\ & i = 1, \dots, N, \end{aligned} \tag{2.28}$$

where $\|\cdot\|_1$ is defined as

$$\|\mathbf{s}\|_1 = |s_1| + \cdots + |s_N|. \tag{2.29}$$

Thus, instead of counting the number of non-zero slack variables, we sum the slack variables instead. Problem (2.28) is an LP, which can be solved efficiently using many existing algorithms [Boyd and Vandenberghe, 2004]. Note that each constraint of the form $\left|\mathbf{a}_i^T \mathbf{x} - b_i\right| \leq \epsilon + s_i$ can be implemented using the two linear constraints

$$
\begin{aligned}
\mathbf{a}_i^T \mathbf{x} - b_i &\leq \epsilon + s_i, \\
-\left(\mathbf{a}_i^T \mathbf{x} - b_i\right) &\leq \epsilon + s_i,
\end{aligned}
\tag{2.30}
$$

where s_i "connects" the two constraints relating to the same datum $(\mathbf{a}_i, b_i)$.

Figure 2.5 illustrates an application of the ℓ_1 approximate technique on a line-fitting problem. On a data instance with approximately 9% outliers, the ℓ_1 solution is close to the desired result and the RANSAC estimate. Figure 2.6 shows the result on a data instance with a much higher level of outlier contamination (67%); on this instance, the ℓ_1 method produces a biased estimate. This suggests that the ℓ_1 minimization technique for approximate maximum consensus should be used only on problem instances with low outlier contamination levels.

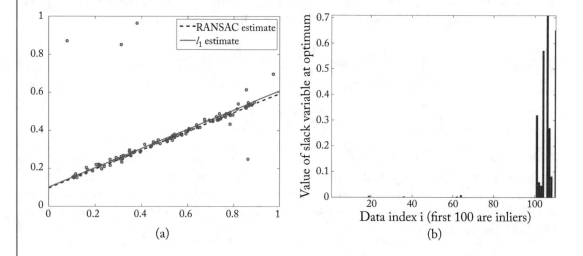

(a)   (b)

Figure 2.5: ℓ_1 minimization for approximate maximum consensus on a line fitting problem. Panel (a) shows the ℓ_1 and RANSAC solutions on a data instance with 100 inliers and 10 outliers ($\approx$ 9% outliers). Both estimates are very similar. Panel (b) shows the values of the slack variables $\mathbf{s}$ at the optimum of (2.28). Observe that the slack variables for the inliers have generally much lower values than the slack variables for the outliers.

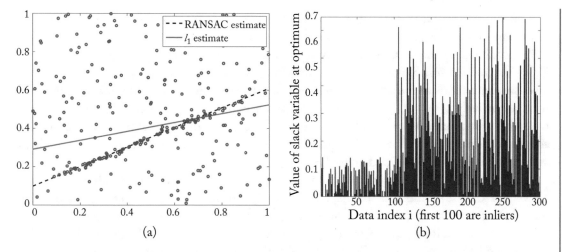

(a)   (b)

Figure 2.6: ℓ_1 minimization for approximate maximum consensus on a line-fitting problem. Panel (a) shows the results on a data instance with 100 inliers and 200 outliers ($\approx 67\%$ outliers). Observe that the ℓ_1 estimate has been biased by the outliers. In contrast, the RANSAC solution is still close to the desired result. In panel (b), a plot of the optimized slack variables $\mathbf{s}$ shows that the inliers have non-negligible slack values.

Relation to Least Absolute Deviations

In contrast to the LS method (2.15), which minimizes the sum of squared errors, the LAD method minimizes the sum of absolute errors

$$\hat{\mathbf{x}} = \arg\min_{\mathbf{x}} \sum_{i=1}^{N} \left| \mathbf{a}_i^T \mathbf{x} - b_i \right|. \tag{2.31}$$

For this reason, the LAD method is also called the *sum of infeasibilities* method. The optimization problem can be re-expressed in matrix form as

$$\hat{\mathbf{x}} = \operatorname*{argmin}_{\mathbf{x} \in \mathbb{R}^d} \left\| \mathbf{b} - \hat{\mathbf{b}} \right\|_1 \quad \text{s.t.} \quad \mathbf{A}\mathbf{x} = \hat{\mathbf{b}}. \tag{2.32}$$

Problem (2.31) can also be formulated and solved as an LP [Wagner, 1959]:

$$\begin{aligned}
\operatorname*{minimize}_{\mathbf{x} \in \mathbb{R}^d, \mathbf{s} \in \mathbb{R}^N} \quad & \|\mathbf{s}\|_1 \\
\text{subject to} \quad & \left| \mathbf{a}_i^T \mathbf{x} - b_i \right| \leq s_i, \\
& s_i \geq 0, \\
& i = 1, \ldots, N.
\end{aligned} \tag{2.33}$$

Comparing (2.33) and (2.28), LAD and the ℓ_1 approximate method for maximum consensus differ only in the allowance of the additional slack ϵ in the latter case.

Traditionally, the LAD estimator is regarded as a robust estimator [Bloomfield and Steiger, 1980]. In contrast to LS, which amplifies the effect of outliers by squaring the residuals, LAD gives smaller weights to the larger outlying residuals. Interpreting LS and LAD as M-estimators with respectively $\rho(r) = r^2/2$ and $\rho(r) = |r|$ (see Section 1.2.2), Figures 2.7a and 2.7b show the weight function $w(r) = \rho'(r)/r$ as defined in (1.22) for both estimators. Observe that LS assigns equal weights to all residuals, regardless of their magnitude. In contrast, larger residuals are progressively down-weighted under LAD.

Figure 2.8a compares the LAD estimate with the maximum consensus estimate obtained by RANSAC. The solutions are comparable in quality. However, as the outlier rate is increased, the LAD estimate becomes biased by the outliers; see Figure 2.8b. This behavior is consistent with the characteristic of the ℓ_1 approximate maximum consensus method (2.28). A reason behind this observation is that, although LAD down-weights the larger residuals due to the outliers, it does not completely discount them. Contrast this to Tukey's biweight (1.21), whose weight function is plotted in Figure 2.7c—only data with a residual less than the threshold is allowed to influence the result.

2.3.1   GENERALIZED FRACTIONAL MODELS

Generalizing the ℓ_1 formulation (2.27) for approximate maximum consensus to nonlinear models is a matter of changing the optimization domain and residual function; that is,

$$
\begin{aligned}
&\underset{\omega \in \Omega, \mathbf{s} \in \mathbb{R}^N}{\text{minimize}} && \|\mathbf{s}\|_1 \\
&\text{subject to} && r_i(\omega) \leq \epsilon + s_i, \\
&&& s_i \geq 0, \\
&&& i = 1, \ldots, N.
\end{aligned}
\tag{2.34}
$$

This creates a nonlinear constrained optimization problem, which has no efficient exact solutions in general, unless there are special properties in $r(\omega)$ that can be exploited.

One such nonlinear residual function, which is frequently encountered in geometric problems in computer vision, and whose form can be fruitfully exploited for efficient optimization, is the *generalized fractional* residual function

$$
r(\mathbf{x}) = \frac{\|\mathbf{A}\mathbf{x} + \mathbf{b}\|_2}{\alpha^T \mathbf{x} + \beta}.
\tag{2.35}
$$

Here, $\mathbf{x} \in \mathbb{R}^d$ is the parameter vector, and $\mathbf{A} \in \mathbb{R}^{2 \times d}$, $\mathbf{b} \in \mathbb{R}^2$, $\alpha \in \mathbb{R}^d$ and $\beta \in \mathbb{R}^1$ are constants that are derived from the input measurements. As can be expected, strict positivity must be imposed on the denominator

$$
\alpha^T \mathbf{x} + \beta > 0
\tag{2.36}
$$

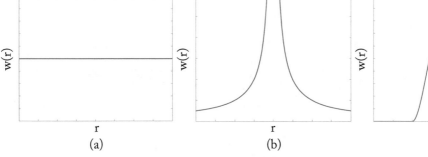

Figure 2.7: Weight function for M-estimator (1.20) corresponding to: (a) least squares, (b) LAD, and (c) Tukey's biweight.

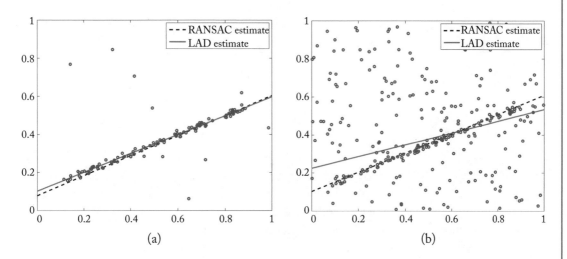

Figure 2.8: Comparing LAD to approximate maximum consensus via RANSAC. On the data in panel (a), where there is a low outlier rate, the LAD estimate is close to the RANSAC estimate. In panel (b), where there is a high outlier rate, the LAD estimate has clearly been biased by the large number of outliers.

to ensure that the residual is defined and positive. The following describes several examples of computer vision problems with generalized fractional residuals. More examples are described in Kahl and Hartley [2008] and Olsson et al. [2007].

Example 2.2   (Triangulation)   The residual function for triangulation (1.16) can be re-expressed as

$$r_i(\mathbf{x}) = \left\| \frac{\mathbf{P}_i^{(1:2)}\tilde{\mathbf{x}}}{\mathbf{P}_i^{(3)}\tilde{\mathbf{x}}} - \mathbf{p}_i \right\|_2 = \frac{\left\| \left[\mathbf{P}_i^{(1:2)} - \mathbf{p}_i \mathbf{P}_i^{(3)} \right] \begin{bmatrix} \mathbf{x} \\ 1 \end{bmatrix} \right\|_2}{\mathbf{P}_i^{(3)} \begin{bmatrix} \mathbf{x} \\ 1 \end{bmatrix}}, \tag{2.37}$$

which has the form (2.35). The condition for the denominator to be strictly positive; that is, $\mathbf{P}_i^{(3)}\tilde{\mathbf{x}} > 0$, naturally corresponds to constraining $\mathbf{x}$ to lie in front of the camera.

Example 2.3   (Homography fitting)   The residual function for homography fitting (1.14) can be re-expressed as

$$r_i(\mathbf{H}) = \left\| \frac{\mathbf{H}^{(1:2)}\tilde{\mathbf{p}}_i}{\mathbf{H}^{(3)}\tilde{\mathbf{p}}_i} - \mathbf{p}_i' \right\|_2 = \frac{\left\| \begin{bmatrix} \tilde{\mathbf{p}}_i^T & \mathbf{0}_{1\times 3} & -\mathbf{p}_{i,1}'\tilde{\mathbf{p}}_i^T \\ \mathbf{0}_{1\times 3} & \tilde{\mathbf{p}}_i^T & -\mathbf{p}_{i,2}'\tilde{\mathbf{p}}_i^T \end{bmatrix} \mathbf{h} \right\|_2}{\begin{bmatrix} \mathbf{0}_{1\times 6} & \tilde{\mathbf{p}}_i^T \end{bmatrix} \mathbf{h}}, \tag{2.38}$$

where $\mathbf{h}$ is the vector obtained by a column-first raster scan of matrix $\mathbf{H}$, and $\mathbf{p}_{i,j}'$ is the j-th element of $\mathbf{p}_i'$. To enable $\mathbf{h}$ to be estimated as a inhomogeneous quantity, Kahl and Hartley [2008] proposed to fix the final element of $\mathbf{h}$ to 1. Taking $\mathbf{h} = [\mathbf{x}^T, 1]^T$ where $\mathbf{x} \in \mathbb{R}^8$ is the remaining unknown, the residual function is modified to become

$$r_i(\mathbf{x}) = \frac{\left\| \begin{bmatrix} \tilde{\mathbf{p}}_i^T & \mathbf{0}_{1\times 3} & -\mathbf{p}_{i,1}'\tilde{\mathbf{p}}_i^T \\ \mathbf{0}_{1\times 3} & \tilde{\mathbf{p}}_i^T & -\mathbf{p}_{i,2}'\tilde{\mathbf{p}}_i^T \end{bmatrix} \begin{bmatrix} \mathbf{x} \\ 1 \end{bmatrix} \right\|_2}{\begin{bmatrix} \mathbf{0}_{1\times 6} & \tilde{\mathbf{p}}_i^T \end{bmatrix} \begin{bmatrix} \mathbf{x} \\ 1 \end{bmatrix}}. \tag{2.39}$$

Clearly (2.39) has the form (2.35).

Estimating $\mathbf{h}$ as the inhomogeneous vector $\mathbf{x}$, however, precludes solutions where the final element of $\mathbf{h}$ is zero. Kahl and Hartley [2008] proposed a preprocessing method for the data $\mathcal{D} = \{(\mathbf{p}_i, \mathbf{p}_i')\}_{i=1}^N$ that prevents such solutions from occurring. Further, to justify the strict positivity constraint on the denominator

$$\begin{bmatrix} \mathbf{0}_{1\times 6} & \tilde{\mathbf{p}}_i^T \end{bmatrix} [\mathbf{x}^T \ 1]^T > 0, \tag{2.40}$$

they appealed to the cheirality condition for 2D homographies to show that a solution $\mathbf{h}$ that satisfies such a condition always exists [Kahl and Hartley, 2008, Section 5.3].

A special case of the generalized fractional model is one where the denominator in (2.35) evaluates to a constant. This leaves the ℓ_2-norm in the numerator, which is a convex function of $\mathbf{x}$, as the residual function. The following is an example.

Example 2.4   (Affine registration) The residual function for affine registration (1.12) can be re-expressed as

$$r_i(\mathbf{\Lambda}) = \|\mathbf{\Lambda}\tilde{\mathbf{p}}_i - \mathbf{p}_i\|_2 = \left\| \begin{bmatrix} \tilde{\mathbf{p}}_i^T & \mathbf{0}_{1\times 3} \\ \mathbf{0}_{1\times 3} & \tilde{\mathbf{p}}_i^T \end{bmatrix} \mathbf{\lambda} - \mathbf{p}_i' \right\|_2, \tag{2.41}$$

where $\mathbf{\lambda} \in \mathbb{R}^6$ is the vector obtained by a column-first raster scan of matrix $\mathbf{\Lambda}$. Clearly (2.41) has the form (2.35), where $\mathbf{\alpha}$ is equivalent to the zero vector and $\beta = 1$.

Of primary interest here is solving maximum consensus with generalized fractional residuals. In such a problem, the data is given in the form $\mathcal{D} = \{(\mathbf{A}_i, \mathbf{b}_i, \mathbf{\alpha}_i, \beta_i)\}_{i=1}^N$, where each tuple $(\mathbf{A}_i, \mathbf{b}_i, \mathbf{\alpha}_i, \beta_i)$ are constants calculated from the measurements corresponding to the i-th "datum" (e.g., in triangulation, a datum consists of a camera matrix $\mathbf{P}_i$ and point measurement $\mathbf{p}_i$). The ℓ_1 approximate technique is formulated as

$$\begin{aligned} \underset{\mathbf{x}\in\mathbb{R}^d, \mathbf{s}\in\mathbb{R}^N}{\text{minimize}} \quad & \|\mathbf{s}\|_1 \\ \text{subject to} \quad & \frac{\|\mathbf{A}_i\mathbf{x} + \mathbf{b}_i\|_2}{\mathbf{\alpha}_i^T\mathbf{x} + \beta_i} \le \epsilon + s_i, \\ & \mathbf{\alpha}_i^T\mathbf{x} + \beta_i > 0, \\ & s_i \ge 0, \\ & i = 1, \dots, N; \end{aligned} \tag{2.42}$$

note the additional constraints $\mathbf{\alpha}_i^T\mathbf{x} + \beta_i > 0$ to ensure validity of the residual.

Observe that for nonnegative ϵ's, the two constraints

$$\frac{\|\mathbf{A}\mathbf{x} + \mathbf{b}\|_2}{\mathbf{\alpha}^T\mathbf{x} + \beta} \le \epsilon, \quad \mathbf{\alpha}^T\mathbf{x} + \beta > 0 \tag{2.43}$$

are equivalent to the *second-order cone* constraint [Boyd and Vandenberghe, 2004, Chap. 4]

$$\|\mathbf{A}\mathbf{x} + \mathbf{b}\|_2 \le \epsilon \left(\mathbf{\alpha}^T\mathbf{x} + \beta\right). \tag{2.44}$$

Problem (2.42) can thus be re-expressed as

$$
\begin{aligned}
\underset{\mathbf{x}\in\mathbb{R}^d,\mathbf{s}\in\mathbb{R}^N}{\text{minimize}} \quad & \|\mathbf{s}\|_1 \\
\text{subject to} \quad & \|\mathbf{A}_i\mathbf{x} + \mathbf{b}_i\|_2 \le \epsilon\left(\boldsymbol{\alpha}_i^T\mathbf{x} + \beta_i\right) + s_i, \\
& s_i \ge 0, \\
& i = 1, \dots, N,
\end{aligned}
\tag{2.45}
$$

which is a *second-order cone program (SOCP)*. Similar to LP, SOCP is convex and there exist efficient solvers for the problem [Boyd and Vandenberghe, 2004].

Figure 2.9 illustrates the result of solving (2.45) to robustly estimate an affine transformation from the input correspondences in Figure 1.2. In this instance, using the same inlier threshold ϵ as in the RANSAC run in Figure 2.3, the SOCP converged to a solution with a consensus of 24. There are two main reasons for the much lower value relative to the consensus of 47 in Figure 2.3: the usage of a transformation model with lower degrees of freedom (6 in an affinity compared with 8 in a homography), and the poor accuracy of the ℓ_1 technique in approximating the maximum consensus solution; cf. Figure 2.6.

Figure 2.9: ℓ_1 approximation of the maximum consensus affine transformation obtained by solving (2.45). With inlier threshold $\epsilon = 3$ pixels, the second-order cone program solution has a consensus of 24.

Using the same input data and inlier threshold, Figure 2.10 shows the result of robustly estimating a homography by (2.45). A much worse solution with a consensus of only 3 was obtained for this instance. This further demonstrates the significant degradation that can occur when a highly nonconvex problem is replaced by a convex substitute.

2.4   CHEBYSHEV APPROXIMATION

We have seen in the beginning of Section 2.3 that ℓ_0 minimization of the excess residuals (i.e., the slack values) is equivalent to consensus maximization, but this is nontrivial to solve. Section 2.3

Figure 2.10: ℓ_1 approximation of the maximum consensus homography obtained by solving (2.45). With inlier threshold $\epsilon = 3$ pixels, the second-order cone program solution has a consensus of 3.

further shows that changing the ℓ_0-norm to ℓ_1-norm yields a drastically simpler problem, but may not give satisfactory estimates. One may rightly ask about the potential of other ℓ_p-norms ($p = 2, 3, \ldots$), but this quickly leads to the realization that increasing p simply raises the non-robustness of the estimate (e.g., $p = 2$ is just LS. See also Section 2.3 on interpreting ℓ_1 as an M-estimator).

Nonetheless, the ℓ_∞-norm—which is maximally non-robust since it effectively fits the outliers—turns out to be quite useful. In essence, this portrays the chicken-and-egg nature of robust fitting: if we knew the outliers, we could easily solve the fitting; conversely, if we knew the fit, we could easily find the outliers. This section explores the fundamental characteristics of ℓ_∞ *minimization* (which leads to so-called *Chebyshev approximation*) and its usage for approximate maximum consensus.

Given data $\mathcal{D} = \{(\mathbf{a}_i, b_i)\}_{i=1}^N$, the Chebyshev approximation technique for the linear model $b = \mathbf{a}^T\mathbf{x}$ obtains $\mathbf{x}$ as the solution to the *minimax* problem

$$\hat{\mathbf{x}} = \operatorname*{argmin}_{\mathbf{x} \in \mathbb{R}^d} \max_i \left| \mathbf{a}_i^T \mathbf{x} - b_i \right|. \tag{2.46}$$

The above problem can be re-expressed in matrix form as

$$\hat{\mathbf{x}} = \operatorname*{argmin}_{\mathbf{x} \in \mathbb{R}^d} \left\| \mathbf{b} - \hat{\mathbf{b}} \right\|_\infty \quad \text{s.t.} \quad \mathbf{A}\mathbf{x} = \hat{\mathbf{b}}, \tag{2.47}$$

where $\| \cdot \|_\infty$ denotes the ℓ_∞ norm. For a vector $\mathbf{v}$ of length N,

$$\|\mathbf{v}\|_\infty = \max(|v_1|, \ldots, |v_N|). \tag{2.48}$$

For this reason, the minimax problem (2.46) is also called the ℓ_∞ minimization problem. In the rest of this book, we may use the terms Chebyshev estimate, minimax estimate and ℓ_∞ estimate interchangeably. The minimax problem can also be formulated as an LP:

$$\begin{aligned}
&\underset{\mathbf{x} \in \mathbb{R}^d, s \in \mathbb{R}}{\text{minimize}} && s \\
&\text{subject to} && \left| \mathbf{a}_i^T \mathbf{x} - b_i \right| \leq s, \\
& && i = 1, \ldots, N, \\
& && s \geq 0,
\end{aligned} \tag{2.49}$$

where in contrast to LAD (2.33), only a single slack variable is involved. The optimized $\hat{s}$ corresponds to the minimized maximum residual; thus, in the rest of this book, we may refer to $\hat{s}$ as the *minimax value*.

However, as alluded to above, the Chebyshev estimator is inherently non-robust because it effectively fits the model onto the most outlying data. Figure 2.11 illustrates the application of the Chebyshev estimator on a line-fitting problem. The optimized line has clearly been biased by the outliers. In particular, observe that the result seems to have been influenced by three points that equally attained the largest residual with respect to the line.

Although it may seem that the Chebyshev approximation is a complete opposite to robust estimation, the fact that the method is easily biased by outliers can actually be exploited to solve maximum consensus. Before we embark on describing the method in Section 2.4.2, we first analyze the properties of the Chebyshev estimate—in particular, is there always a subset of the data that simultaneously attain the largest residual at the optimum?

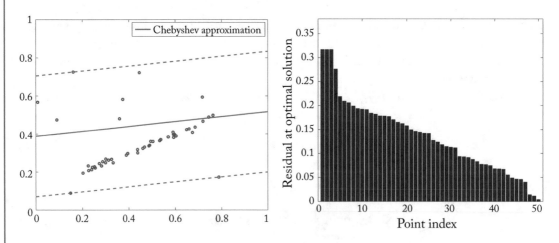

Figure 2.11: Chebyshev approximation (2.46) on line fitting with outliers. In conjunction with the Chebyshev estimate, the dashed lines indicate the optimized minimax residual value. The bar chart on the right shows the sorted residuals at the optimal solution.

2.4.1   CHARACTERIZATION OF THE CHEBYSHEV ESTIMATE

To develop intuition, let us first consider Chebyshev approximation for the simplest case—one-dimensional ($d = 1$) linear model $ax = b$. Given a set of points $\mathcal{D} = \{(a_i, b_i)\}_{i=1}^N$, the corresponding minimax problem is

$$\hat{x} = \underset{x \in \mathbb{R}}{\operatorname{argmin}} \ \max_i \ |a_i x - b_i|. \tag{2.50}$$

Figure 2.12a illustrates the Chebyshev fit on a sample $\mathcal{D}$. Note that the line represented by $a\hat{x} = b$ passes through the origin, in contrast to the line-fitting result, for example, Figure 2.11.

Figure 2.12b illustrates the residual functions $|a_i x - b_i|$ arising from a $\mathcal{D}$, plotted against x. Highlighted in red is the point-wise maximum $\max_i |a_i x - b_i|$ over all the residuals, which is also the objective function in (2.50). Note that the objective function is convex. Further, the minimum of the objective function is attained at the intersection of exactly two of the residual functions, which correspond to the two points which simultaneously attain the minimax residual $\hat{s}$ in Figure 2.12a. In the rest of this section, we attempt to establish this characteristic for the general case $d \geq 1$.

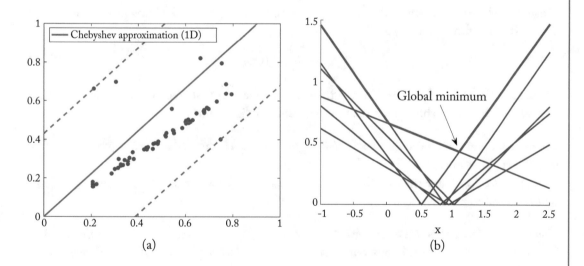

(a)   (b)

Figure 2.12: (a) Chebyshev approximation for the 1D linear relation $ax = b$ on a set of points $\mathcal{D} = \{(a_i, b_i)\}_{i=1}^N$. The equation $ax = b$ defines a line that passes through the origin. The dashed lines indicate the optimized minimax residual value. (b) Illustrating the Chebyshev fit in the parameter space $x \in \mathbb{R}$. Here, each V-shaped curve in blue represents a residual function $|a_i x - b_i|$. The red curve indicates the objective function $\max_i |a_i x - b_i|$.

Consider a problem slightly different than (2.46), whereby given data $\Delta = \{(\alpha_j, \beta_j)\}_{j=1}^M$, solve for

$$\hat{\mathbf{x}} = \operatorname*{argmin}_{\mathbf{x} \in \mathbb{R}^d} \max_j \alpha_j^T \mathbf{x} - \beta_j. \tag{2.51}$$

For general Δ, the problem may not be bounded from below. However, if the input Δ is obtained by "doubling" the data $\mathcal{D}$ in (2.46) in the following manner,

$$(\alpha_i, \beta_i) = (\mathbf{a}_i, b_i), \quad (\alpha_{N+i}, \beta_{N+i}) = (-\mathbf{a}_i, -b_i), \tag{2.52}$$

then Problem (2.51) is always lower bounded by zero. Intuitively, this is because for any pair of hyperplanes $\mathbf{a}_i^T \mathbf{x} - b_i$ and $-\mathbf{a}_i^T \mathbf{x} + b_i$,

$$\min_{\mathbf{x} \in \mathbb{R}^d} \max \left(\mathbf{a}_i^T \mathbf{x} - b_i, -\mathbf{a}_i^T \mathbf{x} + b_i \right) \geq 0, \tag{2.53}$$

thus the minimum of the maximum over N pairs is also bounded below by zero. The following theorem further justifies analyzing (2.46) based on (2.51).

Theorem 2.5 $\hat{\mathbf{x}}$ *is the solution to* (2.46) *if and only if it is the solution to* (2.51), *given that the input Δ to the latter is obtained from the input $\mathcal{D}$ to the former according to* (2.52).

Section A in the Appendix states the proof of the above theorem. Henceforth, we will only consider Problem (2.51) where the data Δ is obtained from $\mathcal{D}$ by the doubling procedure defined above. The cost function of (2.51) is

$$\delta(\mathbf{x}) = \max_j r_j(\mathbf{x}), \tag{2.54}$$

where $r_j(\mathbf{x}) = \alpha_j^T \mathbf{x} - \beta_j$. The following theorem provides the first step in establishing the characteristic of the Chebyshev approximation problem highlighted in Figure 2.11.

Theorem 2.6   *A point $\hat{\mathbf{x}}$ is a minimizer of $\delta(\mathbf{x})$ if and only if the origin $\mathbf{0}$ lies in the convex hull of the set $\{\alpha_k \mid r_k(\hat{\mathbf{x}}) = \delta(\hat{\mathbf{x}})\}$.*

See Section B for the proof of the above theorem. A basic result from convex geometry that is central to the analysis in this section is as follows.

Theorem 2.7   (Carathéodory).   *A point $\mathbf{x} \in \mathbb{R}^d$ lies in the convex hull of a discrete point set $\mathcal{A} \subset \mathbb{R}^d$, if and only if $\mathbf{x}$ can be expressed as a convex linear combination of at most $(d+1)$ elements of $\mathcal{A}$.*

The preceding two theorems provide the foundations to answer the question posed at the end of Section 2.4, viz.:

Theorem 2.8   *If $\hat{\mathbf{x}}$ is a minimizer of*

$$\delta(\mathbf{x}) = \max_{j=1,\dots,M} r_j(\mathbf{x}) \tag{2.55}$$

for input $\Delta = \{(\boldsymbol{\alpha}_j, \beta_j)\}_{j=1}^M$, *then* $\hat{\mathbf{x}}$ *is also the minimizer of*

$$\max_{j \in \mathcal{J}} r_j(\mathbf{x}), \tag{2.56}$$

where $\mathcal{J}$ *indexes a subset of* Δ *of size at most* $(d + 1)$. *Further, the data subset indexed by* $\mathcal{J}$ *simultaneously attain the largest residual with respect to* $\hat{\mathbf{x}}$.

Proof. Let $\mathcal{K} = \{k \mid r_k(\hat{\mathbf{x}}) = \delta(\hat{\mathbf{x}})\}$. By Theorem 2.6, the origin lies in the convex hull of $\{\boldsymbol{\alpha}_k \mid k \in \mathcal{K}\}$. If $|\mathcal{K}| \leq d + 1$, then set $\mathcal{J} = \mathcal{K}$. Otherwise, by Carathéodory's theorem, there is a subset of at most $(d + 1)$ points from $\{\boldsymbol{\alpha}_k \mid k \in \mathcal{K}\}$ such that the origin lies in the convex hull of that subset; then set $\mathcal{J}$ as the index of that subset. By Theorem 2.6, $\hat{\mathbf{x}}$ is also the minimizer of the problem $\max_{j \in \mathcal{J}} r_j(\mathbf{x})$. $\qquad\square$

The previous theorem can then be further extended to cover our target problem (2.46).

Theorem 2.9   *Every solution* $\hat{\mathbf{x}}$ *to the minimax problem* (2.46) *with input* $\mathcal{D} = \{(\mathbf{a}_i, b_i)\}_{i=1}^N$ *is also a solution of the same problem on a subset of* $\mathcal{D}$ *of size at most* $(d + 1)$. *Further, the data in this subset simultaneously attain the largest residual with respect to* $\hat{\mathbf{x}}$.

We refer the reader to Section 2.3 in Cheney [1966] for details of the extension. Looking at Chebyshev approximation for line fitting again, where $d = 2$, Theorem 2.9 predicts that at most three points will simultaneously attain the minimax residual $\hat{s}$. The example in Figure 2.11 corresponds to the case where exactly three attain $\hat{s}$.

2.4.2   OUTLIER REMOVAL WITH ℓ_∞ MINIMIZATION

The observation that the Chebyshev estimator effectively fits the model onto outliers allows us to construct an algorithm for maximum consensus. First, note that the minimax value

$$\min_{\mathbf{x}} \max_{i \in \mathcal{I}} \left| \mathbf{a}_i^T \mathbf{x} - b_i \right| \tag{2.57}$$

for any consensus set $\mathcal{I}$ is less than or equal to the inlier threshold ϵ. An algorithm for maximum consensus based on Chebyshev estimation can be constructed as follows: recursively solve the ℓ_∞ problem (2.49) and remove the data whose residuals equal the minimax value; stop the recursion when the minimax value is not greater than ϵ. From (2.57), the remaining data is guaranteed to be consistent up to ϵ with the Chebyshev estimate $\hat{\mathbf{x}}$. Algorithm 2.4 summarizes this straightforward procedure, where we define $\mathcal{D}(\mathcal{K})$ as the subset of $\mathcal{D}$ indexed by integer subset $\mathcal{K} \subseteq \{1, \ldots, N\}$.

Figure 2.13 illustrates the application of Algorithm 2.4 to line fitting. In this instance, evidently the method is able to find a decent (approximate) maximum consensus solution. A fundamental weakness of this technique, however, is that it implicitly assumes that the structure of interest lies centrally in the spatial extent of the data. Figure 2.14 shows the result of Algorithm 2.4 on a line-fitting problem where the data is unbalanced. Since the outliers are recursively removed

---

Algorithm 2.4 Outlier removal with ℓ_∞ minimization for approximate maximum consensus.

Require: Data $\mathcal{D} = \{(\mathbf{a}_i, b_i)\}_{i=1}^{N}$ and inlier threshold ϵ.

1: **while** true **do**
2:    $(\hat{\mathbf{x}}, \hat{s}) \leftarrow$ Solution of the ℓ_∞ minimization problem (2.49) on $\mathcal{D}$.
3:    **if** $\hat{s} \leq \epsilon$ **then**
4:        Break.
5:    **else**
6:        $N \leftarrow$ Number of data in $\mathcal{D}$.
7:        $\mathcal{K} \leftarrow \{i \mid i \in \{1, \ldots, N\}, |\mathbf{a}_i^T \hat{\mathbf{x}} - b_i| = \hat{s}\}$.
8:        $\mathcal{D} \leftarrow \mathcal{D} \setminus \mathcal{D}(\mathcal{K})$.
9:    **end if**
10: **end while**
11: **return** $\hat{\mathbf{x}}$.

---

starting from the fringes of the data, a large number of inliers are removed before a consensus set is found. This leads to a bad suboptimal solution.

A more fundamental question is the nature of the data that are removed by a scheme such as Algorithm 2.4—specifically, are the data removed at each iteration guaranteed to contain outliers, and in what proportion? Section 2.5.3 discusses these issues.

2.4.3   GENERALISED FRACTIONAL PROGRAMMING

The outlier removal approach (Algorithm 2.4) can be extended to nonlinear models by defining the analogous Chebyshev approximation for the model of interest. This section shows that efficient Chebyshev approximation is possible for generalized fractional models, previously encountered in Section 2.3.1. The corresponding ℓ_∞ minimization problem is

$$
\begin{aligned}
&\underset{\mathbf{x} \in \mathbb{R}^d}{\text{minimize}} \quad \max_i \frac{\|\mathbf{A}_i \mathbf{x} + \mathbf{b}_i\|_2}{\boldsymbol{\alpha}_i^T \mathbf{x} + \beta_i} \\
&\text{subject to} \quad \boldsymbol{\alpha}_i^T \mathbf{x} + \beta_i > 0, \\
&\qquad\qquad\quad i = 1, \ldots, N.
\end{aligned}
\tag{2.58}
$$

Problems of the form above have been studied extensively in economics and operations research under the banner of *generalized fractional programming (GFP)* [Crouzeix and Ferland, 1991]. Well-developed algorithms thus exist for the problem [Agarwal et al., 2008, Olsson et al., 2007], and the basic technique of bisection is described below.

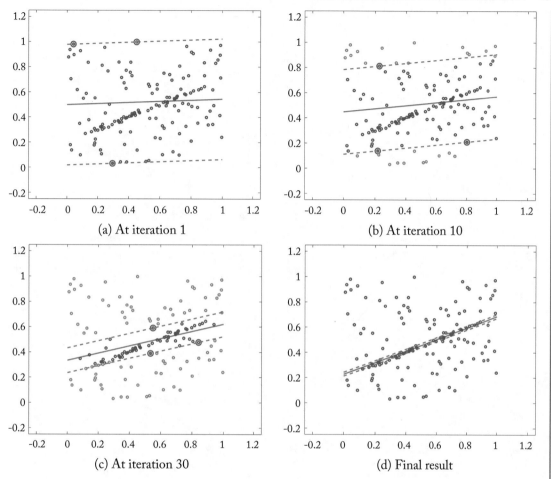

(a) At iteration 1   (b) At iteration 10

(c) At iteration 30   (d) Final result

Figure 2.13: Demonstration of outlier removal with ℓ_∞ minimization (Algorithm 2.4) on a line-fitting problem. Since $d = 2$ for line fitting, at most three points are removed at each iteration.

Bisection

Rewriting (2.58) using a single slack variable yields

$$
\begin{aligned}
& \underset{\mathbf{x}\in\mathbb{R}^d, s\in\mathbb{R}}{\text{minimize}} && s \\
& \text{subject to} && \frac{\|\mathbf{A}_i\mathbf{x} + \mathbf{b}_i\|_2}{\boldsymbol{\alpha}_i^T\mathbf{x} + \beta_i} \leq s, \\
& && \boldsymbol{\alpha}_i^T\mathbf{x} + \beta_i > 0, \\
& && i = 1, \ldots, N, \\
& && s \geq 0.
\end{aligned}
\tag{2.59}
$$

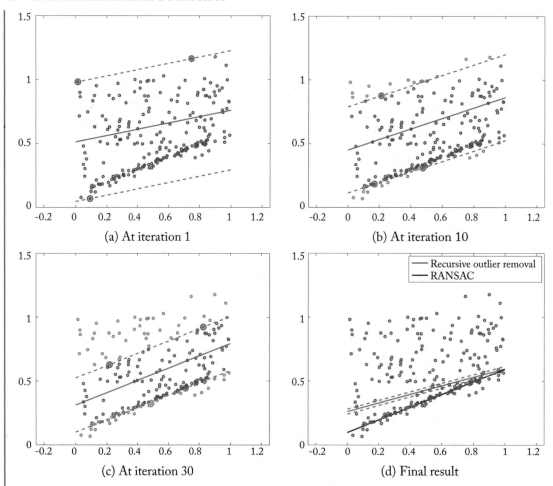

(a) At iteration 1

(b) At iteration 10

(c) At iteration 30

(d) Final result

Figure 2.14: Applying the ℓ_∞ minimization technique for outlier removal (Algorithm 2.4) on a line-fitting problem with unbalanced data, i.e., the structure of interest does not lie centrally in the spatial extent of the data. In such data, the ℓ_∞ technique tends to remove a significant amount of inliers before finding a consensus set. Thus, the maximum consensus solution found is far from ideal. Contrast this with the RANSAC solution, which is much more acceptable.

Applying the thresholding argument (2.43) on the nonnegative slack s, the above problem can expressed equivalently as

$$
\begin{aligned}
& \underset{\mathbf{x}\in\mathbb{R}^d, s\in\mathbb{R}}{\text{minimize}} && s \\
& \text{subject to} && \|\mathbf{A}_i\mathbf{x} + \mathbf{b}_i\|_2 \leq s(\boldsymbol{\alpha}_i^T\mathbf{x} + \beta_i), \\
& && i = 1,\dots,N, \\
& && s \geq 0.
\end{aligned}
\tag{2.60}
$$

Unfortunately, since variable s is multiplied with the other unknowns, the constraints do not define second-order cones, thus (2.60) cannot be solved by convex programming.

The good news is, however, that given s, which must be positive, checking whether all the constraints in (2.60) hold can be achieved efficiently. Specifically, if s is a constant, we can set up the following *convex feasibility test*:

$$
\begin{aligned}
\text{find} \quad & \mathbf{x} \in \mathbb{R}^d \\
\text{such that} \quad & \|\mathbf{A}_i\mathbf{x} + \mathbf{b}_i\|_2 \leq s\left(\boldsymbol{\alpha}_i^T\mathbf{x} + \beta_i\right), \\
& i = 1, \ldots, N,
\end{aligned}
\tag{2.61}
$$

which can be solved using SOCP solvers since the constraints are all second order cones. If the test is successful, a feasible $\mathbf{x}$ is obtained; else, an empty solution is returned.

Armed with an efficient feasibility test, the technique of bisection can be used to solve (2.60); see Algorithm 2.5. Basically, an initial range of $[s_l, s_h]$ is progressively tightened, until the range converges to the optimal value s, or the lower and upper limits are sufficiently close. At each iteration, the decision of which end of the range to revise is informed by the test (2.61) based on the mid-value of the range.

Algorithm 2.5 Bisection for ℓ_∞ minimization of generalized fractional residuals (2.60).

Require: Data $\mathcal{D} = \{(\mathbf{A}_i, \mathbf{b}_i, \boldsymbol{\alpha}_i, \beta_i)\}_{i=1}^N$, accuracy $\gamma \geq 0$.
 1: Initialize s_l to be 0 and s_h to be a large enough value.
 2: **while** $s_h - s_l > \gamma$ **do**
 3:    $s_m = 0.5(s_l + s_h)$.
 4:    $\mathbf{x} \leftarrow$ Solution for feasibility test (2.61) with $s = s_m$.
 5:    **if** $\mathbf{x}$ is non-empty **then**
 6:       $s_h = s_m$.
 7:    **else**
 8:       $s_l = s_m$.
 9:    **end if**
10: **end while**
11: **return** $\mathbf{x}, s_m$.

Algorithm 2.5 can thus be plugged into Algorithm 2.4 to enable approximate maximum consensus on generalized fractional models. Figure 2.15 depicts the result of Algorithm 2.4 on such a problem. As alluded to previously, beyond bisection, other algorithms exist for GFPs. Agarwal et al. [2008] compared several techniques in the context of geometric vision problems. Olsson et al. [2007] also showed that the generalized fractional residual is in fact *pseudoconvex*, which permits the usage of iterative gradient-based minimization to globally solve (2.58). Any of these methods can be used in conjunction with Algorithm 2.4.

Figure 2.15: Result of Algorithm 2.4 with the bisection solver (Algorithm 2.5) for robust homography estimation. The inlier threshold ϵ was set to 3 pixels (same as in Figure 2.3). In this instance, Algorithm 2.4 converged to a consensus set of size 27.

Quasiconvexity

It turns out that the generalized fractional residual function

$$r(\mathbf{x}) = \frac{\|\mathbf{Ax} + \mathbf{b}\|_2}{\boldsymbol{\alpha}^T\mathbf{x} + \beta} \tag{2.62}$$

is *quasiconvex* in the range $\boldsymbol{\alpha}^T\mathbf{x} + \beta > 0$. A function $r : \mathbb{R}^d \mapsto \mathbb{R}_+$ is quasiconvex if every s-sublevel set of r is a convex set [Boyd and Vandenberghe, 2004, Section 3.4]. In more detail, the s-sublevel set of a function r is the set

$$\mathcal{L}_s^r = \left\{ \mathbf{x} \in \mathbb{R}^d \mid r(\mathbf{x}) \leq s \right\}. \tag{2.63}$$

Intuitively, this is simply the region in the domain $\mathbb{R}^d$ where $r(\mathbf{x})$ takes a value that is less than or equal to s. Quasiconvexity is a relaxation of convexity, in that every convex function is quasiconvex, but not all quasiconvex functions are convex. Figure 2.16a depicts a quasiconvex function that is not convex. A nonquasiconvex (and hence, nonconvex) function is shown in Figure 2.16b for comparison.

Quasiconvexity has in fact played a direct part in making the feasibility test (2.61) a tractable problem. First, the point-wise maximum of a set of quasiconvex functions; that is, the objective function in (2.58), is also quasiconvex; see Figure 2.17 for an illustration. Thus, the s-sublevel set of the objective function is convex. This sublevel set is precisely the intersection of the N convex regions defined by the constraints in (2.61).

Comparing Figures 2.17 and 2.12b, it is unsurprising that the solution of (2.58) can also be obtained as the solution of the same problem on a small subset of the data. The following section further examines this aspect of Problem (2.58) from the perspective of LP-type problems.

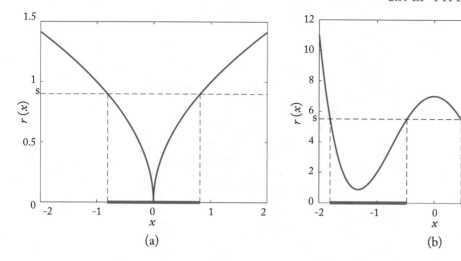

Figure 2.16: (a) A quasiconvex function $r(x)$ with the real line $\mathbb{R}$ as its domain. The s-sublevel set $\mathcal{L}^r_s$ is plotted as a red line segment on the x-axis. For any $s \geq 0$, $\mathcal{L}^r_s$ is a convex set (i.e., a contiguous line segment). Note that this function is not convex. (b) A nonquasiconvex function for comparison; in this function, not all $\mathcal{L}^r_s$ for $s \geq 0$ are convex.

2.5   LP-TYPE PROBLEMS

This slightly lengthier section explores consensus maximization under the framework of *LP-type problems*. The motivation for including this relatively abstract topic is two-fold.

- LP-type problems are a generalization of the Chebyshev approximation problem. As in Section 2.5.3, the LP-type framework allows further theoretical analysis of the outlier removal technique in Section 2.4.2.

- LP-type problems provide a unifying framework and convenient terminology to discuss a class of tractable exact algorithms in Chapter 3.

We begin by defining LP-type problems and describing their common properties.

2.5.1   DEFINITION AND PROPERTIES

LP-type problems were first defined by Matoušek et al. [1996] as a generalization of linear programming problems. In abstract terms, an LP-type problem $(\mathcal{S}, f)$ consists of a set of constraints $\mathcal{S}$, each involving d variables θ, and an objective function f that maps subsets of $\mathcal{S}$ to $\mathbb{R}_+ \cup \{0\}$. Further, f satisfies the following properties.

Property 2.10   (Monotonicity) For every two sets $\mathcal{P} \subseteq \mathcal{Q} \subseteq \mathcal{S}$, the inequalities $f(\mathcal{P}) \leq f(\mathcal{Q}) \leq f(\mathcal{S})$ can be established.

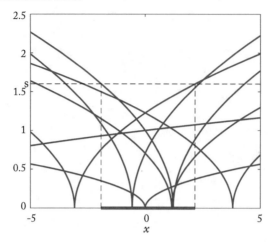

Figure 2.17: A set of quasiconvex functions (in blue) and their point-wise maximum (in red), which is also quasiconvex. Observe that the s-sublevel set for all $s \geq 0$ is a convex set.

Property 2.11 (Locality) For every two sets $\mathcal{P} \subseteq \mathcal{Q} \subseteq \mathcal{S}$ and for every $c \in \mathcal{S}$, if $f(\mathcal{P}) = f(\mathcal{Q}) = f(\mathcal{Q} \cup \{c\})$, then we can establish that $f(\mathcal{P} \cup \{c\}) = f(\mathcal{Q})$.

Define also $\theta(\mathcal{S})$ as the variables θ that extremize $f(\mathcal{S})$ for constraints $\mathcal{S}$. The goal of an LP-type problem is to "calculate" $f(\mathcal{S})$. In practice, this involves finding $\theta(\mathcal{S})$.

Interpreting linear programming as an LP-type problem, $\mathcal{S}$ is a set of half-spaces, and $f(\mathcal{S})$ is the minimum objective value of a linear function of the variables within the intersection of $\mathcal{S}$. The following example describes another classical LP-type problem.

Example 2.12 (Minimum enclosing circle) In MEC, we wish to find the smallest circle that encloses a given set of points $\{\mathbf{p}_i\}_{i=1}^{N}$ on the plane. Formally, MEC can be expressed as

$$\min_{\mathbf{x} \in \mathbb{R}^2} \ \max_{i} \ \|\mathbf{x} - \mathbf{p}_i\|_2, \tag{2.64}$$

where $\mathbf{x}$ is the center of the circle. Figure 2.18a shows the MEC on a set of points. Interpreting MEC as an LP-type problem, set $\mathcal{S}$ as $\{\mathbf{p}_i\}_{i=1}^{N}$ and $f(\mathcal{S})$ as the radius of the smallest circle that encloses $\mathcal{S}$. Further, $\theta(\mathcal{S})$ gives the center $\mathbf{x}^*$ of the MEC on $\mathcal{S}$.

In MEC, the properties of monotonicity and locality can be intuitively appreciated. First, if $\mathcal{P} \subseteq \mathcal{Q} \subseteq \mathcal{S}$, then the MEC($\mathcal{P}$) cannot be larger than the MEC($\mathcal{Q}$.) Also, if $\mathcal{P} \subseteq \mathcal{Q} \subseteq \mathcal{S}$ and $f(\mathcal{P}) = f(\mathcal{Q})$, then MEC($\mathcal{P}$) = MEC($\mathcal{Q}$). Therefore, if the MEC($\mathcal{Q}$) is not enlarged by inserting

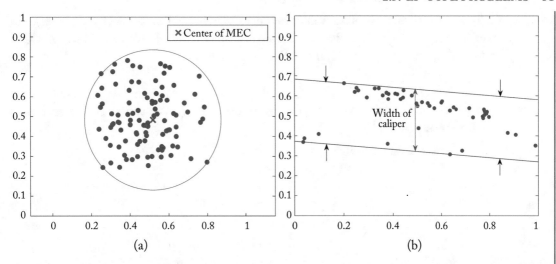

Figure 2.18: (a) Given a set of points on the plane, the goal of the minimum enclosing circle (MEC) is to find the smallest circle that encloses all the points. Observe that, in this example, exactly 3 of the input points lie on the MEC, i.e., are equidistant to the center of the MEC. (b) Interpreting Chebyshev approximation as the minimum width caliper (MWC) problem. The goal is to find a pair of parallel hyperplanes with the smallest width that encloses all the points, where the width of the hyperplane pair is the vertical distance between the hyperplanes.

a point $\mathbf{p}$ into $\mathcal{Q}$ (i.e., $\mathbf{p}$ is already contained within the MEC of $\mathcal{Q}$), then inserting $\mathbf{p}$ into $\mathcal{P}$ will also not enlarge MEC($\mathcal{P}$).

Chebyshev approximation can also be interpreted as an LP-type problem, following the construction in the following example.

Example 2.13   (Chebyshev approximation as an LP-type problem)   Following the notation in Section 2.4, set $\mathcal{S} = \{(\mathbf{a}_i, b_i)\}_{i=1}^{N}$ and $f(\mathcal{S})$ as the minimax value (optimized objective value of Problem 2.49) on $\mathcal{S}$. Then, $\theta(\mathcal{S})$ is the Chebyshev estimate $\hat{\mathbf{x}}$ on $\mathcal{S}$.

Useful geometric intuitions can be gained by interpreting Chebyshev approximation as the *minimum width caliper (MWC)* problem. The goal of MWC is to find a pair of parallel hyperplanes (the caliper) in $\mathbb{R}^{d+1}$ with the smallest width that encloses all the points $\mathcal{S}$. The width of the caliper is the vertical distance (distance along the b-axis) between the hyperplanes; see Figure 2.18b. By drawing analogy between MEC and MWC (i.e., radius of circle is equivalent to width of caliper; interior of circle is equivalent to the "slab" between the parallel hyperplanes), the properties of monotonicity and locality can be easily transferred and shown to hold for MWC.

The following concepts are integral to LP-type problems.

Definition 2.14 (Basis).   A basis of an LP-type problem $(\mathcal{S}, f)$ is a subset $\mathcal{B} \subseteq \mathcal{S}$ such that $f(\mathcal{A}) < f(\mathcal{B})$ for every $\mathcal{A} \subset \mathcal{B}$.

Figures 2.19 and 2.20 illustrate the concept of basis.

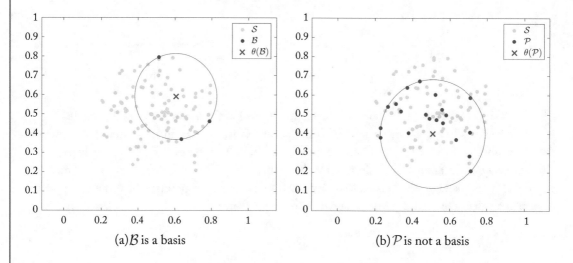

(a) $\mathcal{B}$ is a basis   (b) $\mathcal{P}$ is not a basis

Figure 2.19: Panel (a) shows a basis $\mathcal{B} \subseteq \mathcal{S}$ in the MEC problem. Any proper subset $\mathcal{A}$ of $\mathcal{B}$ will always have an MEC with a strictly smaller radius. Panel (b) shows a subset $\mathcal{P} \subseteq \mathcal{S}$ that is not basis. It is possible to find a proper subset $\mathcal{A}$ of $\mathcal{P}$ such that MEC($\mathcal{A}$) = MEC($\mathcal{P}$).

Definition 2.15 (Support set).   The support set $\mathcal{K}$ of an LP-type problem $(\mathcal{S}, f)$ is a basis of the problem such that $f(\mathcal{S}) = f(\mathcal{K})$. Solving $(\mathcal{S}, f)$ amounts to finding $\mathcal{K}$.

Intuitively, a support set $\mathcal{K}$ is a special type of basis that "holds up" the input constraint set $\mathcal{S}$, in the sense that removing all of $\mathcal{S}$ except $\mathcal{K}$ will still yield the same estimate. To illustrate, observe that there are three points that lie on the MEC of the point set in Figure 2.18a. Further, the MEC on these three points is the same circle. The three points are exactly the support set of the input points. The concept of support set in Chebyshev approximation has been explored in detail in Section 2.4.

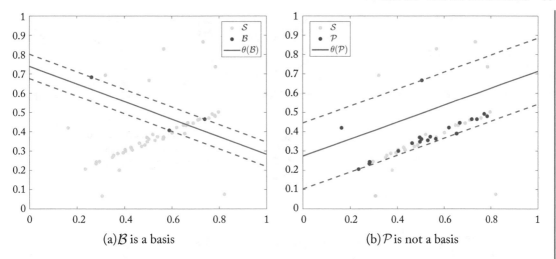

(a) $\mathcal{B}$ is a basis   (b) $\mathcal{P}$ is not a basis

Figure 2.20: Panel (a) shows a basis $\mathcal{B} \subseteq \mathcal{S}$ in Chebyshev approximation. Any proper subset $\mathcal{A}$ of $\mathcal{B}$ will always have a minimax value that is strictly smaller than the minimax value of $\mathcal{B}$. Panel (b) shows a subset $\mathcal{P} \subseteq \mathcal{S}$ that is not basis. It is possible to find a proper subset $\mathcal{A}$ of $\mathcal{P}$ that has the same minimax value (in fact, same Chebyshev estimate) as $\mathcal{P}$.

Quasiconvex Programming

It has been established that *quasiconvex programming*; that is, the problem of minimizing the maximum of a set of quasiconvex functions $r_i(\mathbf{x}), i = 1, \ldots, N$,

$$\min_{\mathbf{x} \in \mathbb{R}^d} \ \max_i \ r_i(\mathbf{x}) \tag{2.65}$$

is an LP-type problem [Amenta et al., 1999, Eppstein, 2005]. Note that Chebyshev approximation (2.46) and MEC (2.64) are subsumed under (2.65), since the corresponding residuals are convex, and hence also quasiconvex. GFP (2.58) is also a specific case of (2.65), hence intimately connecting LP-type problems to geometric estimation in computer vision. The following example interprets a computer vision problem as an LP-type problem.

Example 2.16 (ℓ_∞ **triangulation as an LP-type problem**)   Performing triangulation (Example 1.3) by Chebyshev approximation (2.58) implies minimizing the maximum reprojection error, where reprojection error is as defined in (2.37). This technique is also known as ℓ_∞ triangulation in the literature [Hartley and Schaffalitzky, 2004].

To interpret ℓ_∞ triangulation as an LP-type problem, set $\mathcal{S} = \{(\mathbf{p}_i, \mathbf{P}_i)\}_{i=1}^N$ as the input image measurement/camera matrix pairs, $f(\mathcal{S})$ as the minimized maximum reprojection error (minimax error) on $\mathcal{S}$, and $\theta(\mathcal{S})$ as the ℓ_∞ estimate $\hat{\mathbf{x}}$ from $\mathcal{S}$.

Figure 2.21 illustrates some of the properties of LP-type problems in ℓ_∞ triangulation.

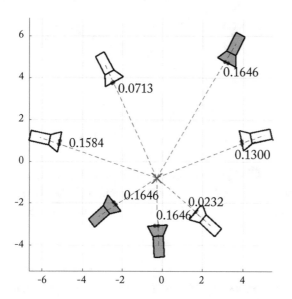

Figure 2.21: A 2D analogy of ℓ_∞ triangulation given an input of 7 noisy observations of a scene point viewed from 7 different cameras. Instead of image planes and 2D measurements, here we have "image lines" and 1D measurements. Similarly, the 2D analogies of the other quantities in the formulation (see Example 2.2) are used (e.g., 2×3 camera matrices). Above, the reprojection errors are simply the distances between the red and blue points, and the values displayed are the errors for each camera w.r.t. the Chebyshev estimate (red cross). The problem remains a GFP and the properties of LP-type problems hold. In particular, since $d = 2$ the combinatorial dimension is 3, and there are 3 views (shaded cameras) that simultaneously attain the minimax error, i.e., the support set.

Another important property of LP-type problems is as follows.

Definition 2.17   (Combinatorial dimension).   The combinatorial dimension of an LP-type problem $(\mathcal{S}, f)$ is the upper bound on the cardinality of its bases.

Amenta et al. [1999] showed that if $r_i(\mathbf{x})$ obeys the property that its ϵ-sublevel sets are *continuously shrinking*; that is, the convex region $r_i(\mathbf{x}) \le \epsilon$ strictly decreases with the reduction in ϵ (Sim and Hartley [2006] called this "strict quasiconvexity"), then the combinatorial dimension of (2.65) is $(d+1)$. Observe, therefore, that in MEC, the support set is at most of size three.

Section 2.4.1 has also established a similar result for Chebyshev approximation. Sim and Hartley [2006] also established the strict quasiconvexity of GFP. Note, therefore, on the 2D triangulation in Figure 2.21, three views attain the minimax error.

To give further illustration of the LP-type properties of quasiconvex programming, Example 2.18 introduces a variant of the triangulation problem.

Example 2.18 (Triangulation with orthogonal error) Following the setup in Example 1.3 for triangulation, but instead of using the reprojection error, we employ the *orthogonal projection error*

$$
\begin{aligned}
r_i(\mathbf{x}) &= \left\| (\mathbf{x} - \mathbf{c}_i) - \hat{\mathbf{p}}_i \hat{\mathbf{p}}_i^T (\mathbf{x} - \mathbf{c}_i) \right\|_2 \\
&= \left\| (\mathbf{I} - \hat{\mathbf{p}}_i \hat{\mathbf{p}}_i^T) \mathbf{x} + (\hat{\mathbf{p}}_i \hat{\mathbf{p}}_i^T - \mathbf{I}) \mathbf{c}_i \right\|_2 ,
\end{aligned}
\tag{2.66}
$$

where $\mathbf{c}_i$ is the coordinates of the camera center in world reference frame, and

$$
\hat{\mathbf{p}}_i = \frac{\mathbf{K}_i^{-1} \mathbf{p}_i}{\| \mathbf{K}_i^{-1} \mathbf{p}_i \|_2}
\tag{2.67}
$$

is the unit norm of the backprojected ray for measurement $\mathbf{p}_i$ using the intrinsic parameter matrix $\mathbf{K}_i \in \mathbb{R}^{3 \times 3}$ of the i-th camera. Intuitively, (2.66) is the distance of the shortest line that joins $\mathbf{x}$ with the ray $\mathbf{c}_i + \alpha \hat{\mathbf{p}}_i$, $\alpha \geq 0$ (the shortest line is the orthogonal projection of $\mathbf{x}$ onto the ray). The corresponding ℓ_∞ triangulation problem is to find $\mathbf{x}$ that minimizes the maximum $r_i(\mathbf{x})$ $\forall i$, i.e., Problem (2.65).

The main purpose of including the variant of triangulation in Example 2.18 is to illustrate its nature as an LP-type problem; observe that the residual function $r_i(\mathbf{x})$ is convex (and hence, quasiconvex). Figure 2.22 shows triangulation with orthogonal error using the data in Figure 2.21. Since in this 2D analogy, $d = 2$, there are 3 views that simultaneously attain the minimax error, i.e., the support set. Note that the estimate in Figure 2.22 differs from the one obtained using the reprojection error in Figure 2.21.

2.5.2 SOLVING LP-TYPE PROBLEMS

Algorithms for LP-type problems exploit the fact that if a new constraint c is added to the constraint set $\mathcal{P}$, either the solution does not change, or the new solution partially depends on c. A well-known method is by Matoušek et al. [1996], which is summarized in Algorithm 2.6. The algorithm is defined recursively, and is executed by inputting an initial basis $\mathcal{C}$. Intuitively, the algorithm recursively removes constraints from the input set $\mathcal{S}$, and then progressively updates the

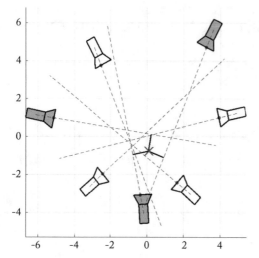

•	Image measurement
✕	Triangulated point
---	Backprojection of measurement

Figure 2.22: A 2D analogy of ℓ_∞ triangulation with orthogonal error (Example 2.18) using the input measurements/cameras in Figure 2.21. The support set is highlighted by shaded cameras, and the minimax error is indicated by the bolded lines around the estimate (red cross).

support set to cover all of $\mathcal{S}$. The output of the algorithm is the support set of the given LP-type problem.

Algorithm 2.6 Method to solve LP-type problem by Matoušek et al. [1996].

---

function solve_lptype($\mathcal{S}, f, \mathcal{C}$):

1: **if** $\mathcal{S} = \mathcal{C}$ **then**
2:     **return** $\mathcal{C}$.
3: **end if**
4: $c \leftarrow$ A random item from $\mathcal{S} \setminus \mathcal{C}$.
5: $\mathcal{B} \leftarrow$ solve_lptype($\mathcal{S} \setminus \{c\}, f, \mathcal{C}$).
6: **if** $f(\mathcal{B}) \neq f(\mathcal{B} \cup \{c\})$ **then**
7:     $\mathcal{B} \leftarrow$ basis($\mathcal{B} \cup \{c\}$).
8:     $\mathcal{B} \leftarrow$ solve_lptype($\mathcal{S}, f, \mathcal{B}$).
9: **end if**
10: **return** $\mathcal{B}$

Two problem-dependent subroutines are required: First, a violation test (Step 6), which checks whether a particular constraint c is satisfied by the solution $\theta(\mathcal{B})$ on the current support set $\mathcal{B}$. This can usually be done quite easily, e.g., for MEC, check if the point $c \in \{\mathbf{p}_i\}$ is within the MEC defined by the current support set $\mathcal{B}$, and for triangulation check if the measurement/camera pair $c \in \{(\mathbf{p}_i, \mathbf{P}_i)\}$ has a reprojection error w.r.t. the current estimate $\theta(\mathcal{B})$ that is lower then the minimax error $f(\mathcal{B})$. The second important subroutine in Algorithm 2.6 is a support set updating step (Step 7), which recalculates the support set $\mathcal{B}$ after including a new constraint c (more below).

Although algorithms for LP-type problems can also be used to solve linear programming, they are not practical for high-dimensional linear programs with many constraints. For such problems, dedicated LP solvers such as the simplex method should be used. For low-dimensional problems, Matoušek et al. [1996] showed that the expected runtime of Algorithm 2.6 is linear in N. To achieve this expected time, the core routine of support set updating must be performed efficiently. For linear constraints (e.g., in Chebyshev approximation), the update can be performed in polynomial time. See also the *feasible set algorithm* of Hawkins [1993], which is similar to Algorithm 2.6, but specialized for the robust fitting of linear models. For general problems within the LP-type framework, however, specialized basis updating routines must be designed.

To see what support set updating entails, we explore support set updating for MEC. In this problem, we need to recalculate the MEC on at most four points (since $|\mathcal{B}| \leq 3$). To do this efficiently, the following facts can be exploited.

- The size of a support set $\mathcal{B}$ can be two or three. In the former case, the two points lie diametrically opposite on the circle; see Figure 2.23a. The latter case has been illustrated in Figure 2.18a.

- If point c violates the current MEC, i.e., $f(\mathcal{B}) \neq f(\mathcal{B} \cup \{c\})$, then c must be in the support set of $\mathcal{B} \cup \{c\}$ [de Berg et al., 2008, Lemma 4.13]. See Figure 2.23b.

Thus, Step 7 in Algorithm 2.6 for MEC can be implemented by checking the combination of c with each point or each pair of points from $\mathcal{B}$. Of course, one cannot assume that the support set of $\mathcal{B} \cup \{c\}$ represents a circle that encloses all the points that are already contained within the circle defined by $\mathcal{B}$. Figure 2.23b provides a clear example of why the assumption is generally untrue. This is why in Step 8 in Algorithm 2.6, another recursive call is made to ensure that the support set is further updated. For higher dimensions d where one is interested in *minimum enclosing balls*, Gärtner [1992] showed that support set updating can be achieved in expected $e^{\mathcal{O}(\sqrt{d})}$ arithmetic operations.

As mentioned above, though support set updating routines can follow some general principles, to perform the updating efficiently, specialized routines should be constructed for specific problems. For example, see Li [2009b] for support set updating for ℓ_∞ triangulation.

2.5.3   OUTLIER REMOVAL FOR LP-TYPE PROBLEMS

In LP-type problems where the input constraint set $\mathcal{S}$ contains outliers, the desired value of $f(\mathcal{S})$ will be biased. Specifically, the outliers in $\mathcal{S}$ will drastically increase the value of $f(\mathcal{S})$. As an example, one may intend to solve MEC on a set of points to estimate the center of the point set.

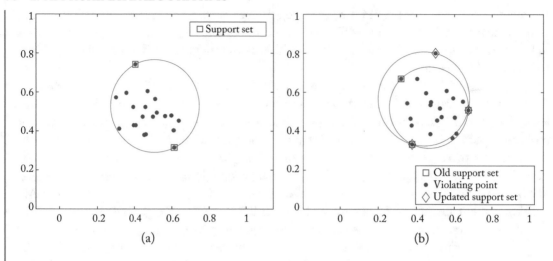

Figure 2.23: (a) MEC problem instance with a support set of size 2. (b) Illustrating Step 7 in Algorithm 2.6. The old support set (blue squares) is updated to become the new support set (red diamonds) after the inclusion of a violating point (red dot). Notice that the violating point must exist in the update support set.

However, if there are outliers, the MEC, and thus the center estimate, will be highly inaccurate. See Figure 2.24a for an illustration of the effects of outliers on MEC.

To obtain a robust solution, a maximum consensus approach can be envisaged where one does not attempt to satisfy all the constraints in $\mathcal{S}$, but only a subset therein. Further, the subset of constraints to obey must yield an f value that is not greater than a predetermined threshold. Formally, this approach is defined as

$$\begin{aligned} \underset{\mathcal{I} \subseteq \mathcal{S}}{\text{maximize}} \quad & |\mathcal{I}| \\ \text{subject to} \quad & f(\mathcal{I}) \le \epsilon, \end{aligned} \tag{2.68}$$

where ϵ is the usual inlier threshold. Figure 2.24a also illustrates the maximum consensus circle for a given ϵ value. An alternative interpretation of maximum consensus MEC is finding the center of a circle of radius ϵ that encloses as many points as possible.

As illustrated in Figure 2.24a, since the support set of an outlier-contaminated $\mathcal{S}$ will consist of outliers, it seems justified to recursively remove support sets until a consensus set is obtained. Algorithm 2.7 summarizes this approach, which is a direct extension of Algorithm 2.4 to the class of LP-type problems. To calculate $f(\mathcal{S})$ and obtain the support set $\mathcal{K}$, any algorithm for the corresponding problem (e.g., linear programming for Chebyshev approximation, bisection for GFP, or Matoušek et al. [1996]'s generic method for LP-type problems) can be applied as a subroutine.

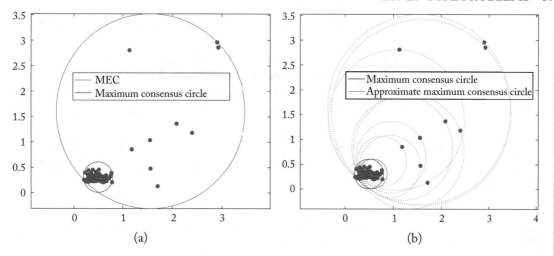

Figure 2.24: (a) If there are outliers, the center estimate of a point set obtained by solving MEC is severely biased; that is, the center of the MEC no longer provides a good estimate of centrality. One must thus estimate the center robustly via (2.68). The maximum consensus circle for $\epsilon = 0.3$ is also shown in the figure, where the consensus (i.e., number of points enclosed by the circle) is 51. The center of the maximum consensus circle gives a better center estimate. (b) The estimated MECs across the iterations of Algorithm 2.7 are shown using dotted lines. The algorithm converges to an approximate maximum consensus circle with consensus value of 47.

Algorithm 2.7 Outlier removal for approximate maximum consensus on LP-type problems.

Require: LP-type problem $(\mathcal{S}, f)$ and inlier threshold ϵ.
 1: **while** true **do**
 2:     $\mathcal{K} \leftarrow$ Support set of $(\mathcal{S}, f)$.
 3:     **if** $f(\mathcal{K}) > \epsilon$ **then**
 4:         $\mathcal{S} \leftarrow \mathcal{S} \setminus \mathcal{K}$.
 5:     **else**
 6:         Break.
 7:     **end if**
 8: **end while**
 9: **return** $\theta(\mathcal{S})$.

Figure 2.24b illustrates the application of Algorithm 2.7 to perform robust MEC (note the close analogy to robust line fitting in Figure 2.13). Figure 2.25 shows the operation of Algorithm 2.7 for robust triangulation with maximum consensus. In triangulation, outliers occur frequently in practice since the observations can be associated wrongly owing to incorrect feature matching. Lastly, the example in Figure 2.15 for robust homography fitting using ℓ_∞ outlier removal is also a special case of the application of Algorithm 2.7.

It is clear from the examples that, in the course of converging to an approximate maximum consensus solution, the algorithm also inadvertently removes inliers, thus leading to a suboptimal maximum consensus solution. Therefore, an important question is whether the algorithm guarantees that outliers are removed in each iteration, or if it is possible that only inliers are discarded.

Definition 2.19   (True inliers and true outliers).   Let $\mathcal{I}^*$ be the optimal solution to (2.68), and $\mathcal{O}^* = \mathcal{S} \setminus \mathcal{I}^*$. The data/constraints in $\mathcal{I}^*$ are the *true inliers*, and the data/constraints in $\mathcal{O}^*$ are the *true outliers*.

Theorem 2.20   *Let $\mathcal{B} \subseteq \mathcal{S}$ be a basis of the LP-type problem $(\mathcal{S}, f)$ with outliers, i.e., $f(\mathcal{S}) > \epsilon$. If $f(\mathcal{B}) > \epsilon$, then $\mathcal{B}$ contains at least one true outlier.*

Proof. If $f(\mathcal{B}) > \epsilon$, then by Property 2.10 (Monotonicity)

$$f(\mathcal{I}^* \cup \mathcal{B}) \geq f(\mathcal{B}) > \epsilon. \tag{2.69}$$

The above shows that the insertion of $\mathcal{B}$ into $\mathcal{I}^*$ causes the maximum consensus set to become inconsistent. Thus, $\mathcal{B}$ must contain at least one constraint that lies in $\mathcal{O}^*$. $\square$

Since the support set $\mathcal{K}$ of any subset $\mathcal{S}' \subseteq \mathcal{S}$ is also a basis of $\mathcal{S}$, then if $f(\mathcal{K}) > \epsilon$, $\mathcal{K}$ must contain at least one true outlier of $\mathcal{S}$, according to Theorem 2.20. Each iteration of Algorithm 2.7 is thus guaranteed to remove a true outlier.

Unfortunately, there is no easy way to tell which of the constraints in $\mathcal{K}$ are the true outliers. Furthermore, depending on the distribution of the data, the majority in $\mathcal{K}$ can be true inliers, and the recursive removal process may remove a significant proportion of true inliers before converging to a consensus set. If an insufficient amount of true inliers remains to define the target model estimate, the approximate maximum consensus estimate from Algorithm 2.7 can be vastly different from the desired result; see Figure 2.14.

In the context of quasiconvex problems where the combinatorial dimension is $(d + 1)$, if in the worst case there is exactly one true outlier in each removed $\mathcal{K}$, then the proportion of true inliers within the total data should ideally be greater than

$$\frac{d}{d + 1} \tag{2.70}$$

for there to be sufficient true inliers left after Algorithm 2.7 to define the desired estimate. Since the ratio (2.70) approaches 1 as d increases, we expect therefore that the outlier removal algorithm is more suited for low-dimensional problems, or problems with small outlier rates for moderate to large d's.

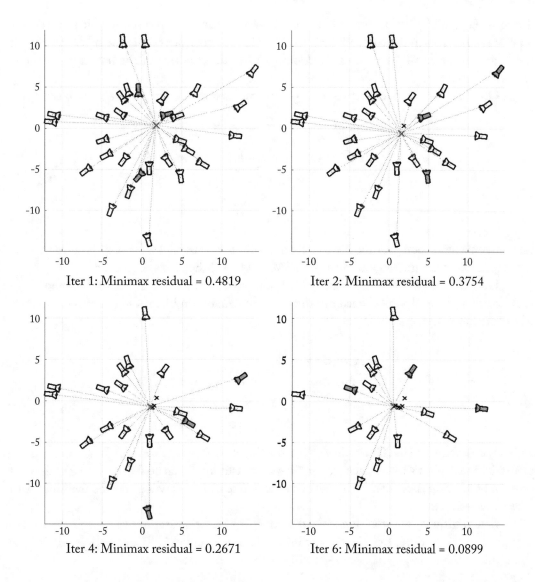

Iter 1: Minimax residual = 0.4819

Iter 2: Minimax residual = 0.3754

Iter 4: Minimax residual = 0.2671

Iter 6: Minimax residual = 0.0899

Figure 2.25: Robust triangulation by conducting outlier removal with Algorithm 2.7 using an inlier threshold of 0.1 "pixels" on the image line (see Figure 2.21). The input is a set of 30 outlier-contaminated observations of a scene point from 30 different views. The support set at each iteration is shown as shaded cameras, and the algorithm converged in 6 iterations.

2.6   THE K-SLACK METHOD

The ℓ_1 and ℓ_∞ minimization problems can be viewed as sitting at two extremes: the former counts all N slack variables in the cost function, whereas the latter considers only the slack variable with the largest value. These two settings overlook the fact that the size of the outlier population is almost always between 1 and N.

One way to moderate the two settings is to consider the K-largest slack variables:

$$\begin{aligned}
\underset{\mathbf{x}\in\mathbb{R}^d, \mathbf{s}\in\mathbb{R}^N}{\text{minimize}} \quad & \underset{\boldsymbol{\pi}\in\{0,1\}^N}{\max} \; \boldsymbol{\pi}^T\mathbf{s} \\
\text{subject to} \quad & \left|\mathbf{a}_i^T\mathbf{x} - b_i\right| \leq \epsilon + s_i, \\
& s_i \geq 0, \\
& i = 1,\ldots,N, \\
& \boldsymbol{\pi}^T\mathbf{1} = K.
\end{aligned} \tag{2.71}$$

The inner maximization over the binary vector $\boldsymbol{\pi}$ with the constraint $\boldsymbol{\pi}^T\mathbf{1} = K$ ensures that only the K-largest slack variables are considered. We call (2.71) the K-slack method.

Here, K is a user-determined constant that attempts to strike a balance between ℓ_1 and ℓ_∞. Clearly if $K = N$, (2.71) becomes the ℓ_1 minimization problem. On the other extreme, if $K = 1$, then (2.71) reduces to

$$\begin{aligned}
\underset{\mathbf{x}\in\mathbb{R}^d, \mathbf{s}\in\mathbb{R}^N}{\text{minimize}} \quad & \underset{i}{\max} \; s_i \\
\text{subject to} \quad & \left|\mathbf{a}_i^T\mathbf{x} - b_i\right| \leq \epsilon + s_i, \\
& s_i \geq 0, \\
& i = 1,\ldots,N,
\end{aligned} \tag{2.72}$$

which is very similar to the Chebyshev approximation problem (2.49), except for the introduction of an additional offset ϵ to the slack amount in each constraint. It can be shown that if the minimax value in (2.49) is greater than ϵ, the optimized estimate of (2.72) will in fact be the same as the Chebyshev estimate.

Before turning our attention toward solving (2.71), let us attempt to gain further insight into the K-slack method. Let $\hat{\mathbf{s}}$ be the optimized slack variables in (2.71), and $\hat{s}_{(K)}$ as the *smallest* entry among the K-largest values in $\hat{\mathbf{s}}$. Define the *potential outlier set* as

$$\mathcal{O} = \left\{i \in \{1,\ldots,N\} \mid \hat{s}_i \geq \hat{s}_{(K)}\right\}. \tag{2.73}$$

Figure 2.26 shows an application of the K-slack method for several K values on a line-fitting problem. Observe that for $K = 1$, exactly three points are in the active set, and as the K is increased, the size of the active set naturally also increases. Although none of the resulting estimates are close to the desired solution, note that for $K = 15$, however, which is close to the number of outliers in the data, most of the points in the active set correspond to outliers. Contrast this to

$K = 38$, where a significant number of inliers are included in the active set. The ability to control the number of outliers in the active set will be useful to construct an outlier removal scheme (Section 2.6.2).

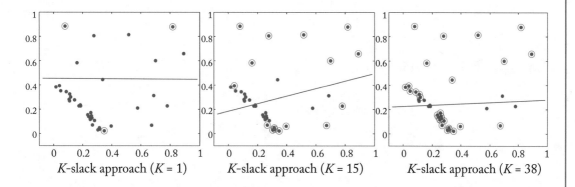

Figure 2.26: Applying the K-slack method (2.71) with $K \in \{1, 15, 38\}$ on a line-fitting problem with $N = 45$ points. The circled points denote the potential outlier sets for each K setting.

2.6.1   A RELAXED MINIMAX FORMULATION

Problem (2.71) seems to be difficult to solve owing to the presence of the discrete constraint on $\boldsymbol{\pi}$. Fortunately, the linearity of (2.71) in $\boldsymbol{\pi}$ allows us to relax the constraint $\boldsymbol{\pi} \in \{0, 1\}^N$ to $\boldsymbol{\pi} \in [0, 1]^N$ without changing the optimal objective value. First, for completeness, the relaxed problem is

$$
\begin{aligned}
\underset{\mathbf{x} \in \mathbb{R}^d, \mathbf{s} \in \mathbb{R}^N}{\text{minimize}} \quad & \max_{\boldsymbol{\pi} \in [0,1]^N} \boldsymbol{\pi}^T \mathbf{s} \\
\text{subject to} \quad & \left| \mathbf{a}_i^T \mathbf{x} - b_i \right| \leq \epsilon + s_i, \\
& s_i \geq 0, \\
& i = 1, \dots, N, \\
& \boldsymbol{\pi}^T \mathbf{1} = K.
\end{aligned}
\tag{2.74}
$$

Observe that if $\mathbf{x}$ and $\mathbf{s}$ are fixed, the inner maximization is simply an LP. This ensures that the optimal $\boldsymbol{\pi}$ can be attained at vertices of the linear constraints on $\boldsymbol{\pi}$. More intuitively, given $\mathbf{x}$ and $\mathbf{s}$, simply set to 1 the K elements in $\boldsymbol{\pi}$ corresponding to the K largest values in $\mathbf{s}$. The constraint $\boldsymbol{\pi}^T \mathbf{1} = K$ will then ensure that the other elements in $\boldsymbol{\pi}$ be set to 0. Thus, the optimized $\boldsymbol{\pi}$ is always integral, and (2.74) is in fact equivalent to (2.71).

To attempt to decouple $\boldsymbol{\pi}$ and $\mathbf{s}$, we analyze the dual of the inner LP. Specifically by introducing Lagrange multipliers $\alpha \in \mathbb{R}$ and $\boldsymbol{\beta} \in \mathbb{R}_+^N$, the dual of the inner LP is

$$
\begin{aligned}
\underset{\alpha \in \mathbb{R}, \boldsymbol{\beta} \in \mathbb{R}^N}{\text{minimize}} \quad & \alpha K + \boldsymbol{\beta}^T \mathbf{1} \\
\text{subject to} \quad & \alpha \mathbf{1} + \boldsymbol{\beta} \geq \mathbf{s}, \\
& \boldsymbol{\beta} \geq \mathbf{0}.
\end{aligned}
\tag{2.75}
$$

Inserting the dual formulation into (2.74) yields

$$
\begin{aligned}
\underset{\mathbf{x} \in \mathbb{R}^d, \mathbf{s} \in \mathbb{R}^N, \alpha \in \mathbb{R}, \boldsymbol{\beta} \in \mathbb{R}^N}{\text{minimize}} \quad & \alpha K + \boldsymbol{\beta}^T \mathbf{1} \\
\text{subject to} \quad & \left| \mathbf{a}_i^T \mathbf{x} - b_i \right| \leq \epsilon + s_i, \\
& s_i \geq 0, \\
& i = 1, \ldots, N, \\
& \alpha \mathbf{1} + \boldsymbol{\beta} \geq \mathbf{s}, \\
& \boldsymbol{\beta} \geq \mathbf{0}.
\end{aligned}
\tag{2.76}
$$

We have thus reformulated (2.71) as an LP. Given the optimized slack $\hat{\mathbf{s}}$ from (2.76), the potential outlier set $\mathcal{O}$ can be constructed by simply following (2.73) again.

Formulation (2.76) can be extended to quasiconvex residuals by following the "tricks" in Section 2.3.1. We thus do not explore this issue further.

2.6.2   OUTLIER REMOVAL WITH THE K-SLACK METHOD

Much like the ℓ_∞ minimization technique for Chebyshev approximation, the K-slack method can be employed as a subroutine in an outlier removal heuristic for approximate maximum consensus. Algorithm 2.8 summarizes the procedure. Unlike Algorithm 2.4, where at most $(d + 1)$ data can be removed in each iteration, Algorithm 2.8 discards K data ($K \geq d + 1$) for each solution of the convex problem (2.76). Thus, Algorithm 2.8 is able to converge to an approximate maximum consensus solution in fewer steps.

Figure 2.27 illustrates the result of applying Algorithm 2.8 with $K = 15$ on the data in Figure 2.13 (the same inlier threshold ϵ was used here). On this data instance, Algorithm 2.8 terminated in 8 iterations. This represents a significant improvement over Algorithm 2.4, which required more than 30 iterations to converge on the same data (see Figure 2.13).

2.7   EXACT PENALTY METHOD

Given an approximate solution $\hat{\mathbf{x}}$ to the maximum consensus problem (2.3) obtained using a fast heuristic such as those described earlier in this chapter, in many applications it is usually of interest to refine $\hat{\mathbf{x}}$. By "refining," we mean making a small local adjustment $\Delta \mathbf{x}$ to $\hat{\mathbf{x}}$, such that $|\mathcal{I}(\hat{\mathbf{x}} + \Delta \mathbf{x})| \geq |\mathcal{I}(\hat{\mathbf{x}})|$. In the context of RANSAC, conducting local refinement is precisely the

---

Algorithm 2.8 Outlier removal with K-slack method for approximate maximum consensus.

Require: Data $\mathcal{D} = \{(\mathbf{a}_i, b_i)\}_{i=1}^{N}$, inlier threshold ϵ and K value.
1: **while** true **do**
2:    $(\hat{\mathbf{x}}, \hat{\mathbf{s}}, \hat{\alpha}, \hat{\boldsymbol{\beta}}) \leftarrow$ Solution of the K-slack problem (2.76) on $\mathcal{D}$.
3:    **if** $\hat{\alpha}K + \hat{\boldsymbol{\beta}}^T \mathbf{1} = 0$ **then**
4:        Break.
5:    **else**
6:        $\mathcal{O} \leftarrow$ Potential outlier set.
7:        $\mathcal{D} \leftarrow \mathcal{D} \setminus \mathcal{D}(\mathcal{O})$.
8:    **end if**
9: **end while**
10: **return** $\hat{\mathbf{x}}$.

---

objective of LO-RANSAC [Chum et al., 2003, Lebeda et al., 2012] (see Section 2.2.1). However, since LO-RANSAC is also a randomized heuristic, there is no guarantee that it is able to drive $\hat{\mathbf{x}}$ toward a better solution.

In this section, we describe a deterministic local refinement algorithm for maximum consensus based on the penalty method [Nocedal and Wright, 2006, Chapter 17]. Though it is more expensive than the algorithms presented earlier, it is able to deterministically adjust $\hat{\mathbf{x}}$ to yield a better solution. This local algorithm is best placed as a postprocessor for the rough initial solution obtained using the fast approximate heuristics.

2.7.1 PENALIZED FORMULATION

The thresholding constraint $|\mathbf{a}_i^T \mathbf{x} - b_i| \leq \epsilon$ can be implemented as two linear constraints

$$\mathbf{a}_i^T \mathbf{x} - b_i \leq \epsilon, \quad -\mathbf{a}_i^T \mathbf{x} + b_i \leq \epsilon. \tag{2.77}$$

Given input data $\mathcal{D} = \{(\mathbf{a}_i, b_i)\}_{i=1}^{N}$, the set of N pairs of constraints of the form (2.77) arising from $\mathcal{D}$ can be summarized as

$$\boldsymbol{\Lambda}^T \mathbf{x} - \boldsymbol{\beta} \leq \mathbf{0}, \tag{2.78}$$

where $\boldsymbol{\Lambda} \in \mathbb{R}^{d \times M}$ and $\boldsymbol{\beta} \in \mathbb{R}^M$ are defined as

$$\boldsymbol{\Lambda} = \left[\mathbf{a}_1, -\mathbf{a}_1, \ldots, \mathbf{a}_N, -\mathbf{a}_N \right], \tag{2.79}$$

$$\boldsymbol{\beta} = \left[\epsilon + b_1, \epsilon - b_1, \ldots, \epsilon + b_N, \epsilon - b_N \right]^T, \tag{2.80}$$

and $M = 2N$. Accordingly, Problem (2.3) can be equivalently expressed as

$$\underset{\mathbf{x} \in \mathbb{R}^d}{\text{maximize}} \quad |\mathcal{J}(\mathbf{x})|, \tag{2.81}$$

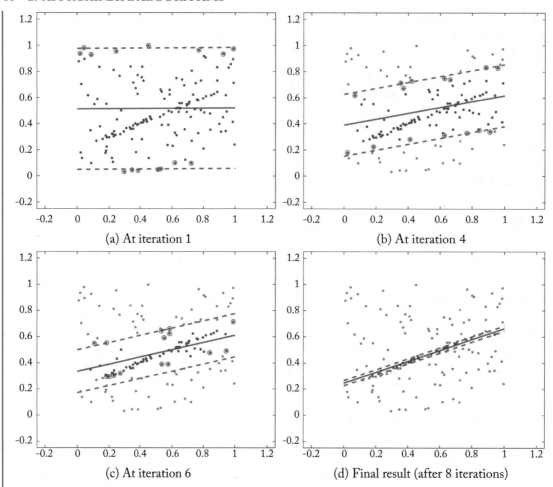

(a) At iteration 1

(b) At iteration 4

(c) At iteration 6

(d) Final result (after 8 iterations)

Figure 2.27: Result of applying Algorithm 2.8 with $K = 15$ on the data in Figure 2.13 (the same inlier threshold ϵ was used here). The circled points are the potential outlier set (2.73) identified at each iteration. The K-slack outlier removal method converged in 8 iterations.

with the consensus set now defined as

$$\mathcal{J}(\mathbf{x}) = \left\{ j \in \{1, \ldots, M\} \mid \boldsymbol{\alpha}_j^T \mathbf{x} - \beta_j \leq 0 \right\}, \tag{2.82}$$

where $\boldsymbol{\alpha}_j$ is the j-th column of $\boldsymbol{\Lambda}$, and β_j is the j-th element of $\boldsymbol{\beta}$. Note that although Problems (2.3) and (2.81) have the same maximizer $\mathbf{x}^*$, the maximum objective values obey the equation

$$|\mathcal{J}(\mathbf{x}^*)| = N + |\mathcal{I}(\mathbf{x}^*)| \tag{2.83}$$

since for any $\mathbf{x}$ at least one of the constraints in (2.77) are satisfied.

In the rest of this section, we regard (2.81) as our target problem. We may thus call $(\boldsymbol{\alpha}_j, \beta_j)$, where $j \notin \mathcal{J}(\mathbf{x})$, an outlier w.r.t. model $\mathbf{x}$.

Complementarity Constraints

Introducing indicator variables $\mathbf{u} \in \{0, 1\}^M$ and slack variables $\mathbf{s} \in \mathbb{R}^M$, we reformulate (2.81) equivalently as an outlier count minimization problem

$$\min_{\mathbf{u}\in\{0,1\}^M, \mathbf{s}\in\mathbb{R}^M, \mathbf{x}\in\mathbb{R}^d} \sum_j u_j \tag{2.84a}$$

$$\text{subject to} \quad s_j - \boldsymbol{\alpha}_j^T \mathbf{x} + \beta_j \geq 0, \tag{2.84b}$$

$$u_j(s_j - \boldsymbol{\alpha}_j^T \mathbf{x} + \beta_j) = 0, \tag{2.84c}$$

$$s_j(1 - u_j) = 0, \tag{2.84d}$$

$$s_j \geq 0. \tag{2.84e}$$

Intuitively, s_j must be non-zero if the j-th datum is an outlier w.r.t. $\mathbf{x}$; in this case, u_j must be set to 1 to satisfy (2.84d). In turn, (2.84c) forces the quantity $(s_j - \boldsymbol{\alpha}_j^T \mathbf{x} + \beta_i)$ to be zero. Conversely, if the j-th datum is an inlier w.r.t. $\mathbf{x}$, then s_j is zero, u_j is zero and $(s_j - \boldsymbol{\alpha}_j^T \mathbf{x} + \beta_j)$ is non-zero. Observe, therefore, that (2.84c) and (2.84d) implement *complementarity* between u_j and $(s_j - \boldsymbol{\alpha}_j^T \mathbf{x} + \beta_j)$.

Note also that, due to the objective function and the condition (2.84d), the indicator variables can be relaxed without impacting the optimum, leading to the equivalent problem

$$\min_{\mathbf{u},\mathbf{s}\in\mathbb{R}^M, \mathbf{x}\in\mathbb{R}^d} \sum_j u_j \tag{2.85a}$$

$$\text{subject to} \quad s_j - \boldsymbol{\alpha}_j^T \mathbf{x} + \beta_j \geq 0, \tag{2.85b}$$

$$u_j(s_j - \boldsymbol{\alpha}_j^T \mathbf{x} + \beta_j) = 0, \tag{2.85c}$$

$$s_j(1 - u_j) = 0, \tag{2.85d}$$

$$1 - u_j \geq 0, \tag{2.85e}$$

$$s_j, u_j \geq 0. \tag{2.85f}$$

This, however, does not make (2.85) tractable to solve exactly, since (2.85c) and (2.85d) are bilinear constraints. By a further modification, (2.85) can be expressed using only positive variables; this will slightly simplify the analysis of optimality and the construction of an algorithm for the problem. Define

$$\mathbf{v} = \begin{bmatrix} \mathbf{x} + \gamma \mathbf{1} \\ \gamma \end{bmatrix} \quad \mathbf{c}_j = \begin{bmatrix} \boldsymbol{\alpha}_j^T & -\boldsymbol{\alpha}_j^T \mathbf{1} \end{bmatrix}^T, \tag{2.86}$$

where both are real vectors of length $(d + 1)$. Problem (2.85) can then be reformulated equivalently as

$$
\min_{\mathbf{u}, \mathbf{s} \in \mathbb{R}^M, \mathbf{v} \in \mathbb{R}^{d+1}} \quad \sum_j u_j
$$

$$
\begin{aligned}
\text{subject to} \quad & s_j - \mathbf{c}_j^T \mathbf{v} + \beta_j \geq 0, \\
& u_j (s_j - \mathbf{c}_j^T \mathbf{v} + \beta_j) = 0, \\
& s_j (1 - u_j) = 0, \\
& 1 - u_j \geq 0, \\
& s_j, u_j, v_j \geq 0.
\end{aligned} \tag{2.87}
$$

Given a solution $\hat{\mathbf{u}}$, $\hat{\mathbf{s}}$ and $\hat{\mathbf{v}}$ to (2.87), the corresponding solution $\hat{\mathbf{x}}$ to (2.85) can be obtained by simply subtracting the last element of $\hat{\mathbf{v}}$ from its first-d elements.

The Penalty Problem

Incorporating the equality constraints in (2.87) into the cost function as a penalty term, we obtain the penalty problem

$$
\begin{aligned}
\min_{\mathbf{u}, \mathbf{s}, \mathbf{v}} \quad & \sum_j u_j + \lambda \left[u_j (s_j - \mathbf{c}_j^T \mathbf{v} + \beta_j) + s_j (1 - u_j) \right] \\
\text{s.t.} \quad & s_j - \mathbf{c}_j^T \mathbf{v} + \beta_j \geq 0, \\
& 1 - u_j \geq 0, \\
& s_j, u_j, v_j \geq 0.
\end{aligned} \tag{2.88}
$$

The constant $\lambda \geq 0$ is called the penalty parameter. Intuitively, the penalty term discourages solutions that violate the complementarity constraints, and the strength of the penalization is controlled by λ.

Henceforth, to reduce clutter and promote clarity in discussion, we sometimes use

$$
\mathbf{z} = \left[\mathbf{u}^T, \ \mathbf{s}^T, \ \mathbf{v}^T \right]^T \tag{2.89}
$$

to group all the unknowns into a single $(2M + d + 1)$-vector. Then, the cost function in (2.88) can be rewritten as

$$
P(\mathbf{z} \mid \lambda) = F(\mathbf{z}) + \lambda Q(\mathbf{z}), \tag{2.90}
$$

where $F(\mathbf{z}) = \|\mathbf{u}\|_1$ and

$$
Q(\mathbf{z}) = \sum_j u_j \left(s_j - \mathbf{c}_j^T \mathbf{v} + \beta_j \right) + s_j \left(1 - u_j \right) \tag{2.91}
$$

$$
= \sum_j s_j - u_j \left(\mathbf{c}_j^T \mathbf{v} - \beta_j \right). \tag{2.92}
$$

In particular, $Q(\mathbf{z})$ is called the *complementarity residual*, since it effectively calculates the amount by which the complementarity conditions are violated under $\mathbf{z}$.

Note also that the remaining constraints in (2.88) can be summarized as

$$
\begin{aligned}
\mathbf{Mz} + \mathbf{q} &\geq \mathbf{0}, \\
\mathbf{z} &\geq \mathbf{0},
\end{aligned}
\tag{2.93}
$$

where

$$
\begin{aligned}
\mathbf{M} &= \begin{bmatrix} \mathbf{0} & \mathbf{I} & -\mathbf{C} \\ -\mathbf{I} & \mathbf{0} & \mathbf{0} \end{bmatrix}, \\
\mathbf{C} &= \begin{bmatrix} \mathbf{c}_1 & \mathbf{c}_2 & \dots & \mathbf{c}_M \end{bmatrix}^T, \\
\mathbf{q} &= \begin{bmatrix} \boldsymbol{\beta}^T & \mathbf{1}^T \end{bmatrix}^T;
\end{aligned}
\tag{2.94}
$$

(the sizes of $\mathbf{I}$, $\mathbf{0}$ and $\mathbf{1}$ are not specified, but this information can be worked out from the context). The constraints (2.93) in fact define a polyhedron

$$
\mathcal{P} = \left\{ \mathbf{z} \in \mathbb{R}^{2M+d+1} \mid \mathbf{Mz} + \mathbf{q} \geq \mathbf{0}, \mathbf{z} \geq \mathbf{0} \right\},
\tag{2.95}
$$

which is a convex set in $\mathbb{R}^{2M+d+1}$. Problem (2.88) can then be very succinctly described as

$$
\min_{\mathbf{z} \in \mathcal{P}} \quad P(\mathbf{z} \mid \lambda)
\tag{2.96}
$$

Exactness of Penalization

Intuitively, by making λ a very large number, we force the solution of (2.96) to lie closer to the feasible region of the original problem (2.87). In fact, it can be established that, for our particular problem, there exists a finite λ where (2.96) has the same solution as (2.87).

First, observe that (2.96) can be seen as an application of the *nonsmooth penalty method* [Nocedal and Wright, 2006, Section 17.2], since the penalty term $Q(\mathbf{z})$ amounts to taking the ℓ_1-norm (a nonsmooth function) of the equality constraints in (2.87). The exactness of the penalization in (2.96) is exhibited in the following theorem.

Theorem 2.21   (Based on Theorem 17.3 in Nocedal and Wright [2006]).   *If $\mathbf{z}^*$ is a local solution of the original problem (2.87), then, there exists $\lambda^* > 0$ such that for all $\lambda \geq \lambda^*$, $\mathbf{z}^*$ is also a local minimizer of $P(\mathbf{z} \mid \lambda)$ subject to $\mathbf{z} \in \mathcal{P}$.*

Intuitively, the theorem states that there is a sufficiently large λ for (2.96), such that any small movement away from $\mathbf{z}^*$ will be penalized strongly enough by $\lambda Q(\mathbf{z})$ to immediately negate any potential reduction to $F(\mathbf{z})$ enabled by violating the complementarity constraints. However, this characteristic is not immediately useful, since although $P(\mathbf{z})$ is quadratic, it is not convex, and hence (2.96) is not amenable for efficient exact solutions. A follow-up theorem will prove more useful for our aims.

Theorem 2.22 (Based on Theorem 17.4 in Nocedal and Wright [2006]). *Let $\hat{\mathbf{z}}$ be a Karush-Kuhn-Tucker (KKT) point of the penalized problem (2.96) for λ greater than λ^*. Then, $Q(\hat{\mathbf{z}}) = 0$, and $\hat{\mathbf{z}}$ is also a KKT point of (2.87).*

Recall that a KKT point of a constrained optimization problem is a point that satisfies the first-order necessary conditions (FONC) for a local solution [Nocedal and Wright, 2006, Chapter 12]. Theorem 2.22 thus justifies solving the target problem (2.87) up to FONC optimality by finding a KKT point of the penalty problem (2.96) with a sufficiently large λ. In the next subsection, we capitalize on this result to construct a deterministic local refinement algorithm for maximum consensus.

2.7.2   DETERMINISTIC LOCAL REFINEMENT ALGORITHM

In this section, first an algorithm for solving the penalty problem under a fixed λ is described. Then, a broader algorithm that subsumes the penalty problem and progressively increases λ is developed to achieve the aim of deterministic local improvement.

Solving the Penalty Problem

As alluded to earlier, although $P(\mathbf{z} \mid \lambda)$ is quadratic, it is not convex. Interestingly, however, it can be shown that (2.96) has a vertex solution—in fact, the KKT points of $P(\mathbf{z} \mid \lambda)$ for $\mathbf{z} \in \mathcal{P}$ are extreme points of the convex set $\mathcal{P}$. This phenomenon is due to the fact that the variables are uncoupled in the bilinear constraints (2.84c) and (2.84d) [Mangasarian, 1994], i.e., only products between disjoint subsets of the variables $\mathbf{z}$ appear in the constraints. See Section C in the Appendix for a proof.

To solve (2.96), observe that if $\mathbf{u}$ is fixed, (2.96) reduces to an LP. Conversely, if $\mathbf{s}$ and $\mathbf{v}$ are fixed, (2.96) is also an LP. This advocates alternating between optimizing subsets of the variables using LPs. Algorithm 2.9 summarizes the method, which is in fact a special case of the method of Frank and Wolfe [1956] for nonconvex quadratic minimization. The following theorem shows that Algorithm 2.9 returns a KKT point of (2.96).

Theorem 2.23   *In a finite number of steps, Algorithm 2.9 converges to a KKT point of Problem (2.96).*

Proof. The set of constraints $\mathcal{P}$ can be decoupled into the two disjoint subsets

$$\mathcal{P} = \mathcal{P}_1 \times \mathcal{P}_2, \tag{2.97}$$

where $\mathcal{P}_1$ involves only $\mathbf{s}$ and $\mathbf{v}$, and $\mathcal{P}_2$ is the complement of $\mathcal{P}_1$. With $\mathbf{u}$ fixed in Line 5, the LP converges to a vertex of $\mathcal{P}_1$. Similarly, with $\mathbf{s}$ and $\mathbf{v}$ fixed in Line 6, the LP converges to a vertex

---

Algorithm 2.9 Frank-Wolfe method for penalty Problem (2.96).

Require: Data $\{(\mathbf{c}_j, \beta_j)\}_{j=1}^M$, penalty value λ, initial solution $\mathbf{u}^{(0)}, \mathbf{v}^{(0)}, \mathbf{s}^{(0)}$, threshold δ.

1: $P^{(0)} \leftarrow P(\mathbf{u}^{(0)}, \mathbf{s}^{(0)}, \mathbf{v}^{(0)} \mid \lambda)$.
2: $t \leftarrow 0$.
3: **while** true **do**
4:    $t \leftarrow t + 1$.
5:    $\mathbf{s}^{(t)}, \mathbf{v}^{(t)} \leftarrow \operatorname{argmin}_{\mathbf{s},\mathbf{v}} P(\mathbf{u}^{(t-1)}, \mathbf{s}, \mathbf{v} \mid \lambda)$ s.t. $\mathcal{P}$.
6:    $\mathbf{u}^{(t)} \leftarrow \operatorname{argmin}_{\mathbf{u}} P(\mathbf{u}, \mathbf{s}^{(t)}, \mathbf{v}^{(t)} \mid \lambda)$ s.t. $\mathcal{P}$.
7:    $P^{(t)} \leftarrow P(\mathbf{u}^{(t)}, \mathbf{s}^{(t)}, \mathbf{v}^{(t)} \mid \lambda)$.
8:    **if** $|P^{(t-1)} - P^{(t)}| \leq \delta$ **then**
9:       Break.
10:   **end if**
11: **end while**
12: **return** $\mathbf{u}^{(t)}, \mathbf{v}^{(t)}, \mathbf{s}^{(t)}$.

---

in $\mathcal{P}_2$. Each intermediate solution $\mathbf{u}^{(t)}, \mathbf{v}^{(t)}, \mathbf{s}^{(t)}$ is thus a vertex of $\mathcal{P}$ or a KKT point of (2.96). Since each LP must reduce or maintain $P(\mathbf{z} \mid \lambda)$, which is bounded below, the process terminates in finite steps. $\qquad\square$

A closer look reveals the LP in Line 5 to be

$$\min_{\mathbf{s},\mathbf{v}} \quad \sum_j s_j - u_j \left(\mathbf{c}_j^T \mathbf{v} - \beta_j\right)$$
$$\text{s.t.} \quad s_j - \mathbf{c}_j^T \mathbf{v} + \beta_j \geq 0, \tag{LP1}$$
$$s_j, v_j \geq 0,$$

and the LP in Line 6 to be

$$\min_{\mathbf{u}} \quad \sum_j u_j \left[1 - \lambda(\mathbf{c}_j^T \mathbf{v} - \beta_j)\right]$$
$$\text{s.t.} \quad 0 \leq u_j \leq 1. \tag{LP2}$$

Observe that LP2 can be solved in closed form and it also drives $\mathbf{u}$ to integrality: if $[1 - \alpha(\mathbf{c}_j^T \mathbf{v} - \beta_j)] \leq 0$, set $u_j = 1$, else, set $u_j = 0$. Further, LP1 can be seen as "weighted" ℓ_1-norm minimization, with $\mathbf{u}$ being the weights. Intuitively, therefore, Algorithm 2.9 alternates between residual minimization (LP1) and inlier-outlier dichotomization (LP2).

Main Algorithm

In practice a one-shot approach that solves a single instance of the penalty problem under a very high λ is unlikely to be successful, since by penalizing violations to complementarity more heavily, the movement of $\mathbf{z}$ is restricted. A more practical method is to progressively increase

λ and solve multiple instances of the penalty problem, where the converged solution under a λ is used to initialize the solution under the next λ. The overall process is terminated when the complementarity residual $Q(\mathbf{z})$ is sufficiently small. Algorithm 2.10 describes the procedure.

Algorithm 2.10 Deterministic local refinement algorithm for (2.87).

Require: Data $\{(\mathbf{c}_j, \beta_j)\}_{j=1}^M$, initial solution $\mathbf{u}, \mathbf{s}, \mathbf{v}$, initial penalty parameter λ, increment rate κ, threshold δ.

1: **while** true **do**
2:      $\mathbf{u}, \mathbf{s}, \mathbf{v} \leftarrow \text{fw}(\{(\mathbf{c}_j, \beta_j)\}_{j=1}^M, \lambda, \mathbf{u}, \mathbf{s}, \mathbf{v})$.   /*Algorithm 2.9.*/
3:      **if** $Q([\mathbf{u}^T, \mathbf{s}^T, \mathbf{v}^T]^T) \leq \delta$ **then**
4:          Break.
5:      **end if**
6:      $\lambda \leftarrow \kappa \cdot \lambda$.
7: **end while**
8: **return** $\mathbf{u}, \mathbf{s}, \mathbf{v}$.

Algorithm 2.10 requires the initialization of $\mathbf{u}$, $\mathbf{s}$ and $\mathbf{v}$. For consensus maximization, it is more natural to initialize the more familiar model parameters $\mathbf{x}$—as mentioned previously, $\mathbf{x}$ can be taken as the output of a fast approximate heuristic. Given $\mathbf{x}$, $\mathbf{v}$ can be obtained based on the relationship (2.86) as

$$\mathbf{v} = \begin{bmatrix} (\mathbf{x} + |\min_i(x_i)|\mathbf{1}) \\ |\min_i(x_i)| \end{bmatrix}. \tag{2.98}$$

This in turn provides initial values to $\mathbf{s}$ and $\mathbf{u}$ as follows:

$$\begin{aligned} \mathbf{u} &= \mathbb{I}(\mathbf{Cv} - \boldsymbol{\beta} > 0), \\ \mathbf{s} &= \mathbf{u} \odot (\mathbf{Cv} - \boldsymbol{\beta}), \end{aligned} \tag{2.99}$$

where $\odot$ indicates element-wise multiplication.

Other required inputs are the initial penalty parameter λ, and the increment rate κ for the penalty parameter. These values affect the convergence speed of Algorithm 2.10. To avoid bad minima, λ and κ should be set conservatively, e.g. $\lambda \in [1, 10]$, $\kappa \in [1, 5]$.

Figure 2.28 illustrates the application of Algorithm 2.10 to line fitting. In this example, the local refinement algorithm was initialized respectively using RANSAC and ordinary LS. In both cases, Algorithm 2.10 was able to adjust the initial solution to a result with higher consensus. The improvement on the LS initial solution was particularly significant, owing to LS having been heavily biased by the outliers. In the next section, a broader evaluation of Algorithm 2.10, which includes different kinds of input data and comparisons with other approximate algorithms, is provided.

Although the derivations behind Algorithms 2.9 and 2.10 were based on the linear model, the algorithms can be easily extended to generalized fractional models by following essentially

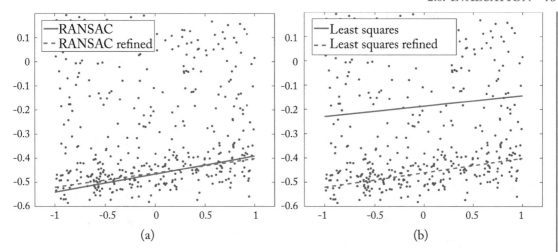

Figure 2.28: The results of RANSAC, least squares, and the deterministic local improvement method (Algorithm 2.10) initialized with the former two methods. Observe that least squares was heavily biased, but the refinement algorithm was able to recover from the bad initialization.

the same tricks in Section 2.3 for the ℓ_1 minimization method. We thus do not further discuss this matter, and refer the interested reader to Le et al. [2017] for details.

2.8 EVALUATION

This section reports the evaluation results of some the algorithms described in this chapter, as well as several other methods that are well known in the literature, on common input instances. It is not the intention of this section here to identify the best algorithm—such an endeavor will require a significantly more comprehensive benchmark (e.g., involving the usage of large-scale benchmark datasets and multiple target applications). The aim of this section is to provide a rough indication of the relative performance and accuracy; the reader should be mindful that the conclusions here may not generalize to other settings.

List of Algorithms
The following is the list of algorithms included in the experiments.

- RANSAC: The confidence of $\rho = 0.99$ was used in the stopping criterion (see Algorithm 2.3). On each data instance, RANSAC was executed 10 times, and the average consensus and runtime were reported.

- Locally Optimized RANSAC (LO-RANSAC) by Chum et al. [2003]: The maximum number of iterations in the inner sampling of the best consensus set was set to 100.

- Improved LO-RANSAC by Lebeda et al. [2012]: Following the originators' proposal, the inner sampling for local refinement will only be executed if the new consensus size is higher than a pre-defined threshold (set to 10% of the data size in the experiments).

- ℓ_1 minimization: As described in Section 2.3.

- ℓ_∞ outlier removal: As described in Sections 2.4.2 and 2.5.3.

- Deterministic local refinement algorithm: As described in Section 2.7.2. Initialization with RANSAC and least squares were both tested.

In segments of the experiments involving image feature correspondences as input, two other RANSAC variants—Guided MLESAC [Tordoff and Murray, 2005] and PROSAC [Chum and Matas, 2005]—were executed. Both methods take advantage of feature-matching scores to guide the sampling of minimal subsets to speed up convergence.

All the methods and experiments were implemented in MATLAB and run on a standard desktop machine with 3.5 GHz processor and 8 GB of RAM.

Robust Linear Regression

Synthetically generated data were used in this segment. Each input instance was generated as follows: $N = 500$ points $\{(\mathbf{a}_i, b_i)\}_{i=1}^N$ in $\mathbb{R}^9$ were produced following a linear trend $b_i = \mathbf{a}_i^T \mathbf{x}$, where $\mathbf{x}$ and $\mathbf{a}_i$ were sampled randomly from $[-1, 1]^8$. Each b_i was perturbed by Normal noise with standard deviation 0.1. To simulate outliers, a percentage of the b_i's were further randomly selected and corrupted. Two different corruption strategies were used:

- Balanced: b_i was added with Gaussian noise of standard deviation 1. This evenly distributed the outliers on both sides of the hyperplane $b = \mathbf{a}^T \mathbf{x}$.

- Unbalanced: b_i was also added with Gaussian noise of standard deviation 1, but the sign of the additive noise was forced to be positive. Thus, outliers were distributed only on one side of the hyperplane. Figure 2.28 gives a 2D analogy of the unbalanced data generated in this manner.

The inlier threshold ϵ for maximum consensus was set to $\epsilon = 0.1$. For the deterministic local refinement method (Algorithm 2.10), the initial α was set to 0.5 and $\kappa = 5$ for all the runs. Figures 2.29 and 2.30 plot the consensus at termination and runtime of the above algorithms against percentage of data selected for corruption (up to 60% corruption). Note that the runtime of the deterministic local refinement algorithm includes the duration of its initialization technique.

On data with both balanced and unbalanced outliers, the solution quality of all the methods naturally decreased with percentage of outlier corruption. However, on data with unbalanced outliers, ℓ_1 and ℓ_∞ decreased at a faster rate than the other methods, indicating their tendencies to converge to suboptimal results under unbalanced outliers—this undesirable behavior was highlighted in the earlier sections.

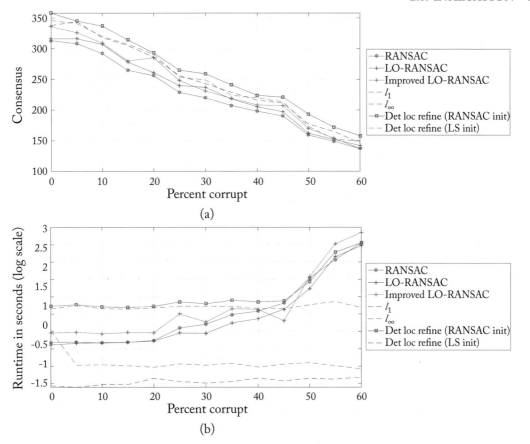

Figure 2.29: (a) Solution quality and (b) runtime of various maximum consensus algorithms on 8-dimensional robust linear regression with *balanced* outliers.

On all the input instances, the deterministic local refinement method returned the estimate with the highest consensus. The attainment of the highest quality even under LS initialization on unbalanced outliers suggests that the deterministic local refinement method is able to recover from bad initialization (cf. Figure 2.28). Also, the fact that the solution of RANSAC was consistently improved by the local refinement algorithms demonstrates that it is usually possible to locally refine the RANSAC estimate.

The downside of deterministic local refinement, however, is its higher runtime compared with the RANSAC variants. Nonetheless, as the percentage of corrupted data was increased over 35%, the runtime of the RANSAC variants started to increase rapidly (recall that the number of samples increases exponentially with outlier rate—see Section 2.2), to the extent that the RANSAC initialization cost overwhelmed the deterministic local refinement cost. The variant

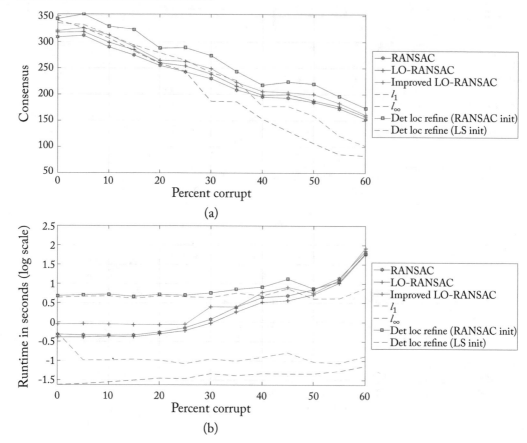

Figure 2.30: (a) Solution quality and (b) runtime of various maximum consensus algorithms on 8-dimensional robust linear regression with *unbalanced* outliers.

of deterministic local refinement with LS initialization maintained a discernibly lower rate of increase in runtime.

Robust Estimation of Image Warping Functions

In this segment of the experiments, the approximate algorithms were evaluated on robust estimation of image warping functions, specifically 2D homography and affine transformations, from outlier-contaminated feature correspondences. Given two overlapping images, the scale-invariant feature transform (SIFT) method [Lowe, 2004] (based on the implementation of Vedaldi and Fulkerson [2010]) was used to automatically detect and match local features between the images. The parameters in the SIFT routine were chosen such that ≈ 500 correspondences were extracted. The parameters of the warping function were then estimated via maximum consensus using the transfer error as residual function and inlier threshold of 4 pixels.

For homography estimation, five image pairs from Oxford's Visual Geometry Group (VGG), namely University Library, Christ Church, Valbonne, Kapel, and Paris's Invalides, were chosen for testing. For affinity estimation, a different set of five image pairs from VGG, namely, Bikes, Graff, Bark, Tree, and Boat, were selected. Figure 2.31 shows sample data for Christ Church and Trees, as well as the inlier/outlier dichotomization based on the consensus set returned by the deterministic local refinement method (Algorithm 2.10), with initial $\alpha = 10$ and $\kappa = 1.5$. The local refinement technique increased the consensus of the initial solution respectively from 235–280 and from 372–396.

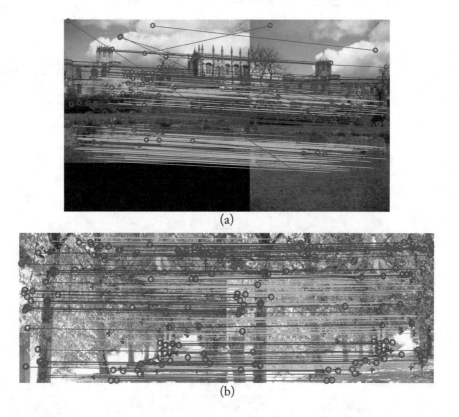

(a)

(b)

Figure 2.31: Result of applying the deterministic local refinement method (Algorithm 2.10) to (a) homography fitting ($N = 445$ input correspondences) and (b) affine registration ($N = 568$ input correspondences). Green and red lines represent inliers and outliers based on the output consensus set. For clarity, only 100 inliers/outliers are plotted above. In both cases, RANSAC was applied as the initializer. Algorithm 2.10 increased the consensus of the RANSAC solution, respectively, from 235–280 and from 372–396.

Table 2.1 lists the optimized consensus and runtime of the different methods. Among the RANSAC variants, PROSAC and Guided MLESAC were able to speed up convergence due to the usage of feature-matching scores for guided sampling. PROSAC, in fact, returned higher-quality solutions than RANSAC in all instances. In some of the instances, the LO-RANSAC methods were able to significantly increase the consensus of RANSAC. Generally, the randomized heuristics terminated in a matter of seconds. Although the ℓ_1 and ℓ_∞ techniques were much faster, the quality of their estimate was on the whole lower.

Table 2.1: Quantitative results for robust estimation of image warping functions. Legend: $|\mathcal{I}|$ = consensus at convergence, RS = RANSAC, PS = PROSAC, GMLE = Guided MLESAC, LOR1 = LO-RANSAC, LOR2 = Improved LO-RANSAC, ℓ_1 = ℓ_1 minimization (Section 2.3), ℓ_∞ = ℓ_∞ outlier removal (Section 2.4.2), DLocR = deterministic local refinement algorithm with RANSAC initialization (Section 2.7.2). Time for DLocR inclusive of initialization.

		Method	RS	PS	GMLE	LOR1	LOR2	ℓ_1	ℓ_∞	DLocR
Homography Estimation	University Library	$|\mathcal{I}|$	251	269	251	294	294	120	53	**301**
	N = 545	time (s)	0.73	0.62	0.69	1.90	1.89	3.10	2.49	12.76
	Christ Church	$|\mathcal{I}|$	235	236	227	250	246	246	160	**280**
	N = 445	time (s)	0.47	0.47	0.43	1.33	1.61	1.23	2.44	10.37
	Valbonne	$|\mathcal{I}|$	131	134	117	156	136	24	22	**158**
	N = 434	time (s)	3.17	2.39	5.76	3.04	5.80	1.36	1.27	17.20
	Kapel	$|\mathcal{I}|$	163	167	130	167	168	28	161	**170**
	N = 449	time (s)	1.19	1.15	9.89	2.18	2.70	1.62	1.16	8.46
	Invalides	$|\mathcal{I}|$	144	159	140	149	156	84	142	**178**
	N = 413	time (s)	1.36	0.90	1.60	2.17	2.94	1.04	0.71	10.20
	Bikes	$|\mathcal{I}|$	424	427	425	426	424	387	431	**437**
	N = 557	time (s)	6.09	6.09	5.79	6.28	11.8	1.77	1.77	15.26
	Graff	$|\mathcal{I}|$	126	129	127	134	126	147	274	**276**
	N = 327	time (s)	3.51	3.35	3.14	4.07	6.61	0.99	0.23	5.94
Affinity Estimation	Bark	$|\mathcal{I}|$	279	288	270	284	279	298	439	**442**
	N = 458	time (s)	4.89	4.93	4.68	5.11	9.54	1.31	0.19	10.19
	Tree	$|\mathcal{I}|$	372	367	371	372	372	277	370	**396**
	N = 568	time (s)	5.70	6.01	5.73	6.93	11.50	4.81	0.81	15.96
	Boat	$|\mathcal{I}|$	476	477	476	477	476	469	464	**483**
	N = 574	time (s)	6.32	6.29	6.02	7.18	12.32	4.12	1.02	14.86

The converged solutions of deterministic local refinement (with RANSAC initialization) were of superior quality relative to the estimates of the other algorithms. However, the runtime of deterministic local refinement was higher than the others, though not by a significant margin (note that the reported runtimes are inclusive of the RANSAC initialization step). Note that LS initialization was not invoked here, since finding LS estimates based on geometric distances is intractable in general. The results support the usage of Algorithm 2.10 in settings where slight additional runtime is a worthwhile expense for deterministic convergence to a higher-quality maximum consensus estimate.

2.9   BIBLIOGRAPHICAL REMARKS

A brief outline of the invention of RANSAC and its adoption into computer vision has been given in Section 1.4. The LAD method for robust estimation in geometric applications was first proposed by Seo et al. [2009], though they couched their technique as an extension of the framework of ℓ_∞ outlier removal, instead of a bona fide robust estimation approach. The relaxation of the ℓ_0-norm in the maximum consensus objective criterion to the ℓ_1-norm (see Section 2.3) was first proposed by Olsson et al. [2010].

The usage of the (non-robust) Chebyshev approximation technique in geometric vision is attributed to Hartley and Schaffalitzky [2004], who first targeted the problem of triangulation. This was later extended to other vision problems by Kahl [2005] and Ke and Kanade [2005]. Li [2007] later pointed out the connection of Chebyshev approximation in geometric vision to LP-type methods. The relation to GFP was established by Agarwal et al. [2008], though Olsson et al. [2007] were the first to propose an algorithm in the spirit of GFP.

The application of Chebyshev estimation as a subroutine in outlier removal was first proposed by Sim and Hartley [2006]. Yu et al. [2011] later proposed a generalized formulation for approximation by minimizing the sum of infeasibilities (i.e., the K-slack method), where LAD and Chebyshev estimation are two extremes of the same method. Yu et al. also proposed the usage of their approximation scheme as a subroutine for outlier removal, to extend the technique of Sim and Hartley.

At the time of writing, the topic of deterministic local improvement methods for consensus maximization was relatively new. The technique based on exact penalization of complementarity constraints was proposed by Le et al. [2017].

CHAPTER 3

Exact Algorithms

3.1 INTRODUCTION

Exact algorithms for maximum consensus aim to find the globally optimal solution $\mathbf{x}^*$ to the problem. Associated with $\mathbf{x}^*$ is the maximum consensus set $\mathcal{I}(\mathbf{x}^*)$. As discussed in Section 1.3, owing to its combinatorial nature, maximum consensus is intractable in general. Therefore, to find the global solution, some form of search must be conducted. The main topic in this chapter is how to conduct the search efficiently.

   Most of the algorithms contained here have runtimes that scale nontrivially with the input size (recall the $\Omega(N^d)$ lower bound in Conjecture 1 in Section 1.3). Thus, except for lower-dimensional problems, the exact algorithms will unlikely be faster than the approximate algorithms in Chapter 2; the main benefit of exact algorithms is guaranteed global optimality. Also, relative to the approximate algorithms, the exact algorithms here are more "bespoke," i.e., they are usually specialized for a target model/application. This also makes it more difficult to compare exact algorithms in a common benchmark.

3.2 OPTIMAL LINE FITTING

Let us begin with the line-fitting problem, in which we are given a set of points $\mathcal{D} = \{(p_i, q_i)\}_{i=1}^{N}$ on the plane, and the aim is to robustly fit a line onto the points. To recap, a line is defined by parameter vector $\mathbf{x} = [m, c]^T$, and the i-th residual is

$$r_i(\mathbf{x}) = |mp_i + c - q_i|. \tag{3.1}$$

Under the maximum consensus framework, we seek the line $\mathbf{x}^*$ with the largest consensus set, given inlier threshold ϵ. Ideally, we want to avoid searching over $\mathbb{R}^2$ to find this line.

3.2.1 CHARACTERIZATION OF THE SOLUTION

What properties does $\mathbf{x}^*$ hold? Intuitively, one expects that it is possible to perturb $\mathbf{x}^*$ slightly without changing the consensus set; see Figure 1.7. In this section, we seek to formalize this intuition, and to construct a technique to remove the non-uniqueness of $\mathbf{x}^*$.

Definition 3.1 (Sidedness).   A point (p_i, q_i) is above (respectively, below) the line represented by parameter vector $\mathbf{x}$ if $[p_i, 1]^T \mathbf{x} - q_i < 0$ (respectively, $[p_i, 1]^T \mathbf{x} - q_i > 0$). Trivially, for two points (p_i, q_i) and (p_j, q_j), if the following quantity is positive,

$$\left([p_i, 1]^T \mathbf{x} - q_i\right) \left([p_j, 1]^T \mathbf{x} - q_j\right) \tag{3.2}$$

then the two points lie on the same side of the line represented by parameter vector $\mathbf{x}$.

We revisit Chebyshev approximation for line fitting. See Definition 2.15 for the meaning of the support set of a set of points under Chebyshev approximation.

Lemma 3.2   *Let $\hat{\mathbf{x}}$ by the Chebyshev line estimate for the points $\mathcal{D}$. If $\mathcal{K}$ is a support set of $\mathcal{D}$, then the points in $\mathcal{K}$ cannot all lie on the same side of line $\hat{\mathbf{x}}$.*

Proof. If all of the points in $\mathcal{K}$ lie on the same side of $\hat{\mathbf{x}}$, then it is possible to translate the line in a way that simultaneously reduces the residuals of the points in $\mathcal{K}$. This contradicts that $\hat{\mathbf{x}}$ is the Chebyshev estimate. □

The following theorem provides a way to resolve the non-uniqueness of the optimal line $\mathbf{x}^*$. For simplicity, we assume that no points in $\mathcal{D}$ have the same coordinates.

Theorem 3.3   *Given an optimal maximum consensus line $\mathbf{x}^*$, it is always possible to find another line $\mathbf{x}^{**}$ with the same consensus set as $\mathbf{x}^*$, and where there are two points on the same side of the line $\mathbf{x}^{**}$ with residuals equal to ϵ.*

Proof. Let $\hat{\mathbf{x}}$ be the Chebyshev estimate with minimax value $\hat{s}$ on the maximum consensus set $\mathcal{I}(\mathbf{x}^*)$, and $\mathcal{K}$ be the support set of $\mathcal{I}(\mathbf{x}^*)$. By construction, $\hat{s} \leq \epsilon$, and $\mathcal{I}(\hat{\mathbf{x}}) = \mathcal{I}(\mathbf{x}^*)$. Also, since we have assumed that no points in $\mathcal{D}$ have the same coordinates, then $|\mathcal{K}| > 1$.

- Case 1: $\hat{s} = \epsilon$ and $|\mathcal{K}| \geq 3$.
  In this case, $\hat{\mathbf{x}} = \mathbf{x}^*$, and it is not possible to adjust $\mathbf{x}^*$ without reducing its consensus size. From Lemma 3.2, there will be at least two points on the same side of $\hat{\mathbf{x}}$ with residual ϵ as measured to $\hat{\mathbf{x}}$. Hence, set $\mathbf{x}^{**}$ as $\hat{\mathbf{x}}$.

- Case 2: $\hat{s} = \epsilon$ and $|\mathcal{K}| = 2$.
  This corresponds to the situation where $\mathcal{K}$ contains two points (p_i, q_i) and (p_j, q_j), with $p_i = p_j$, and $\hat{\mathbf{x}}$ is a non-unique Chebyshev estimate; see Figure 3.1a. Then, it is always possible to rotate the line $\hat{\mathbf{x}}$ about the point $(p_i, 0.5 * (q_i + q_j))$, until the residual of another point in $\mathcal{I}(\hat{\mathbf{x}})$ becomes ϵ, without changing the consensus set of the rotated line. Set $\mathbf{x}^{**}$ as the rotated line.

- Case 3: $\hat{s} < \epsilon$ and $|\mathcal{K}| \geq 3$.
  From Lemma 3.2, there are at least two points on the same side of $\hat{\mathbf{x}}$ with residual $\hat{s}$. Without loss of generality, we assume that two such points lie below $\hat{\mathbf{x}}$. Then, it is always possible to translate $\hat{\mathbf{x}}$ by adding $(\epsilon - \hat{s})$ to the intercept of $\hat{\mathbf{x}}$, without changing the consensus set of the line; see Figure 3.1b. Set $\mathbf{x}^{**}$ as the translated line.

- Case 4: $\hat{s} < \epsilon$ and $|\mathcal{K}| = 2$.
  First, rotate $\hat{\mathbf{x}}$ following Case 2 until the residual of another point becomes $\hat{s}$, without changing the consensus set of $\hat{\mathbf{x}}$. Then translate the line following Case 3. Set $\mathbf{x}^{**}$ as the resulting line.

Note that since $\mathcal{I}(\hat{\mathbf{x}}) = \mathcal{I}(\mathbf{x}^*)$ is already the maximum consensus set, it is not possible for the adjustments on line $\hat{\mathbf{x}}$ above to expand its consensus set. □

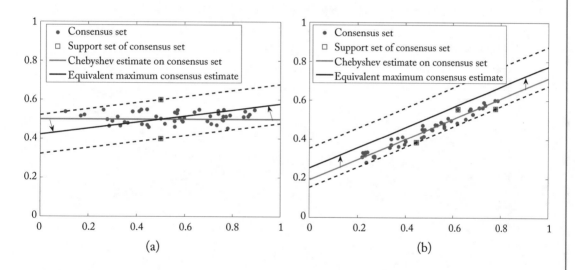

Figure 3.1: Finding equivalent maximum consensus solutions via: (a) rotating or (b) translating the Chebyshev estimate on the maximum consensus set. Observe that for the equivalent maximum consensus solutions, there are two points on the same side of the line with residual ϵ.

Theorem 3.3 suggests that the maximum consensus line $\mathbf{x}^*$ can be found as a line that lies vertically with distance ϵ above another line defined by two points. Algorithm 3.11 describes a simple method to achieve this. The algorithm has runtime complexity $\mathcal{O}(N^3)$, because for each pair of points examined, it checks the consensus size of the candidate solutions generated by iterating over all N points in $\mathcal{D}$. We discuss a more efficient algorithm in Section 3.2.2 that exploits a form of linear ordering of the points $\mathcal{D}$.

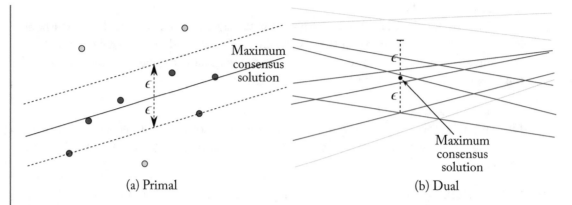

(a) Primal   (b) Dual

Figure 3.2: Characterization of the maximum consensus solution according to Theorem 3.3 in the primal and dual space, where the dual transform is as described in Definition 3.4.

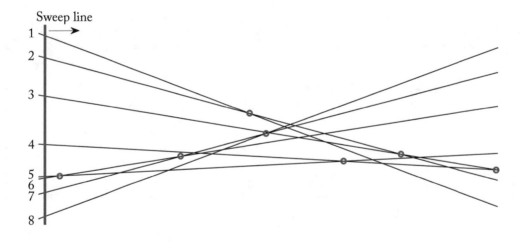

Figure 3.3: Plane sweep method in the dual space with 8 lines, where each line corresponds to a point in the primal. The sweep line is shown in its initial position, and the red circles indicate the initial events.

Conceptual Differences with RANSAC

An ostensible similarity between Algorithm 3.11 and RANSAC (Algorithm 2.3) is that they both examine subsets of the data (of size 2 for line fitting) to find the maximum consensus solution. However, although RANSAC takes estimates directly from the minimal subsets as candidate solutions, Algorithm 3.11 translates the minimal estimates according to Theorem 3.3 to guarantee that a globally optimal solution can be reached; no such assurance can be made, however, that an optimal result will always coincide with a minimal estimate. Therefore, even if one changes the

Algorithm 3.11 A simple method to fine the optimal maximum consensus line.

Require: Point set $\mathcal{D} = \{(p_i, q_i)\}_{i=1}^N$ where no two points are the same, inlier threshold ϵ.

1: $\Psi^* \leftarrow 0$, $\mathbf{x}^* \leftarrow$ *NULL*.
2: **for** every pair (i, j) with $i \neq j$ **do**
3:     $\tilde{\mathbf{x}} \leftarrow$ line defined by (p_i, q_i) and (p_j, q_j).
4:     $\tilde{\mathbf{x}}_a \leftarrow$ line obtained by adding ϵ to the intercept of $\tilde{\mathbf{x}}$.
5:     **if** $\Psi(\tilde{\mathbf{x}}_a) > \Psi^*$ **then**
6:        $\Psi^* \leftarrow \Psi(\tilde{\mathbf{x}}_a)$, $\mathbf{x}^* \leftarrow \tilde{\mathbf{x}}_a$.
7:     **end if**
8:     $\tilde{\mathbf{x}}_b \leftarrow$ line obtained by subtracting ϵ from the intercept of $\tilde{\mathbf{x}}$.
9:     **if** $\Psi(\tilde{\mathbf{x}}_b) > \Psi^*$ **then**
10:       $\Psi^* \leftarrow \Psi(\tilde{\mathbf{x}}_b)$, $\mathbf{x}^* \leftarrow \tilde{\mathbf{x}}_b$.
11:     **end if**
12: **end for**
13: **return** $\mathbf{x}^*$.

---

sample-and-test procedure in RANSAC to complete enumeration of minimal subsets, it does not yield the optimal solution in general.

After introducing a more efficient variant of Algorithm 3.11 in the next section, we experimentally compare an optimal line-fitting algorithm with RANSAC.

3.2.2   PLANE SWEEP METHOD

It is often the case that computational gains may be extracted by considering a low-dimensional problem in dual space [Chazelle et al., 1983]. This section shows how the following kind of duality can be exploited for maximum consensus line fitting.

Definition 3.4 (A point and line duality). A point (p, q) in the primal space is mapped to the line $c = pm + q$ in the dual space. A line $q = mp + c$ in the primal space is mapped to the point $(-m, c)$ in the dual space.

Under this duality, a point that lies at the intersection of two lines in the primal space is mapped to a line that is defined by two points in the dual space. Similarly, a line that passes through two points in the primal space is transformed to a point that lies at the intersection of two lines in the dual space. The ordering and vertical distance between point and line are also preserved. Namely, if point (p, q) is above line ℓ with distance r in the primal, then the dual line of (p, q) is also above the dual point of ℓ with distance r.

Souvaine and Steele [1987] applied the above duality to construct an $\mathcal{O}(N^2 \log N)$ method for LMedS line fitting. We repurpose their technique for maximum consensus.

Casting Theorem 3.3 in the dual, the maximum consensus solution is a point lying vertically above or below the intersection of two lines with distance ϵ, and exactly $|\mathcal{I}(\mathbf{x}^*)|$ lines have vertical distance less than or equal to ϵ to the maximum consensus point; see Figure 3.2. More intuitively, the "slab" that contains the maximum consensus set in the primal becomes a vertical line segment of length 2ϵ in the dual. Further, since the slab rests upon two points in one of its edges, an end of the segment is at the intersection of two lines.

In the dual space, the point set $\mathcal{D} = \{(p_i, q_i)\}_{i=1}^N$ becomes an *arrangement* of lines; see Figure 3.3. The classical plane sweep method for finding line segment intersections [Shamos and Hoey, 1976] can be converted to find the maximum consensus set. Conceptually, a vertical line continuously sweeps the dual plane from left to right. As the sweep line moves, it maintains an ordered list of the nonvertical lines that it intersects with; this list is called *status*. For example, at the sweep line position in Figure 3.3, status $= [1, 2, 3, 4, 5, 6, 7, 8]$.

The key insight in plane sweep is that the ordering in status changes only at the intersection of two lines; these intersection points are called *events*. For example, at the leftmost event in Figure 3.3, lines 5 and 6 are about to swap positions in status. In practice, therefore, the sweep line need only visit $\mathcal{O}(N^2)$ of these discrete positions.

More importantly, for maximum consensus, the events are precisely the locations in dual space that we must visit (cf. the outer loop in Algorithm 3.11). At each event, we are interested to determine the number of lines that are vertically above and below the event within distance 2ϵ. These lines correspond to two candidate consensus sets in the primal; see Figure 3.2. For example, in the leftmost event in Figure 3.3, we ask how many of the lines among $[1, 2, 3, 4, 5, 6]$ are above the event within 2ϵ, and how many among $[5, 6, 7, 8]$ are below within 2ϵ. Since the lines are already sorted by their vertical distances along the sweep line, these questions can be answered in $\mathcal{O}(\log N)$ time using bisection.

Algorithm 3.12 summarizes the plane sweep method. For simplicity, the algorithm assumes nondegenerate data (i.e., no two points in $\mathcal{D}$ have the same coordinates).

To initialize the sweep line such that it lies to the left of all possible events, the algorithm takes advantage of the fact that the dual lines sorted by their slope values (which correspond to $\{p_i\}_{i=1}^N$ in the primal) give the desired status. The set of initial events are generated by finding intersections between adjacent dual lines in the initial status. In Figure 3.3, the initial events are circled in red. The leftmost event must exist in this set.

On each visited event, two pairs of indices swap positions in status, and new events are generated by intersecting newly adjacent dual lines. The new events are then appended to the existing set. This guarantees that the next leftmost event will now exist. For example, on visiting the first event in Figure 3.3, lines 4 and 6 are newly adjacent, as are lines 5 and 7; the latter pair produces the next leftmost event. After updating the current best solution, the algorithm retrieves and advances to the next leftmost in the set of events.

Algorithm 3.12 Plane sweep method for maximum consensus line fitting.

Require: Points $\mathcal{D} = \{(p_i, q_i)\}_{i=1}^{N}$, inlier threshold ϵ.

1: $v \leftarrow 0, \mathbf{x}^* \leftarrow NULL$.

2: Re-order $\mathcal{D}$ based on increasing $\{p_i\}$ values.

3: $status \leftarrow [1, 2, \ldots, N]$.

4: $events \leftarrow$ Intersection in dual space for each adjacent pair in $status$.

5: **while** $events$ is not empty **do**

6:    $\mathbf{x} \leftarrow$ Retrieve and remove leftmost point in $events$.

7:    $(i, j) \leftarrow$ Indices of the two dual lines that intersect at $\mathbf{x}$.

8:    // Find more events.

9:    Swap positions of i and j in $status$.

10:    $events \leftarrow events \cup \{$intersections from newly adjacent pairs in $status\}$.

11:    // Update current best solution.

12:    $bef \leftarrow$ Items before i and j in $status$.

13:    $k \leftarrow$ bisection$(\mathbf{x}, [bef, i, j], \epsilon)$

14:    **if** $k > v$ **then**

15:       $v \leftarrow k, \mathbf{x}^* \leftarrow \mathbf{x}$ with ϵ added to the second element.

16:    **end if**

17:    $aft \leftarrow$ Items after i and j in $status$.

18:    $k \leftarrow$ bisection$(\mathbf{x}, \text{flip}([i, j, aft]), \epsilon)$ // flip reverses the ordering.

19:    **if** $k > v$ **then**

20:       $v \leftarrow k, \mathbf{x}^* \leftarrow \mathbf{x}$ with ϵ subtracted from the second element.

21:    **end if**

22: **end while**

23: **return** $\mathbf{x}^*$.

   bisection$(\mathbf{x}, arr, \epsilon)$

1: $a \leftarrow 1, b \leftarrow len(arr)$.

2: **while** $b - a > 1$ **do**

3:    $c \leftarrow floor(0.5 * (a + b))$.

4:    If $r_{arr(c)}(\mathbf{x}) \leq \epsilon$, then $b \leftarrow c$, else $a \leftarrow c$.

5: **end while**

6: If $r_{arr(a)}(\mathbf{x}) \leq \epsilon$, then return $(len(arr) - a + 1)$, else return $(len(arr) - b + 1)$.

Runtime Analysis

To implement the above operations efficiently, appropriate supporting algorithms and data structures must be used. The status can be initialized in $\mathcal{O}(N \log N)$ time. Pointers that map each existing event to the two lines that form it can be stored such that updates to the status can be done in constant time. The set of events can be stored in a heap, which facilitates constant time retrieval of the leftmost event, and $\mathcal{O}(\log N)$ deletions/insertions. Overall, since $\mathcal{O}(N^2)$ events must be visited, and each visit incurs operations (updating status and events list, bisection to check consensus size) that take $\mathcal{O}(\log N)$ time, the worst case computational complexity for Algorithm 3.12 is $\mathcal{O}(N^2 \log N)$.

To compare the performance of RANSAC and the plane sweep method, two experiments were performed; see Figure 3.4 for the results. In the first experiment, the outlier rate was fixed while the input size N was varied. Expectedly the runtime of plane sweep increased with N, whereas the runtime of RANSAC was roughly the same since the outlier rate was constant. In the second experiment, the input size N was fixed, while the outlier rate was varied. As anticipated, plane sweep exhibited a roughly constant trend, whereas the runtime of RANSAC increased with the outlier rate. On all the experiments, the maximum consensus size found by plane sweep was always larger than the one returned by RANSAC.

Edelsbrunner and Souvaine [1990] have since improved the runtime of the LMedS method of Souvaine and Steele [1987] to $\mathcal{O}(N^2)$ using topological plane sweep. Possibly a similarly efficient algorithm for maximum consensus line fitting can be devised. We leave this as future work.

3.3   INTEGER LINEAR PROGRAMMING METHOD

We say that a system of linear inequalities $\{\boldsymbol{\alpha}_i^T \mathbf{x} + \beta_i \leq 0\}_{i=1}^N$ is *infeasible* or *inconsistent* if there does not exist an $\mathbf{x} \in \mathbb{R}^d$ such that all the inequalities in the system can be simultaneously satisfied. An inconsistent linear system may represent a set of design or operational choices that are desirable, but ultimately cannot be satisfied at the same time. To enable optimization (e.g., using an LP solver) given an inconsistent linear system as the input constraints, the system must be repaired before optimization can begin.

One way of repairing is to remove the least number of linear inequalities to yield a consistent linear system. This creates the problem of maximum feasible subsystem or MaxFS, i.e., find the largest subsystem of linear inequalities that is feasible [Chinneck, 2007, Chapter 7]. The problem can be succinctly defined as

$$
\begin{aligned}
\underset{\mathbf{x} \in \mathbb{R}^d, \mathbf{z} \in \{0,1\}^N}{\text{minimize}} \quad & \sum_{i=1}^N z_i \\
\text{subject to} \quad & \boldsymbol{\alpha}_i^T \mathbf{x} + \beta_i \leq z_i M, \\
& i = 1, \ldots, N,
\end{aligned}
\tag{3.3}
$$

where M is a large positive constant. Setting indicator z_i to 1 effectively switches off the i-th linear inequality since this introduces a large slack M to the right hand side (RHS). The objective of minimizing the sum of the indicators thus aligns with the goal of MaxFS of finding a feasible $\mathbf{x}$ by deleting as few linear inequalities as possible.

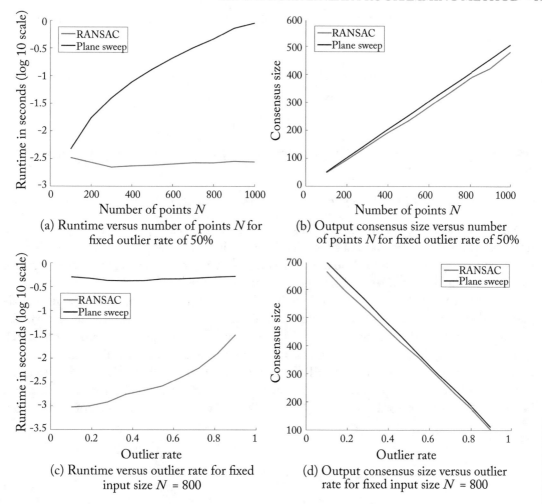

Figure 3.4: Performance comparison of RANSAC and plane sweep methods for line fitting on a 1.7 GHz Intel Core i7 machine. Results are averaged over 100 randomly generated point sets $\mathcal{D}$ containing a line with outliers. Panels (a) and (b) show runtime and output consensus size for increasing input size N and a fixed outlier rate of 50%. Panels (c) and (d) show the runtime and output consensus size for increasing outlier rate and a fixed input size $N = 800$.

Problem (3.3) is an instance of an integer linear program (ILP). Observe that the objective function and constraints are all linear, and the variables are a mix of integers and continuous numbers. The astute reader may surmise at this stage that the value of M plays a major role in the solution of Problem (3.3). We discuss this matter later in this section.

Of immediate relevance is the possibility of writing maximum consensus as an ILP:

$$
\begin{aligned}
\underset{\mathbf{x}\in\mathbb{R}^d,\mathbf{z}\in\{0,1\}^N}{\text{minimize}} \quad & \sum_{i=1}^{N} z_i \\
\text{subject to} \quad & \left| \mathbf{a}_i^T \mathbf{x} - b_i \right| \le \epsilon + z_i M, \\
& i = 1, \dots, N.
\end{aligned}
\tag{3.4}
$$

Recall the trick from (2.30) that allows the constraint $\left| \mathbf{a}_i^T \mathbf{x} - b_i \right| \le \epsilon + z_i M$ to be implemented as two linear constraints

$$
\mathbf{a}_i^T \mathbf{x} - b_i \le \epsilon + z_i M, \qquad -\left(\mathbf{a}_i^T \mathbf{x} - b_i \right) \le \epsilon + z_i M.
\tag{3.5}
$$

The (not unexpected) bad news is that ILPs are *NP*-hard in general [Conforti et al., 2014]. The (somewhat) good news is that ILPs are very common in real-life applications, thus there exist many industry-grade solvers that can be applied on (3.4). Currently the more prominent software packages include IBM ILOG CPLEX and Gurobi Optimizer.

Many state-of-the-art ILP solvers are based on the BnB technique. BnB is a general algorithm design paradigm to solve *NP*-hard optimization problems [Horst and Tuy, 2003]. The technique systematically enumerates candidate solutions by partitioning and pruning the search space $\mathbb{R}^d$. Pruning is achieved by bounding the objective value over a region of the space. Section 3.4 further explores the concept of BnB. In the context of solving (3.4), it suffices to mention that BnB recursively partitions $\mathbb{R}^d$ into axis aligned rectangular regions, and the required lower bound over a rectangular region $\mathbb{B} \subseteq \mathbb{R}^d$ is obtained via a convex relaxation of (3.4), which amounts to the LP

$$
\begin{aligned}
\underset{\mathbf{x}\in\mathbb{B},\mathbf{z}\in[0,1]^N}{\text{minimize}} \quad & \sum_{i=1}^{N} z_i \\
\text{subject to} \quad & \left| \mathbf{a}_i^T \mathbf{x} - b_i \right| \le \epsilon + z_i M, \\
& i = 1, \dots, N.
\end{aligned}
\tag{3.6}
$$

The *cutting plane* technique is used to introduce additional linear constraints in (3.6) to further tighten the bound, so as to improve the chances of pruning $\mathbb{B}$. For this reason, BnB-based ILP algorithms are often called *branch-and-cut (BnC)* methods. Since we are using ILP solvers as a "black box" (much like how we have used LP and SOCP solvers in Chapter 2), we will not further dwell on BnC. The interested reader is referred to Conforti et al. [2014] for a recent exposition of ILP algorithms.

Figure 3.5 illustrates the robust fitting of an affine plane by solving (3.4). An affine plane is defined by a 3-vector $\mathbf{x}$ and parametrized by the equation $q = [\mathbf{p}^T, 1]\mathbf{x}$, where $(\mathbf{p}, q)$ is a point in $\mathbb{R}^3$ that lies on the plane; thus, $\mathbf{a} = [\mathbf{p}^T, 1]^T$ and $b = q$. The input instance $\mathcal{D}$ in Figure 3.5 was synthetically generated with $N = 100$ points and 30% outliers. Executed on a 2.7 GHz Intel Core i7 processor, the state-of-the-art Gurobi Optimizer required approximately 420 s to converge to the globally optimal result. This outcome underlines the significant computational hardness of maximum consensus—line fitting $(d = 2)$ and plane fitting $(d = 3)$ differ by only one variable in $\mathbf{x}$, however, the latter takes several orders of magnitude more time to solve given the same number of measurements N.

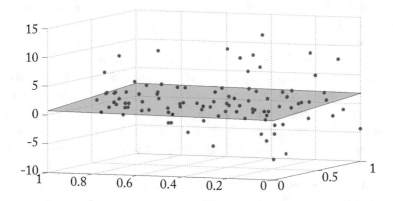

Figure 3.5: Robustly fitting an affine plane on outlier-contaminated data by solving the ILP defined in (3.4). Here, the input size N is 100, and the outlier rate is 30%. On a standard 2.7 GHz Intel Core i7 machine, Gurobi Optimizer took approximately 420 s to converge.

3.3.1   NUMERICAL ACCURACY AND PERFORMANCE

A vital input to the MaxFS formulation (3.3) is the positive constant M. The role of M is to provide a large slack amount to enable the exclusion of constraints, based on the indicator values. Using a large constant to ignore infeasible constraints is a standard practice in the optimization literature called the *big-M* method [Padberg, 1999]. Intuitively, M must be greater than the largest amount of violation among all N constraints at the optimal $\mathbf{x}$. If M is not big enough, the ILP solution for $\mathbf{x}$ will be erroneous, or the ILP itself may be infeasible. For problems where the values for $\mathbf{x}$ are known to be bounded as $\mathbf{0} \leq \mathbf{x} \leq \mathbf{u}$, Amaldi et al. [2008] suggest that a reasonable choice for M is

$$\max_{i=1,\dots,N} \left(b_i - \sum_{j:a_{i,j}<0} a_{i,j} u_j \right),\tag{3.7}$$

where $a_{i,j}$ is the j-th element of $\mathbf{a}_i$, and u_j is the j-th element of $\mathbf{u}$.

It may thus seem that a safe strategy is to make M as large as practicable. Using a very large M, however, raises at least two issues. The first is that inaccuracies will creep into the optimization if M is extremely large, since the effects of fractional values will be significantly amplified, leading to loss of integrality of the integer variables $\mathbf{z}$ and degradation of precision to parameters $\mathbf{x}$. Amaldi et al. [2005] provide clear evidence of numerical inaccuracies of the ILP formulation of MaxFS.

Using an extremely large M is also problematic, since it reduces the tightness of the LP relaxation as a lower bound. Observe that if M is very large, the relaxed indicator variable $z_i \in [0, 1]$ need only be activated slightly to obtain sufficient slack for the corresponding constraints. Thus, the optimal value of the LP tends to be close to zero, which weakens its ability to conduct pruning and significantly slows down convergence.

A heuristic is thus required to obtain an M that is big enough, but not too big. In the context of the ILP formulation for maximum consensus (3.4), M must be greater than the largest residual (take ϵ) at the optimal $\mathbf{x}$. Although in general this knowledge is unavailable *a priori*, if one is allowed to re-scale the data coordinates, or equivalently if the maximum range of the data is known beforehand, a suitable M can be guesstimated. For the plane fitting data in Figure 3.5, for example, the response measurements $\{q_i\}_{i=1}^{N}$ are known to lie within ± 100, thus one may reasonably expect $M = 100$ to be an appropriate choice; indeed, this was the value used to obtain the presented result.

Another heuristical procedure to select M is to first apply a fast approximate algorithm such as RANSAC to obtain a good suboptimal maximum consensus solution. This provides a ballpark estimate of the maximum residual. One could then inflate the maximum residual by several factors to obtain M.

3.3.2   GENERALIZED FRACTIONAL MODELS

Extending (3.4) to general nonlinear models creates integer nonlinear programs (INLP), which are even more challenging than ILPs. For models with generalized fractional residuals (Section 2.3.1), however, ILP formulations are still possible.

First, the definition of the p-norm $\|\mathbf{x}\|_p$ of a vector $\mathbf{x}$ is

$$\|\mathbf{x}\|_p = (|x_1|^p + |x_2|^p + \cdots + |x_d|^p)^{1/p} . \tag{3.8}$$

Next, note that for $p \geq 1$, the nonlinear residual function

$$r(\mathbf{x}) = \frac{\|\mathbf{Ax} + \mathbf{b}\|_p}{\boldsymbol{\alpha}^T \mathbf{x} + \beta} \tag{3.9}$$

remains quasiconvex in the region $\boldsymbol{\alpha}^T \mathbf{x} + \beta > 0$. In the context of maximum consensus, changing the p-norm in the numerator of (3.9) from $p = 2$ to other values has the effect of modifying the shape of the inlier neighborhood; see Figure 3.6. Since the outlier residuals are typically much greater than the inlier residuals, we would expect that any $p \geq 1$ would be suitable for the purpose of separating inliers from outliers.

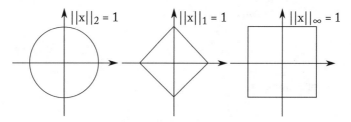

Figure 3.6: Unit-circle for three different p-norms.

The big-M formulation for maximum consensus with residuals of the form (3.9) is

$$
\begin{aligned}
&\underset{\mathbf{x}\in\mathbb{R}^d,\mathbf{z}\in\{0,1\}^N}{\text{minimize}} && \sum_{i=1}^{N} z_i \\
&\text{subject to} && \|\mathbf{A}_i\mathbf{x} + \mathbf{b}_i\|_p \le \epsilon\left(\boldsymbol{\alpha}_i^T\mathbf{x} + \beta_i\right) + z_i M \\
&&& i = 1,\ldots,N,
\end{aligned}
\tag{3.10}
$$

where we have applied the same trick as in Section 2.3.1 to move the denominator of the generalized fractional function (3.9) to the right hand side.

Let the elements in $\mathbf{A}_i \in \mathbb{R}^{2\times d}$ and $\mathbf{b}_i \in \mathbb{R}^{2\times 1}$ be represented as

$$
\mathbf{A}_i = \begin{bmatrix} \mathbf{a}_{i,1}^T \\ \mathbf{a}_{i,2}^T \end{bmatrix}, \quad \mathbf{b}_i = \begin{bmatrix} b_{i,1} \\ b_{i,2} \end{bmatrix}.
\tag{3.11}
$$

For $p = 1$, the inequality in (3.10) can be re-expressed as

$$
\left|\mathbf{a}_{i,1}^T\mathbf{x} + b_{i,1}\right| + \left|\mathbf{a}_{i,2}^T\mathbf{x} + b_{i,2}\right| \le \epsilon\left(\boldsymbol{\alpha}_i^T\mathbf{x} + \beta_i\right) + z_i M.
\tag{3.12}
$$

Recursively applying the expansion rule in (2.30) enables inequality (3.12) to be implemented as four linear constraints

$$
\begin{aligned}
\mathbf{a}_{i,1}^T\mathbf{x} + b_{i,1} + \mathbf{a}_{i,2}^T\mathbf{x} + b_{i,2} &\le \epsilon\left(\boldsymbol{\alpha}_i^T\mathbf{x} + \beta_i\right) + z_i M, \\
-\mathbf{a}_{i,1}^T\mathbf{x} - b_{i,1} + \mathbf{a}_{i,2}^T\mathbf{x} + b_{i,2} &\le \epsilon\left(\boldsymbol{\alpha}_i^T\mathbf{x} + \beta_i\right) + z_i M, \\
\mathbf{a}_{i,1}^T\mathbf{x} + b_{i,1} - \mathbf{a}_{i,2}^T\mathbf{x} - b_{i,2} &\le \epsilon\left(\boldsymbol{\alpha}_i^T\mathbf{x} + \beta_i\right) + z_i M, \\
-\mathbf{a}_{i,1}^T\mathbf{x} - b_{i,1} - \mathbf{a}_{i,2}^T\mathbf{x} - b_{i,2} &\le \epsilon\left(\boldsymbol{\alpha}_i^T\mathbf{x} + \beta_i\right) + z_i M,
\end{aligned}
\tag{3.13}
$$

where the constraints relating to the same datum $(\mathbf{A}_i, \mathbf{b}_i.\boldsymbol{\alpha}_i, \beta_i)$ are "chained" together by the same indicator variable z_i. Plugging the constraints back into the big-M formulation (3.10) thus yields an ILP.

For $p = \infty$, the p-norm reduces to

$$
\|\mathbf{x}\|_p = \max\left(|x_1|, |x_2|, \ldots, |x_d|\right).
\tag{3.14}
$$

The inequality in (3.10) thus becomes

$$\max\left(\left|\mathbf{a}_{i,1}^T\mathbf{x} + b_{i,1}\right|, \left|\mathbf{a}_{i,2}^T\mathbf{x} + b_{i,2}\right|\right) \le \epsilon(\boldsymbol{\alpha}_i^T\mathbf{x} + \beta_i) + z_i M, \qquad (3.15)$$

which is equivalent to simultaneously imposing

$$\left|\mathbf{a}_{i,1}^T\mathbf{x} + b_{i,1}\right| \le \epsilon\left(\boldsymbol{\alpha}_i^T\mathbf{x} + \beta_i\right) + z_i M,$$
$$\left|\mathbf{a}_{i,2}^T\mathbf{x} + b_{i,2}\right| \le \epsilon\left(\boldsymbol{\alpha}_i^T\mathbf{x} + \beta_i\right) + z_i M. \qquad (3.16)$$

Applying the expansion rule in (2.30) on the above, we obtain the four linear constraints

$$\mathbf{a}_{i,1}^T\mathbf{x} + b_{i,1} \le \epsilon\left(\boldsymbol{\alpha}_i^T\mathbf{x} + \beta_i\right) + z_i M,$$
$$-\mathbf{a}_{i,1}^T\mathbf{x} - b_{i,1} \le \epsilon\left(\boldsymbol{\alpha}_i^T\mathbf{x} + \beta_i\right) + z_i M,$$
$$\mathbf{a}_{i,2}^T\mathbf{x} + b_{i,2} \le \epsilon\left(\boldsymbol{\alpha}_i^T\mathbf{x} + \beta_i\right) + z_i M,$$
$$-\mathbf{a}_{i,2}^T\mathbf{x} - b_{i,2} \le \epsilon\left(\boldsymbol{\alpha}_i^T\mathbf{x} + \beta_i\right) + z_i M. \qquad (3.17)$$

Again, z_i connects the constraints that relate to the i-th datum. Substituting (3.17) into the big-M formulation (3.10), we obtain again an ILP.

Figure 3.7 illustrates the result of robustly estimating an affine transformation (a $d = 6$ dimensional model) from a set of outlier-contaminated feature correspondences between two images. The data in this example consists of $N = 85$ feature correspondences obtained using the SIFT method [Lowe, 2004]. See Example 2.4 for the definition of the residual function for maximum consensus. Setting $p = \infty$, $\epsilon = 1$ and $M = 1000$ in the ILP (3.10), on a standard 2.7 GHz Intel Core i7 machine, Gurobi Optimizer took approximately 1028 s to find the globally optimal solution.

3.4 ROBUST POINT SET REGISTRATION

As alluded to in Section 3.3, the technique of BnB offers a general framework to devise exact solutions for *NP*-hard optimization problems such as maximum consensus. In this section, we illustrate the principle of BnB by describing a robust point set registration algorithm based on maximum consensus. In particular, we aim to solve *Euclidean registration* of 3D point sets, which requires estimating a 6DOF rigid transformation. The Euclidean registration problem is encountered very frequently in computer vision and robotics tasks, such as hand-eye calibration, 3D reconstruction and modeling, and recognition of 3D objects. Further, outliers almost always exist in the data, thus necessitating robust estimation (the precise notion of an "outlier" in point set registration is defined below).

Two main design choices must be made to adapt the generic framework of BnB to solve robust point set registration:

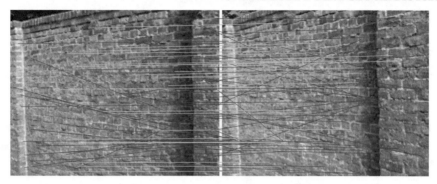

Figure 3.7: Robustly estimating an affine transformation ($d = 6$) via maximum consensus from a set of outlier-contaminated SIFT feature correspondences [Lowe, 2004]. There are a total of $N = 85$ feature correspondences. With $p = \infty$, $\epsilon = 1$ pixel and $M = 1000$ in (3.10), on a standard 2.7 GHz Intel Core i7 machine, Gurobi Optimizer took approximately 1028.07 s to solve the ILP. Green and red lines respectively denote inliers and outliers at the optimum.

- defining a suitable representation or parametrization of the transformation model to form the search space of BnB; and

- constructing an upper bound function for the maximum consensus criterion to enable pruning of subregions of the search space.

In the rest of this section, the two concepts are progressively teased out by first focusing on rotational alignment (3DOF), and then extending to full 6DOF Euclidean registration.

3.4.1 ROTATIONAL ALIGNMENT

Given two point sets $\{\mathbf{p}_i\}_{i=1}^{N}$ and $\{\mathbf{p}'_j\}_{j=1}^{M}$, we wish to estimate a rotation $\mathbf{R}$ that can align the points. Note that the two point sets differ in cardinality in general, thus; not all the points in a set will have a matching point in the other set. Such non-matching points behave as outliers to the estimation. It is thus sensible to estimate $\mathbf{R}$ with a maximum consensus approach, where the consensus score is defined as

$$\Psi(\mathbf{R}) = \sum_{i=1}^{N} \max_{j} \mathbb{I}\left(\left\|\mathbf{R}\mathbf{p}_i - \mathbf{p}'_j\right\|_2 \leq \epsilon\right), \tag{3.18}$$

and ϵ is the usual inlier threshold. The existence of the inner maximization in (3.18), however, sets robust point set registration apart from the typical robust estimation problems seen previously in this book. Basically, for each point $\mathbf{p}_i$ that is acted upon by $\mathbf{R}$, a separate test must be conducted to see if a matching point exists in the second set. Registering point sets according to criterion (3.18) is also called *geometric matching* [Breuel, 2003].

Branch-and-Bound Algorithm

The set of rotations form a group called the special orthogonal group $SO(3)$. The parametrization of $SO(3)$ (i.e., numerically representing members of the group to facilitate calculus, search, etc.) is a nontrivial topic by itself (see Hartley et al. [2013] for a recent exposition of this topic). For the purpose of BnB search over $SO(3)$, the *axis-angle* parametrization is commonly used. Specifically, a rotation is represented as a 3-vector $\mathbf{r} = \theta \hat{\mathbf{r}}$, whose direction specified by the unit vector $\hat{\mathbf{r}}$ gives the axis of rotation, and whose length $\|\mathbf{r}\|_2 = \theta$ represents the angle of rotation; see Figure 3.8a. Let $\mathbf{R_r}$ refer to the rotation matrix corresponding to the axis-angle vector $\mathbf{r}$. Via Rodrigues' rotation formula,

$$\mathbf{R_r} = \mathbf{I} + \sin\theta [\hat{\mathbf{r}}]_\times + (1 - \cos\theta)[\hat{\mathbf{r}}]_\times^2, \tag{3.19}$$

where $[\hat{\mathbf{r}}]_\times$ is the skew symmetric cross-product matrix

$$[\hat{\mathbf{r}}]_\times = \begin{bmatrix} 0 & -\hat{r}_3 & \hat{r}_2 \\ \hat{r}_3 & 0 & -\hat{r}_1 \\ -\hat{r}_2 & \hat{r}_1 & 0 \end{bmatrix}. \tag{3.20}$$

A solid ball of radius π thus encompasses $SO(3)$. Note, however, that diametrically opposing vectors on the surface of the ball represent the same rotation.

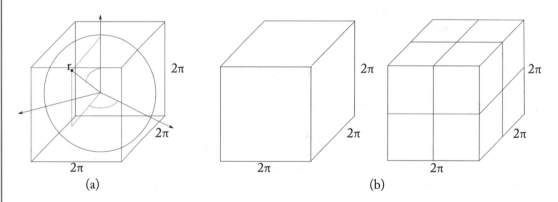

(a)   (b)

Figure 3.8: (a) In the axis-angle representation of rotations, the direction $\hat{\mathbf{r}}$ of vector $\mathbf{r}$ indicates the axis of rotation, while its length $\|\mathbf{r}\|_2$ indicates the angle of rotation. All rotations are thus contained in a solid ball of radius π. (b) Illustrating the octal subdivision of the initial cube that encloses the π-ball.

Algorithm 3.13 summarizes a BnB algorithm to maximize (3.18) over $SO(3)$, based on the axis-angle parametrization for rotations. To initialize BnB, we enclose the π-ball with the tightest bounding solid cube. Then, we recursively subdivide the cube into smaller cubes—octal subdivision; see Figure 3.8b. Given a cube $\mathbb{B}$, the algorithm attempts to reject it (i.e., prevent from further subdivision) by means of a *bounding function* $\hat{\Psi}$ (to be defined later), or seeks within $\mathbb{B}$ a rotation with higher consensus than the incumbent. Eventually, the algorithm searches all of the π-ball, or is able to terminate early from concluding that no other yet-to-be explored rotations can give a higher objective value than the incumbent.

Algorithm 3.13 BnB method to maximize (3.18) for robust rotational registration.

Require: Point sets $\{\mathbf{p}_i\}_{i=1}^N$ and $\{\mathbf{p}_j'\}_{j=1}^M$, inlier threshold ϵ.
 1: Initialize priority queue q.
 2: $\mathbb{B} \leftarrow$ Solid cube of side length 2π, centered at the origin.
 3: $\Psi^* \leftarrow 0$, $\mathbf{R}^* \leftarrow NULL$.
 4: Insert $\mathbb{B}$ into q.
 5: **while** q is not empty **do**
 6:   $\mathbb{B} \leftarrow$ Remove from q the cube with the highest priority.
 7:   $\mathbf{c} \leftarrow$ Center point of $\mathbb{B}$.
 8:   **if** $\Psi(\mathbf{R_c}) = \Psi^*$ **then**
 9:     Break.
10:   **else if** $\Psi(\mathbf{R_c}) > \Psi^*$ **then**
11:     $\Psi^* \leftarrow \Psi(\mathbf{R_c})$, $\mathbf{R}^* \leftarrow \mathbf{R_c}$.
12:   **end if**
13:   Subdivide $\mathbb{B}$ into 8 cubes $\mathbb{B}_1, \ldots, \mathbb{B}_8$.
14:   **for** $i = 1, \ldots, 8$ **do**
15:     **if** $\hat{\Psi}(\mathbb{B}_i) > \Psi^*$ **then**
16:       Insert $\mathbb{B}_i$ with priority $\hat{\Psi}(\mathbb{B}_i)$ into q.
17:     **end if**
18:   **end for**
19: **end while**
20: **return** $\mathbf{R}^*$.

Enclosing a ball with a cube inevitably raises boundary issues. If a cube $\mathbb{B}$ resulting from a partition does not lie in the π-ball, it is immediately rejected (this obvious step is not displayed in Algorithm 3.13). If the cube $\mathbb{B}$ lies partially in the π-ball, no special treatment is required, though this implies that the search will cover redundant regions.

Bounding Function

Clearly, the bounding function $\hat{\Psi}$ plays a critical role in BnB. The value $\hat{\Psi}(\mathbb{B})$ evaluated by the bounding function over cube $\mathbb{B}$ must satisfy

$$\hat{\Psi}(\mathbb{B}) \geq \max_{\mathbf{r} \in \mathbb{B}} \Psi(\mathbf{R_r}). \tag{3.21}$$

Further, to ensure convergence to the global optimum, $\hat{\Psi}(\mathbb{B})$ must converge to $\Psi(\mathbf{R_r})$ if $\mathbb{B}$ collapses into the single point $\mathbf{r}$.

A fundamental result of the axis-angle representation toward constructing bounds for rotation estimation is

$$\angle(\mathbf{R_u p}, \mathbf{R_v p}) \leq \|\mathbf{u} - \mathbf{v}\|_2. \tag{3.22}$$

(See, for example, Section 3.1 of Hartley and Kahl [2009] for a discussion on the basis of this result.) Let $\mathbf{c}$ be the center point of a cube $\mathbb{B}$ in the axis-angle rotation space. Then, for any $\mathbf{r} \in \mathbb{B}$,

$$\angle(\mathbf{R_c p}, \mathbf{R_r p}) \leq \max_{\mathbf{r} \in \mathbb{B}} \|\mathbf{c} - \mathbf{r}\|_2 = \alpha_{\mathbb{B}}, \tag{3.23}$$

where we define $\alpha_{\mathbb{B}}$ as half of the diagonal length of $\mathbb{B}$. It thus follows that

$$\|\mathbf{R_c p} - \mathbf{R_r p}\|_2 \leq \delta_{\mathbf{p}}, \tag{3.24}$$

where $\delta_{\mathbf{p}}$ is obtained using the cosine rule as

$$\delta_{\mathbf{p}} = \sqrt{2\|\mathbf{p}\|_2^2(1 - \cos\alpha_{\mathbb{B}})}. \tag{3.25}$$

Intuitively, (3.24) states that, given all rotations $\mathbf{r}$ in $\mathbb{B}$, the point $\mathbf{R_r p}$ lies within a ball of radius $\delta_{\mathbf{p}}$ with center at $\mathbf{R_c p}$. Figure 3.9 illustrates this bound.

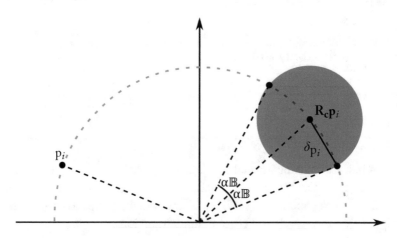

Figure 3.9: A 2D view of the uncertainty region (3.24).

Based on (3.24), an upper bound function for (3.18) can be constructed as

$$\hat{\Psi}_{\text{ball}}(\mathbb{B}) = \sum_{i=1}^{N} \max_{j} \mathbb{I}\left(\left\|\mathbf{R_c p}_i - \mathbf{p}'_j\right\|_2 \leq \epsilon + \delta_{\mathbf{p}_i}\right). \tag{3.26}$$

Intuitively, since the point $\mathbf{R_r p}_i$ for all possible $\mathbf{r} \in \mathbb{B}$ lies within a ball of radius $\delta_{\mathbf{p}_i}$ centerd at $\mathbf{R_c p}_i$, we conservatively allow any point $\mathbf{p}'_j$ with distance not greater than $\epsilon + \delta_{\mathbf{p}_i}$ to $\mathbf{R_c p}_i$ to match with $\mathbf{p}_i$. We can thus conclude that $\hat{\Psi}_{\text{ball}}(\mathbb{B})$ satisfies the requirements of the bounding function, as summarized below.

Theorem 3.5   *For any cube $\mathbb{B}$ in the axis-angle space,*

$$\hat{\Psi}_{ball}(\mathbb{B}) \geq \max_{\mathbf{r} \in \mathbb{B}} \Psi(\mathbf{R_r}), \tag{3.27}$$

and $\hat{\Psi}_{ball}(\mathbb{B}) = \Psi(\mathbf{R_r})$ if $\mathbb{B}$ is a single point $\mathbf{r}$.

A formal proof of the theorem is given in Section D in the Appendix.

Tightening the Bound
The uncertainty predicted by (3.24) is unnecessarily conservative. Intuitively, the point $\mathbf{Rp}$ for all $\mathbf{R} \in SO(3)$ can only lie on a sphere with radius $\|\mathbf{p}\|_2$. The uncertainty defined in (3.24), however, includes regions off the sphere. In general, a tighter bounding function enables BnB to terminate more quickly, since the bounding function is able to more aggressively prune the search space. It is thus of interest to construct a tighter $\hat{\Psi}$.

Define $S_\theta(\mathbf{p})$ as the *spherical patch* centerd at $\mathbf{p}$ with angular radius θ; that is,

$$S_\theta(\mathbf{p}) = \left\{ \mathbf{x} \in \mathbb{R}^3 \mid \|\mathbf{x}\|_2 = \|\mathbf{p}\|, \angle(\mathbf{p}, \mathbf{x}) \leq \theta \right\}. \tag{3.28}$$

$S_{2\pi}(\mathbf{p})$ is thus the sphere of radius $\|\mathbf{p}\|_2$ centerd at the origin, and $S_\theta(\mathbf{p}) \subseteq S_{2\pi}(\mathbf{p})$. Further, the outline of $S_\theta(\mathbf{p})$ is a circle on $S_{2\pi}(\mathbf{p})$. Result (3.23) can thus be re-expressed as

$$\mathbf{R_r p} \in S_{\alpha_\mathbb{B}}(\mathbf{R_c p}), \tag{3.29}$$

where $\mathbf{c}$ is the center of rotation cube $\mathbb{B}$, and $\mathbf{r}$ is any point in $\mathbb{B}$. See Figure 3.10. As can be readily appreciated, this uncertainty region is less wasteful than (3.24).

To construct a bounding function based on (3.29), first, let $l_\epsilon(\mathbf{p})$ denote the *solid ball* of radius ϵ centered at $\mathbf{p}$:

$$l_\epsilon(\mathbf{p}) = \left\{ \mathbf{p} \in \mathbb{R}^3 \mid \|\mathbf{p} - \mathbf{x}\|_2 \leq \epsilon \right\}. \tag{3.30}$$

The objective function (3.18) can thus be re-written as

$$\Psi(\mathbf{R}) = \sum_{i=1}^{N} \max_j \mathbb{I}\left(\mathbf{Rp}_i \in l_\epsilon(\mathbf{p}'_j) \right). \tag{3.31}$$

From (3.29), determining if $\mathbf{R_r p}_i$ can possibly match with $\mathbf{p}'_j$ under all $\mathbf{r} \in \mathbb{B}$ amounts to checking whether whether $S_{\alpha_\mathbb{B}}(\mathbf{R_c p}_i)$ intersects $l_\epsilon(\mathbf{p}'_j)$; see Figure 3.10. This suggests the following upper

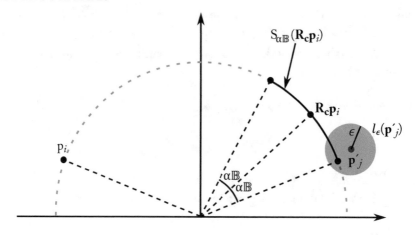

Figure 3.10: A 2D view of the uncertainty region (3.29).

bound function:

$$\hat{\Psi}_{\text{patch}}(\mathbb{B}) = \sum_{i=1}^{N} \max_{j} \; \mathbb{I}\left(S_{\alpha_{\mathbb{B}}}(\mathbf{R_c}\mathbf{p}_i) \cap l_{\epsilon}(\mathbf{p}'_j) \neq \emptyset\right). \tag{3.32}$$

By the construction process, we can intuitively appreciate the validity of $\hat{\Psi}_{\text{patch}}$ as a bounding function for BnB, as summarized in the following result.

Theorem 3.6   *For any cube $\mathbb{B}$ in the axis-angle space,*

$$\hat{\Psi}_{patch}(\mathbb{B}) \geq \max_{\mathbf{r} \in \mathbb{B}} \Psi(\mathbf{R_r}), \tag{3.33}$$

and $\hat{\Psi}_{patch}(\mathbb{B}) = \Psi(\mathbf{R_r})$ if $\mathbb{B}$ is a single point $\mathbf{r}$.

A formal proof of the above theorem is available in Section E in the Appendix.

Intuitively, $\hat{\Psi}_{\text{patch}}$ imposes a tighter bound than $\hat{\Psi}_{\text{ball}}$, since the former encloses $\mathbf{R_r}\mathbf{p}_i$ in a spherical patch, whereas the latter encloses $\mathbf{R_r}\mathbf{p}_i$ in a ball that subsumes the spherical patch. A formal proof is as follows.

Theorem 3.7   *For any cube $\mathbb{B}$ in the axis-angle space,*

$$\hat{\Psi}_{ball}(\mathbb{B}) \geq \hat{\Psi}_{patch}(\mathbb{B}). \tag{3.34}$$

In words, $\hat{\Psi}_{patch}$ is a tighter bounding function than $\hat{\Psi}_{ball}$.

Proof. First, it is trivial to see that any pair $\mathbf{p}_i$ and $\mathbf{p}'_j$ that contribute 1 to $\hat{\Psi}_{\text{patch}}(\mathbb{B})$ must also contribute 1 to $\hat{\Psi}_{\text{ball}}(\mathbb{B})$; observe that if $S_{\alpha_{\mathbb{B}}}(\mathbf{R_c p}_i)$ and $l_{\epsilon}(\mathbf{p}'_j)$ have a non-empty intersection, then necessarily $\|\mathbf{R_c p}_i - \mathbf{p}'_j\|_2 \leq \epsilon + \delta_{\mathbf{p}_i}$.

The reverse, however, is not necessarily true; there are hypothetical pairs $\mathbf{p}_i$ and $\mathbf{p}'_j$ that contribute 1 to $\hat{\Psi}_{\text{ball}}(\mathbb{B})$ but 0 to $\hat{\Psi}_{\text{patch}}(\mathbb{B})$. To construct such a pair, set $\mathbf{p}'_j = \mathbf{R_c p}_i(1 + \frac{\epsilon + \delta_{\mathbf{p}_i}}{\|\mathbf{p}_i\|})$. Clearly the condition $\|\mathbf{R_c p}_i - \mathbf{p}'_j\| \leq \epsilon + \delta_{\mathbf{p}_i}$ holds and $\mathbf{p}_i$ and $\mathbf{p}'_j$ contribute 1 to $\hat{\Psi}_{\text{ball}}(\mathbb{B})$. However, then $\|\mathbf{p}'_j\| - \|\mathbf{p}_i\| > \epsilon$ and $l_{\epsilon}(\mathbf{p}'_j)$ cannot intersect with $S_{\alpha_{\mathbb{B}}}(\mathbf{R_c p}_i)$, thus the pair $\mathbf{p}_i$ and $\mathbf{p}'_j$ contribute 0 to $\hat{\Psi}_{\text{patch}}(\mathbb{B})$. $\qquad\square$

Efficient Objective and Bound Evaluation

Another vitally important aspect of Algorithm 3.13 is the efficiency in evaluating the objective and bounding functions, since these are repeatedly called during BnB. In the version of rotation estimation without *a priori* determined correspondences, a separate search, defined by the inner maximization in (3.31) and (3.32), must be conducted for each $\mathbf{p}_i$ to find matching point in the second set $\{\mathbf{p}'_j\}_{j=1}^M$. Ideally we would like to avoid iterating over all j to answer each such query; though this has linear complexity, it becomes a significant computational bottleneck if the functions are repeatedly evaluated.

First, observe that under pure rotational motion, a point $\mathbf{p}_i$ is restricted to lie on the sphere $S_{2\pi}(\mathbf{p}_i)$. Thus, we can preclude beforehand the points $\mathbf{p}'_j$ that lie too far away from $S_{2\pi}(\mathbf{p}_i)$, since these will never be matched with $\mathbf{p}_i$ regardless of the rotation applied. The geometric matching objective function (3.31) can thus be re-written as

$$\Psi(\mathbf{R}) = \sum_{i=1}^N \max_{j \in \mathcal{B}_i} \mathbb{I}\left(\mathbf{R p}_i \in l_{\epsilon}(\mathbf{p}'_j)\right), \tag{3.35}$$

where

$$\mathcal{B}_i = \left\{ j \in \{1, \ldots, M\} \mid \left| \|\mathbf{p}_i\|_2 - \|\mathbf{p}'_j\|_2 \right| \leq \epsilon \right\} \tag{3.36}$$

indexes the points in the second set that lie close enough to $S_{2\pi}(\mathbf{p}_i)$ to bear any hope of matching with $\mathbf{p}_i$. Similarly, the upper bound function $\hat{\Psi}_{\text{patch}}$ (3.32) can be re-written as

$$\hat{\Psi}_{\text{patch}}(\mathbb{B}) = \sum_{i=1}^N \max_{j \in \mathcal{B}_i} \mathbb{I}\left(S_{\alpha_{\mathbb{B}}}(\mathbf{R_c p}_i) \cap l_{\epsilon}(\mathbf{p}'_j) \neq \emptyset\right). \tag{3.37}$$

Second, the question of whether $\mathbf{p}_i$ has a matching point in the second set can be answered by means of a nearest neighbor search. In particular, the value of

$$\max_{j \in \mathcal{B}_i} \mathbb{I}\left(\mathbf{R p}_i \in l_{\epsilon}(\mathbf{p}'_j)\right) \tag{3.38}$$

must be 0 if the point from $\mathcal{B}_i$ that is nearest to $\mathbf{R}\mathbf{p}_i$ has a distance that is greater than ϵ; else, the value of (3.38) must be 1. Similarly, the value of

$$\max_{j \in \mathcal{B}_i} \mathbb{I}\left(S_{\alpha_{\mathbb{B}}}(\mathbf{R_c}\mathbf{p}_i) \cap l_\epsilon(\mathbf{p}'_j) \neq \emptyset\right) \tag{3.39}$$

must be 0 if the point from $\mathcal{B}_i$ that is nearest to $\mathbf{R_c}\mathbf{p}_i$ has a distance that is greater than $\epsilon + \delta_{\mathbf{p}_i}$. If the distance of the nearest neighbor is not greater than $\epsilon + \delta_{\mathbf{p}_i}$, however, the intersection test between $S_{\alpha_{\mathbb{B}}}(\mathbf{R_c}\mathbf{p}_i)$ and $l_\epsilon(\mathbf{p}'_j)$ for the nearest neighbor $\mathbf{p}'_j$ must be carried out to determine if (3.39) evaluates to 1.

The search for the nearest neighbor can be conducted more efficiently than linear scanning by using kd-trees. Specifically, the points indexed by $\mathcal{B}_i$ is stored in a kd-tree data structure, which is a balanced binary tree that partitions the 3D Euclidean space according to the spatial distribution of the points [de Berg et al., 2008, Chapter 5]. Given the kd-tree, finding the nearest neighbor of a query point can be accomplished in $\mathcal{O}(\log M)$ average time (see Friedman et al. [1977] for details of the search algorithm). Although N kd-trees need to be built (one for each $\mathcal{B}_i$), and the kd-tree construction takes $\mathcal{O}(M \log^2 M)$ time in the worst case, the cost of constructing kd-trees for Algorithm 3.13 is of minor concern since the kd-trees can be built offline prior to BnB search.

Based on the essential principles above, a much more efficient method based on stereo-graphic projection and circular R-tree indexation to evaluate $\hat{\Psi}_{\text{patch}}$ has been proposed by Parra Bustos et al. [2016]. We refer the reader to that paper for details.

Evaluation

To test the BnB algorithm for 3D rotational alignment, data from the Stanford 3D Scanning Repository[1] were used. Two of the objects in the repository are shown in Figures 3.11a and 3.11b. For each object, two partially overlapping scans $\mathcal{V}_1$ and $\mathcal{V}_2$ were retrieved. For each pair $\mathcal{V}_1$ and $\mathcal{V}_2$, 100 point correspondences were extracted using the ISS3D keypoint detector Zhong [2009] and PFH descriptor Rusu et al. [2008] as implemented on Point Cloud Library.[2] For each correspondence $\mathbf{k} \leftrightarrow \mathbf{k}'$, points in the δ_{loc}-neighborhood of $\mathbf{k}$ and $\mathbf{k}'$ were extracted and re-centered respectively on the keypoints. The extracted points were then used as the input $\{\mathbf{p}_i\}_{i=1}^N$ and $\{\mathbf{p}'_j\}_{j=1}^M$ for rotational alignment.

By swapping the input point sets if necessary, assume that $N \leq M$. The actual size N depends on the neighborhood size δ_{loc}, i.e., increasing δ_{loc} also increases N. Figure 3.11c plots the median runtime of Algorithm 3.13 (on a standard 3.7 GHz Intel Core i7 machine) across all the generated input instances $\{\mathbf{p}_i\}_{i=1}^N$ and $\{\mathbf{p}'_j\}_{j=1}^M$, as the size N of the problems were increased. Note that the recorded durations include time for all data structure preparations (kd-tree construction, etc.). Observe that the runtime of BnB using $\hat{\Psi}_{\text{patch}}$ (indicated as "patch bound") as much shorter

---

[1] http://graphics.stanford.edu/data/3Dscanrep/
[2] http://pointclouds.org/

than the runtime using $\hat{\Psi}_{\text{ball}}$ (indicated as "ball bound"). In particular, for $N \geq 1500$, the runtime using $\hat{\Psi}_{\text{patch}}$ is an order of magnitude smaller than the runtime using $\hat{\Psi}_{\text{ball}}$.

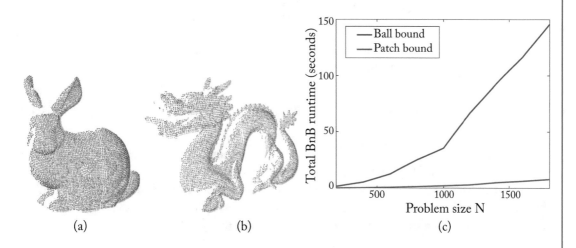

(a)   (b)   (c)

Figure 3.11: (a, b) Sample objects from the Stanford 3D Scanning Repository used in this evaluation. (c) The median runtimes of Algorithm 3.13 using respectively $\hat{\Psi}_{\text{ball}}$ (ball bound) and $\hat{\Psi}_{\text{patch}}$ (patch bound) as the bounding function.

This result is a clear validation of Theorem 3.7, and it suggests that there is much to gain by closely examining the underlying geometry of a maximum consensus problem.

3.4.2 EUCLIDEAN REGISTRATION

A 6DOF rigid transformation $\mathbf{Rp} + \mathbf{t}$ is defined by a rotation $\mathbf{R} \in SO(3)$ and a translation $\mathbf{t} \in \mathbb{R}^3$. Extending the maximum consensus criterion (3.18) for rotational alignment to Euclidean registration yields the following objective function:

$$\Psi(\mathbf{R}, \mathbf{t}) = \sum_{i=1}^{N} \max_{j} \, \mathbb{I} \left(\left\| \mathbf{Rp}_i + \mathbf{t} - \mathbf{p}'_j \right\|_2 \leq \epsilon \right). \tag{3.40}$$

The space of all rigid transformations $(\mathbf{R}, \mathbf{t})$ defines a group called the special Euclidean group $SE(3)$. Although it is possible to globally maximize (3.40) by conducting a BnB search directly over $SE(3)$, a more convenient approach that uses the robust rotational alignment algorithm (Algorithm 3.13) as a subroutine can be constructed.

First, for reasons that will be clear later, we depart slightly from convention to define a rigid transformation as $\mathbf{R}(\mathbf{p} + \mathbf{t})$; with straightforward manipulation, the traditional version can be recovered without loss of generality. Function (3.40) is then modified to become

$$\Psi(\mathbf{R}, \mathbf{t}) = \sum_{i=1}^{N} \max_{j} \, \mathbb{I} \left(\left\| \mathbf{R}(\mathbf{p}_i + \mathbf{t}) - \mathbf{p}'_j \right\|_2 \le \epsilon \right). \tag{3.41}$$

By "nesting" the rotational parameters, the problem of maximizing (3.41) can be formulated equivalently as maximizing the function

$$\Psi(\mathbf{t}) = \max_{\mathbf{R} \in SO(3)} \sum_{i=1}^{N} \max_{j} \, \mathbb{I} \left(\left\| \mathbf{R}(\mathbf{p}_i + \mathbf{t}) - \mathbf{p}'_j \right\|_2 \le \epsilon \right). \tag{3.42}$$

Now, evaluating (3.42) given $\mathbf{t}$ amounts to solving the rotational alignment problem on the point sets $\{\mathbf{p}_i + \mathbf{t}\}_{i=1}^{N}$ and $\{\mathbf{p}'_j\}_{j=1}^{M}$, which can be achieved via Algorithm 3.13.

Our goal of robust Euclidean registration can now be achieved by devising a BnB algorithm that globally maximizes (3.42). To this end, an upper bound function $\hat{\Psi}(\mathbb{T})$ that takes as input a cube $\mathbb{T} \subset \mathbb{R}^3$ in the translation space, and which satisfies the condition

$$\hat{\Psi}(\mathbb{T}) \ge \max_{\mathbf{t} \in \mathbb{T}} \Psi(\mathbf{t}), \tag{3.43}$$

must be constructed. Defining $\mathbf{c}$ as the center of $\mathbb{T}$, and δ as half of the diagonal length of $\mathbb{T}$, the following function:

$$\hat{\Psi}(\mathbb{T}) = \max_{\mathbf{R} \in SO(3)} \sum_{i=1}^{N} \max_{j} \, \mathbb{I} \left(\left\| \mathbf{R}(\mathbf{p}_i + \mathbf{c}) - \mathbf{p}'_j \right\|_2 \le \epsilon + \delta \right) \tag{3.44}$$

satisfies the required properties of an upper bound function. Intuitively, the additional slack δ is incorporated to account for the uncertainty in translation. Further, as $\mathbb{T}$ collapses to a single point $\mathbf{t}$, δ becomes 0 and $\hat{\Psi}(\mathbb{T})$ reduces to $\Psi(\mathbf{t})$. For brevity, we do not provide a formal proof; in any case, a proof can be easily developed along the lines in Section 3.4.1. A more important practical detail is that $\hat{\Psi}(\mathbb{T})$ can be evaluated by rotationally aligning $\{\mathbf{p}_i + \mathbf{c}\}_{i=1}^{N}$ and $\{\mathbf{p}'_j\}_{j=1}^{M}$, with the inflated inlier threshold $\epsilon + \delta$.

Algorithm 3.14 outlines the BnB algorithm for maximizing (3.42). As can be readily observed, it is largely similar to Algorithm 3.13 for rotation estimation. Although the main body of Algorithm 3.14 appears to optimize only the translation, the rotation is implicitly optimized by the evaluation of Ψ (Step 8) and $\hat{\Psi}$ (Step 16). This leads to globally optimal Euclidean point set registration under the maximum consensus criterion.

Evaluation

Figure 3.12 illustrates the results of applying Algorithm 3.14 on downsampled versions of two of the objects from the Stanford 3D Scanning Repository. Specifically, for the "bunny" object, $N = 358$ and $M = 343$, and for the "dragon" object, $N = 358$ and $M = 343$. The maximized

---

Algorithm 3.14 BnB method to maximize (3.42) for robust Euclidean point set registration.

Require: Point sets $\{\mathbf{p}_i\}_{i=1}^N$ and $\{\mathbf{p}'_j\}_{j=1}^M$, inlier threshold ϵ.

1: Initialize priority queue q.
2: $\mathbb{T} \leftarrow$ Initial cube in $\mathbb{R}^3$ containing globally optimal translation.
3: $\Psi^* \leftarrow 0, \mathbf{t}^* \leftarrow NULL$.
4: Insert $\mathbb{T}$ into q.
5: **while** q is not empty **do**
6:     $\mathbb{T} \leftarrow$ Remove from q the cube with the highest priority.
7:     $\mathbf{c} \leftarrow$ Center point of $\mathbb{T}$.
8:     $\Psi_\mathbf{c} \leftarrow$ Value of $\Psi(\mathbf{c})$ obtained using rotation search (Algorithm 3.13); see Sec. 3.4.2.
9:     **if** $\Psi_\mathbf{c} = \Psi^*$ **then**
10:         Break.
11:     **else if** $\Psi_\mathbf{c} > \Psi^*$ **then**
12:         $\Psi^* \leftarrow \Psi_\mathbf{c}, \mathbf{t}^* \leftarrow \mathbf{c}$.
13:     **end if**
14:     Subdivide $\mathbb{T}$ into 8 cubes $\mathbb{T}_1, \ldots, \mathbb{T}_8$.
15:     **for** $i = 1, \ldots, 8$ **do**
16:         $\hat{\Psi}_i \leftarrow$ Value of $\hat{\Psi}(\mathbb{T}_i)$ obtained using rotation search (Algorithm 3.13); see Sec. 3.4.2.
17:         **if** $\hat{\Psi}_i > \Psi^*$ **then**
18:             Insert $\mathbb{T}_i$ with priority $\hat{\Psi}_i$ into q.
19:         **end if**
20:     **end for**
21: **end while**
22: **return** $\mathbf{t}^*$ (Optional: obtain $\mathbf{R}^*$ by evaluating $\Psi(\mathbf{t}^*)$).

---

consensus $\Psi(\mathbf{t}^*)$, where $\Psi(\mathbf{t})$ is as defined in (3.42), are respectively 176 and 305, indicating a larger ratio of overlap in the dragon point clouds. In terms of actual runtime, on a standard 3.7 GHz Intel Core i7 machine, Algorithm 3.14 required approximately 16,000 and 6,000 s to terminate for the bunny and dragon point clouds. This indicates that Euclidean registration (a 6DOF problem) is a significantly more challenging optimization task than rotational alignment (a 3DOF problem).

Figure 3.13 illustrates a run of Algorithm 3.14 on the data in Figure 3.12a. Specifically, Figure 3.13 plots the lower bound Ψ^* and the upper bound (i.e., the upper bound of the cube $\mathbb{T}$ at the front of q) at each iteration of the algorithm. Observe that a good incumbent solution was found quickly (in approximately 200 iterations), and most of the optimization effort was devoted to lowering the upper bound, i.e., to pruning the search space. This is characteristic of the BnB technique.

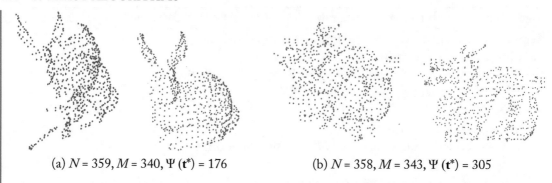

(a) $N = 359, M = 340, \Psi(\mathbf{t}^*) = 176$ (b) $N = 358, M = 343, \Psi(\mathbf{t}^*) = 305$

Figure 3.12: Input point clouds and results of applying Algorithm 3.14 to perform Euclidean registration on the point clouds. Here, the point clouds are downsampled versions of the original from the Stanford 3D Scanning Repository. The actual size of the point clouds and maximized consensus value by Algorithm 3.14 are displayed in the sub-captions above.

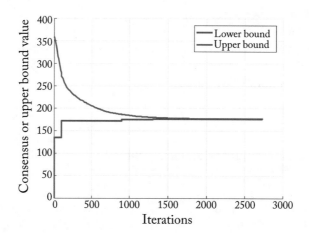

Figure 3.13: Progression of the lower and upper bounds in a run of Algorithm 3.14 on a downsampled version the "bunny" 3D scans in Figure 3.12a.

3.5 TRACTABLE ALGORITHMS WITH SUBSET SEARCH

We now come back to the familiar problem of maximum consensus fitting of linear models. Recall the definition of the maximum consensus problem introduced in Section 2.1:

$$\underset{\mathbf{x} \in \mathbb{R}^d}{\text{maximize}} \quad |\mathcal{I}(\mathbf{x})| \tag{3.45}$$

where $\mathcal{I}(\mathbf{x})$ is the consensus set corresponding to parameter vector $\mathbf{x}$

$$\mathcal{I}(\mathbf{x}) = \left\{ i \in \{1, \ldots, N\} \mid |\mathbf{a}_i^T \mathbf{x} - b_i| \leq \epsilon \right\}. \tag{3.46}$$

In particular, $\mathbf{x}^*$ is the optimal solution, and $\mathcal{I}(\mathbf{x}^*)$ is the maximum consensus set.

For the special case of line fitting ($d = 2$), Section 3.2.1 showed that in general the optimal line $\mathbf{x}^*$ is not unique, and it is possible to perturb $\mathbf{x}^*$ without changing its consensus set $\mathcal{I}(\mathbf{x}^*)$. In fact, Theorem 3.3 established that one can always find an optimal solution that is supported by a small subset of the data of known maximum cardinality. Based on that characterization, Algorithm 3.11 presented a simple $\mathcal{O}(N^3)$ method to find $\mathbf{x}^*$.

Is it possible to devise an algorithm based on similar ideas for $d > 2$? Before embarking on designing such an algorithm, let us first investigate the properties of $\mathcal{I}(\mathbf{x}^*)$.

3.5.1 CHARACTERIZATION OF THE SOLUTION

As in the case of line fitting, the solution of (3.45) for $d > 2$ is also non-unique. The following theorem is a direct extension of Theorem 3.3.

Theorem 3.8   *Given an optimal solution $\mathbf{x}^*$ to* (3.45), *it is always possible to find another estimate $\mathbf{x}^{**}$ with the same consensus set as $\mathbf{x}^*$, and where there are at most $(d + 1)$ data whose residuals to $\mathbf{x}^{**}$ are equal and of at most ϵ in value.*

Proof. Take $\mathbf{x}^{**}$ as the Chebyshev approximation (2.46) on the data indexed by $\mathcal{I}(\mathbf{x}^*)$:

$$\mathbf{x}^{**} = \operatorname*{argmin}_{\mathbf{x} \in \mathbb{R}^d} \max_{i \in \mathcal{I}(\mathbf{x}^*)} \left| \mathbf{a}_i^T \mathbf{x} - b_i \right|. \tag{3.47}$$

It is trivial to see that

$$\max_{i \in \mathcal{I}(\mathbf{x}^*)} \left| \mathbf{a}_i^T \mathbf{x}^{**} - b_i \right| \leq \epsilon, \tag{3.48}$$

by virtue of $\mathcal{I}(\mathbf{x}^*)$ being a consensus set. It thus follows that

$$\mathcal{I}(\mathbf{x}^{**}) = \mathcal{I}(\mathbf{x}^*); \tag{3.49}$$

that is, $\mathbf{x}^{**}$ is also a maximum consensus solution. Note that $\mathcal{I}(\mathbf{x}^{**})$ cannot be larger than $\mathcal{I}(\mathbf{x}^*)$, since the latter is already the maximum consensus set.

Assume that $\mathcal{I}(\mathbf{x}^*)$ is nondegenerate, based on the notion of degeneracy in Definition 3.13. From the characterization theorem of the Chebyshev estimate (Theorem 2.9), we know that $\mathbf{x}^{**}$ can equivalently be obtained as the Chebyshev estimate on the *support set* $\mathcal{K}^*$ of $\mathcal{I}(\mathbf{x}^*)$, where $|\mathcal{K}^*| \leq (d + 1)$; that is,

$$\mathbf{x}^{**} = \min_{\mathbf{x} \in \mathbb{R}^d} \max_{i \in \mathcal{K}^*} \left| \mathbf{a}_i^T \mathbf{x} - b_i \right|. \tag{3.50}$$

Further, the data $\{(\mathbf{a}_i, b_i)\}_{i \in \mathcal{K}^*}$ attain the same residual as measured to $\mathbf{x}^{**}$, and the residual value is less than or equal to ϵ. See Definition 2.15 for the notion of a support set. $\square$

The above theorem provides justification to solve maximum consensus by finding the support set $\mathcal{K}^*$ of the maximum consensus set, where the cardinality of $\mathcal{K}^*$ is not greater than $(d + 1)$. In the rest of this section, we describe algorithms to conduct this search.

Observe also that Theorem 3.3 further rotates and/or translates the Chebyshev estimate on the maximum consensus set, such that there exists two points with residual ϵ to the optimal line. Primarily, this was to enable the plane sweep technique to perform the search. Since the algorithms described in this section do not apply the plane sweep technique, Theorem 3.8 does not include the additional rotation and/or translation steps (Figure 3.1 already depicts the two normalization techniques on line fitting).

3.5.2   SUBSET ENUMERATION

Based on Theorem 3.8, Algorithm 3.15 presents a simple method that enumerates all $(d + 1)$-subsets of the data to solve maximum consensus. The solution $\mathbf{x}^*$ is taken as the Chebyshev estimate $\mathbf{y}$ of the $(d + 1)$-subset $\mathcal{K}$ that satisfies the necessary condition

$$\max_{i \in \mathcal{K}} \left| \mathbf{a}_i^T \mathbf{y} - b_i \right| \leq \epsilon, \tag{3.51}$$

and whose consensus $\Psi(\mathbf{y})$ is the highest. Note that, whereas the size of the optimal support set $\mathcal{K}^*$ can be less than $(d + 1)$, Algorithm 3.15 enumerates subsets of size exactly $(d + 1)$ only. This is justified since there is always a $(d + 1)$-subset $\mathcal{K}$, where $\mathcal{K}^* \subseteq \mathcal{K} \subseteq \mathcal{I}^*$, that also satisfies condition (3.51), and where

$$\operatorname*{argmin}_{\mathbf{x} \in \mathbb{R}^d} \max_{i \in \mathcal{K}^*} \left| \mathbf{a}_i^T \mathbf{x} - b_i \right| = \operatorname*{argmin}_{\mathbf{x} \in \mathbb{R}^d} \max_{i \in \mathcal{K}} \left| \mathbf{a}_i^T \mathbf{x} - b_i \right|. \tag{3.52}$$

This feature is related to the *locality* property of the minimax problem (Property 2.11 in Section 2.5), which we touch upon again in Section 3.6.

Obviously Algorithm 3.15 requires $\binom{N}{d+1}$ iterations. Overall, including the effort to calculate the consensus value (Step 5), the algorithm runs in $\mathcal{O}(N^{d+2})$ time. Although seemingly finding the Chebyshev estimate $\mathbf{y}$ on each iteration (Step 3) is expensive, as detailed in (2.49), the minimax problem can be formulated as an LP, which can be solved cheaply in practice, and more so because each minimax problem is only of size $(d + 1)$.

In fact, a closed-form method, from de la Vallée-Poussin [Cheney, 1966, Chapter 2], can be used to obtain the Chebyshev estimate on $(d + 1)$ cases. Let $\mathbf{A}(\mathcal{K})$ be the $(d + 1) \times d$ matrix obtained by vertically stacking the vectors $\{\mathbf{a}_j^T\}_{j=\mathcal{K}}$, and $\mathbf{b}(\mathcal{K})$ be the $(d + 1)$-vector obtained by vertically stacking the values $\{b_j\}_{j \in \mathcal{K}}$. Assuming that the rows of $\mathbf{A}(\mathcal{K})$ are linearly independent, let

$$\mathbf{r} = \mathbf{b}(\mathcal{K}) - \mathbf{A}(\mathcal{K})\mathbf{x}_{LS} \tag{3.53}$$

be the signed residual vector of data $\{(\mathbf{a}_j, b_j)\}_{j \in \mathcal{K}}$ with respect to its LS estimate

$$\mathbf{x}_{LS} = \left[\mathbf{A}(\mathcal{K})^T \mathbf{A}(\mathcal{K}) \right]^{-1} \mathbf{A}(\mathcal{K})^T \mathbf{b}(\mathcal{K}). \tag{3.54}$$

Algorithm 3.15 Subset enumeration method for the maximum consensus problem (3.45).

Require: Input data $\mathcal{D} = \{(\mathbf{a}_i, b_i)\}_{i=1}^N$, inlier threshold ϵ.

1: $\Psi^* \leftarrow 0, \mathbf{x}^* \leftarrow NULL$.

2: **for** each subset $\mathcal{K} \subseteq \{1, \dots, N\}$ of size $(d+1)$ **do**

3:      $\mathbf{y} \leftarrow$ Chebyshev estimate on data indexed by $\mathcal{K}$.

4:      **if** $\max_{j \in \mathcal{K}} \left| \mathbf{a}_j^T \mathbf{y} - b_j \right| \leq \epsilon$ **then**

5:          **if** $\Psi(\mathbf{y}) > \Psi^*$ **then**

6:              $\Psi^* \leftarrow \Psi(\mathbf{y}), \mathbf{x}^* \leftarrow \mathbf{y}$.

7:          **end if**

8:      **end if**

9: **end for**

10: **return** $\mathbf{x}^*$.

Also, define

$$S = \frac{\mathbf{r}^T \mathbf{r}}{\|\mathbf{r}\|_1}. \tag{3.55}$$

Then, the Chebyshev estimate on the $(d+1)$-subset is

$$\hat{\mathbf{x}} = \left(\mathbf{A}(\mathcal{K})^T \mathbf{A}(\mathcal{K})\right)^{-1} \mathbf{A}(\mathcal{K})^T \left(\mathbf{b}(\mathcal{K}) - S \cdot \text{sign}(\mathbf{r})\right), \tag{3.56}$$

where $\text{sign}(\mathbf{r})$ returns a vector of signs of the values in $\mathbf{r}$. See Cheney [1966, Chapter 2] for more details and proof of this method.

If d is regarded as a constant, Algorithm 3.15 is polynomial with respect to the number of measurements N. In this sense, the algorithm can be regarded as tractable or efficient. In reality, however, even for moderate d and N, the number of $(d+1)$-subsets that the algorithm needs to examine is hopelessly large. Therefore, the algorithm is practical only for small d. In Section 3.6, we describe a method that avoids complete enumeration by conducting a more structured search for the optimal subset.

For completeness, it is worthwhile to compare Algorithm 3.15, which derives candidate solutions from Chebyshev estimates on $(d+1)$-subsets, with the approach of RANSAC that examines minimal estimates on subsets of size d (Section 2.2). In general, the optimal solution does not coincide with a minimal estimate; thus, even if all minimal subsets are enumerated, there is no guarantee of finding the globally optimal solution.

LP-type Problems

Maximum consensus estimation for the class of LP-type problems has been touched upon in Section 2.5.3. For convenience, we write again the maximum consensus formulation below (recall that an LP-type problem $(\mathcal{S}, f)$ consists of a set of constraints $\mathcal{S}$ and an objective function f that satisfies the properties outlined in Section 2.5.1):

$$\underset{\mathcal{I} \subseteq \mathcal{S}}{\text{maximize}} \quad |\mathcal{I}|$$
$$\text{subject to} \quad f(\mathcal{I}) \leq \epsilon, \tag{3.57}$$

where ϵ is the usual inlier threshold. Section 2.5.1 also established Chebyshev approximation (for both linear and generalized fractional models) as an instance of an LP-type problem. It is therefore possible to conduct a subset search for exact maximum consensus estimation for a broader class of problems than fitting linear models. Before describing the details of the method, we define the following terminologies.

Definition 3.9   (Violation set and coverage set).   For LP-type problem $(\mathcal{S}, f)$, the *violation set* $\mathcal{V}(\mathcal{P})$ of a subset $\mathcal{P} \subseteq \mathcal{S}$ are the constraints that violate $\mathcal{P}$; that is,

$$\mathcal{V}(\mathcal{P}) = \{c \in \mathcal{S} \mid f(\mathcal{P}) \neq f(\mathcal{P} \cup \{c\})\}. \tag{3.58}$$

Also, if $\mathcal{K}$ is the support set of $\mathcal{P}$, then obviously $\mathcal{V}(\mathcal{K}) = \mathcal{V}(\mathcal{P})$. The *coverage set* $\mathcal{C}(\mathcal{P})$ is simply the complement of the violation set $\mathcal{V}(\mathcal{P})$; also, $\mathcal{C}(\mathcal{K}) = \mathcal{C}(\mathcal{P})$.

Definition 3.10   (Feasibility).   A basis $\mathcal{B}$ is *feasible* w.r.t. the maximum consensus problem (3.57) if $f(\mathcal{B}) \leq \epsilon$.

By exploiting the nature of LP-type problems, problem (3.57) can be solved by searching for the support set $\mathcal{K}^*$ of the maximum consensus set $\mathcal{I}^*$. Since $\mathcal{K}^*$ is also a particular basis $\mathcal{B}$ of the input constraint set $\mathcal{S}$, this permits us to solve (3.57) by checking only the bases. Specifically, our goal is to find the feasible basis with the largest coverage set:

$$\underset{\mathcal{B} \text{ is a basis of } \mathcal{S}}{\text{maximize}} \quad |\mathcal{C}(\mathcal{B})|$$
$$\text{subject to} \quad f(\mathcal{B}) \leq \epsilon. \tag{3.59}$$

This avoids searching over the power set of $\mathcal{S}$ since the basis size is known and bounded from above. In particular, for the class of models with quasiconvex residuals, the cardinality of $\mathcal{B}$ is at most $(d + 1)$ (see Section 2.5.1). Algorithm 3.16 presents a subset enumeration procedure (a direct extension of Algorithm 3.15) to find $\mathcal{K}^*$ for models with quasiconvex residuals.

A candidate $\mathcal{B}$ admits a feasible solution if $f(\mathcal{B}) \leq \epsilon$, where the corresponding consensus set is simply $\mathcal{C}(\mathcal{B})$. The core subroutine in Algorithm 3.16 is thus calculating $f(\mathcal{B})$; that is, solving the LP-type problem on a $(d + 1)$-subset of the constraints. This can be done efficiently using the algorithms discussed in Sections 2.4 and 2.5.2 (e.g., LP, bisection).

3.6   TREE SEARCH

In Section 3.2.2, the concepts of point-and-line duality and plane sweep were employed to devise a more efficient $\mathcal{O}(N^2 \log N)$ algorithm for maximum consensus line fitting. The algorithm

---

Algorithm 3.16 Subset enumeration method for LP-type maximum consensus (3.57).

Require: Input constraint set $\mathcal{S}$, inlier threshold ϵ.

 1: $\Psi^* \leftarrow 0, \mathcal{K}^* \leftarrow NULL$.
 2: **for** each subset $\mathcal{B} \subseteq \{1, \ldots, N\}$ of size $(d + 1)$ **do**
 3:    **if** $f(\mathcal{B}) \leq \epsilon$ **then**
 4:       **if** $|\mathcal{C}(\mathcal{B})| > \Psi^*$ **then**
 5:          $\Psi^* \leftarrow |\mathcal{C}(\mathcal{B})|, \mathcal{K}^* \leftarrow \mathcal{B}$.
 6:       **end if**
 7:    **end if**
 8: **end for**
 9: **return** $\theta(\mathcal{K}^*)$.

---

exploits the linear ordering of the dual lines along a sweep line to improve efficiency. Sweeping an arrangement of lines is a special case of sweeping an arrangement of hyperplanes, for which efficient algorithms exist [Edelsbrunner et al., 1986]. Possibly a sweep-based algorithm can be constructed for higher-dimensional maximum consensus ($d > 2$), although such an algorithm is unlikely to be more efficient than $\mathcal{O}(N^d)$.

In this section, instead of point-to-hyperplane duality, we exploit another fundamental arrangement of the data—a *tree structure* that is induced by the minimax problem (2.46)—to derive an exact algorithm for maximum consensus.

The Intuition

Consider again the simple case of estimating a 1D linear relation $b = ax$ from measurements $\mathcal{D} = \{(a_i, b_i)\}_{i=1}^N$. The i-th residual w.r.t. candidate solution x is

$$r_i(x) = |a_i x - b_i|. \qquad (3.60)$$

Figure 2.12b in Chapter 2 displays $r_i(x)$ in the parameter space $x \in \mathbb{R}$ for a sample $\mathcal{D}$ of size $N = 6$. Figure 3.14a provides a close-up of Figure 2.12b. In addition to highlighting the Chebyshev estimate on $\mathcal{D}$, which is defined by the residual of two points (i.e., the support set), Figure 3.14a also shows the ℓ_∞ solution on other subsets of $\mathcal{D}$ of size two. These subsets are precisely the bases $\mathcal{B}$ of the problem (recall Definition 2.14). Observe that each $\theta(\mathcal{B})$ corresponds to the Chebyshev estimate on a subset $\mathcal{P} \subseteq \mathcal{D}$, i.e., $\mathcal{C}(\mathcal{B}) = \mathcal{P}$.

Now, Figure 3.14b shows the outcome of deleting a point in the support set, and recalculating the Chebyshev estimate on the remaining data. Obviously a new support set is obtained, and the corresponding Chebyshev estimate has a lower minimax value. Figures 3.14c and 3.14d depict the outcomes if the above process is carried out two more times. The crucial idea here is that, by recursively removing a point from the support set and re-estimating, we are able to arrive at one of the $\theta(\mathcal{B})$. Further, the $\theta(\mathcal{B})$ for all bases $\mathcal{B}$ seem to be reachable from such a recursive removal process.

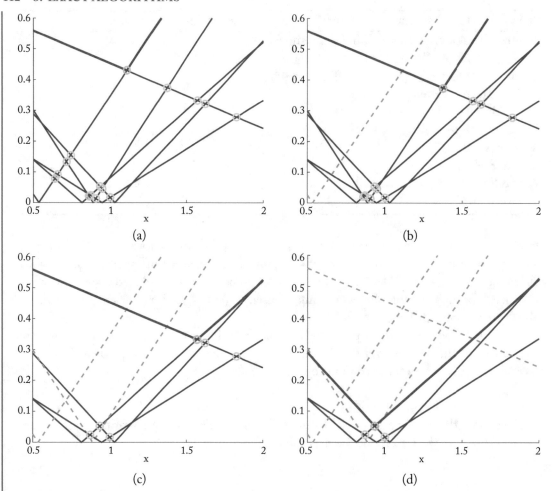

Figure 3.14: Panel (a) plots the residual function $r_i(x) = |a_i x - b_i|$ for a sample dataset $\mathcal{D} = \{(a_i, b_i)\}_{i=1}^{N}$ of size $N = 6$. The Chebyshev estimate is highlighted with a green circle, whereas the ℓ_∞ estimate on other bases $\mathcal{B}$ are marked with a cyan circle. Panels (b), (c), and (d) show the results of recursively removing a point from the support set and solving the Chebyshev estimate on the remaining data.

The above observation suggests that the ℓ_∞ estimates $\theta(\mathcal{B})$ on the bases $\mathcal{B}$ are arranged in a tree structure. Further, the set of estimates also includes the Chebyshev estimate $\mathbf{x}^*$ on the maximum consensus set $\mathcal{I}^*$, by the simple fact that $\mathcal{I}^*$ is a subset of $\mathcal{D}$. More importantly, the tree structure can be exploited to conduct a guided search for $\mathbf{x}^*$. Before describing algorithms to do so, we first formalize and generalize the above observation.

3.6.1   EXISTENCE OF TREE STRUCTURE

Definition 3.11   (Level of basis).   The level $l(\mathcal{B})$ of a basis $\mathcal{B} \subseteq \mathcal{S}$ of LP-type problem $(\mathcal{S}, f)$ is the cardinality of its violation set; that is, $l(\mathcal{B}) = |\mathcal{V}(\mathcal{B})|$.

Based on the above definition, the support set of $\mathcal{S}$ is the level-0 basis. Define also

$$\mathcal{B}^{(k)} = \{\mathcal{B} \text{ is a basis} \mid l(\mathcal{B}) = k\}, \tag{3.61}$$

i.e., $\mathcal{B}^{(k)}$ is the set of all bases of level k.

Definition 3.12   (Basis adjacency).   Two bases $\mathcal{B} \in \mathcal{B}^{(k)}$ and $\mathcal{B}' \in \mathcal{B}^{(k+1)}$ are adjacent if $\mathcal{V}(\mathcal{B}') = \mathcal{V}(\mathcal{B}) \cup \{c\}$ for some $c \in \mathcal{V}(\mathcal{B})$.

Equivalently, we say that two bases $\mathcal{B}$ and $\mathcal{B}'$ are adjacent, if $\mathcal{B}'$ is the support set of the data $\mathcal{C}(\mathcal{B})$ *after* removing a constraint c from $\mathcal{B}$, i.e., $\mathcal{C}(\mathcal{B}) = \mathcal{C}(\mathcal{B}') \cup \{c\}$. For example, the Chebyshev estimates in each pair of successive panels in Figure 3.14 are adjacent bases.

Definition 3.13   (Nondegeneracy).   An LP-type problem $(\mathcal{S}, f)$ is non-degenerate if $f(\mathcal{B}) \neq f(\mathcal{B}')$ for any two distinct bases $\mathcal{B}$ and $\mathcal{B}'$.

Figure 3.15 illustrates an instance of the Chebyshev approximation problem (2.46) and an instance of the MEC problem (2.64) that do not satisfy the condition described above; they are *degenerate* LP-type problems. In particular, these example problems have non-unique support sets; there is more than one subset of three points that can act as the support set.

The following theorem from Matoušek [1995], establishes the existence of the tree structure alluded to above, assuming that the LP-type problem $(\mathcal{S}, f)$ is nondegenerate.

Theorem 3.14   *Every basis $\mathcal{B} \in \mathcal{B}^{(k)}$ can be reached from the level-0 basis (the support set of $\mathcal{S}$) by a directed path.*

For completeness, the proof of the theorem from Matoušek [1995] is restated in Section F in the Appendix.

The theorem above establishes that the set of bases of a nondegenerate LP-type problem can be arranged in a tree structure; Figure 3.16 illustrates. Each node in the tree corresponds to a basis $\mathcal{B}$. The vertical height of a basis indicates the value of $f(\mathcal{B})$. A downward edge from a basis represents the removal of a particular item from the basis. In this example, the combinatorial dimension of the problem is two (cf. the 1D linear regression problem in Figure 3.14), thus there are at most two downward edges attached to each node. Observe that, starting from the level-0 basis, it is possible to descend to any of the bases in the higher levels by following a directed path.

A precondition for the existence of the tree structure is nondegeneracy. In practice, this cannot always be assumed. Matoušek [1995] showed how a degenerate LP-type problem can be refined into a nondegenerate one, without drastically changing the combinatorial structure of the tree. Henceforth, for simplicity, we assume that all data are nondegenerate.

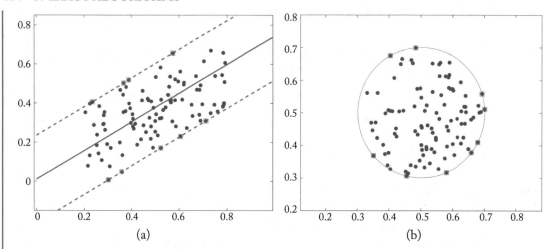

(a)   (b)

Figure 3.15: A Chebyshev approximation problem instance and a MEC problem instance that represent degenerate LP-type problems. Observe that there is more than one subset of three points that can act as the support set.

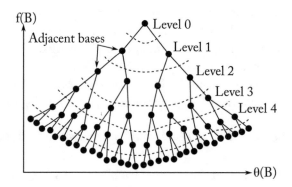

Figure 3.16: A tree structure induced by an LP-type problem. Each node in the tree corresponds to a basis. In this example, the combinatorial dimension of the problem is two.

Maximum Consensus as Tree Search

Taking advantage of the tree structure, we redefine problem (3.59) as

$$\begin{array}{ll} \underset{\mathcal{B} \text{ is a basis of } \mathcal{S}}{\text{minimize}} & l(\mathcal{B}) \\ \text{subject to} & f(\mathcal{B}) \le \epsilon. \end{array} \qquad (3.62)$$

Here, instead of maximizing its coverage, we minimize the level of the basis. Formulation (3.62) thus seeks the *shallowest* basis that is feasible. Figure 3.17 illustrates this version of maximum consensus. The set of feasible bases are the nodes situated below the horizontal line of height ϵ. Among the feasible bases, the ones with the lowest level (level 4 in this example) are colored in green—these are the global minimizers of problem (3.62). Intuitively, for this example, the maximum consensus set must exclude exactly four constraints.

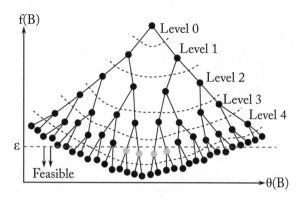

Figure 3.17: Maximum consensus as tree search. The set of feasible bases are situated below the horizontal line of height ϵ. The feasible bases with the lowest level are the nodes in green.

In the following, we describe methods to solve (3.62) that exploit the tree structure.

3.6.2 BREADTH FIRST SEARCH

A simple method is to traverse the tree in a breadth-first manner, or test for feasibility and expand (generate adjacent bases of) all the bases at a particular level before going to the next level; see Figure 3.18. Algorithm 3.17 summarizes the breadth-first search (BFS) method. Such a search regime guarantees that the first feasible basis found has the lowest possible level.

A direct breadth-first traversal, however, ignores the fact that there are multiple paths for arriving at the same level-k basis. This corresponds to the fact that as long as the same set of data are removed, the order of the removal is not important. This phenomenon can be observed clearly in Figure 3.14. Significant redundancy thus exists in the tree (note that in the tree diagrams shown thus far, this redundancy is not illustrated).

To avoid unnecessary traversals, therefore, "seen before" or repeated bases should be avoided in BFS. This is implemented in Step 11 in Algorithm 3.17. Depending on the actual distribution of the data, however, two equal bases can have different coverage sets, or equivalently, violation sets. Therefore, two bases $\mathcal{B}_1$ and $\mathcal{B}_2$ are declared the same only if $\mathcal{V}(\mathcal{B}_1) = \mathcal{V}(\mathcal{B}_2)$. To enable this comparison to be done efficiently, the technique of *hashing* is employed in Algorithm 3.17. To be specific, the indices of the constraints in $\mathcal{V}(\mathcal{B})$ are sorted to yield a sequence of integers, which are then converted to ASCII characters and hashed into a hash table T [Ramakrishna and Zobel, 1997]. For example, the set $\mathcal{V}(\mathcal{B}) = \{c_{71}, c_{10}, c_5, c_4, c_{28}\}$ is converted to the string 0405102871

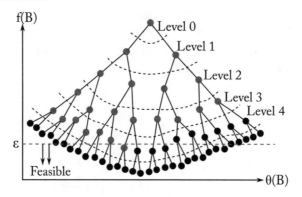

Figure 3.18: BFS method to solve maximum consensus.

Algorithm 3.17 Breadth-first search (BFS) for maximum consensus.

Require: LP-type problem $(\mathcal{S}, f)$, inlier threshold ϵ.
 1: Initialize queue q.
 2: Initialize hash table T.
 3: $\mathcal{B} \leftarrow$ Support set of $\mathcal{S}$.
 4: Insert $\mathcal{B}$ into q.
 5: **while** q is not empty **do**
 6:    $\mathcal{B} \leftarrow$ Remove front item of q.
 7:    **if** $f(\mathcal{B}) \le \epsilon$ **then**
 8:        Return with $\theta(\mathcal{B})$ as the maximum consensus estimate.
 9:    **end if**
10:    **for** each $c \in \mathcal{B}$ **do**
11:        **if** indices of $\mathcal{V}(\mathcal{B}) \cup \{c\}$ do not exist in T **then**
12:            Hash indices of $\mathcal{V}(\mathcal{B}) \cup \{c\}$ into T.
13:            $\mathcal{B}' \leftarrow$ Support set of $[\mathcal{C}(\mathcal{B}) \setminus \{c\}]$.
14:            Insert $\mathcal{B}'$ into q.
15:        **end if**
16:    **end for**
17: **end while**
18: Return error (no feasible basis).

---

before hashing. If $\mathcal{V}(\mathcal{B})$ is encountered again later in the search, hashing the indices of $\mathcal{V}(\mathcal{B})$ into T would result in a collision. This simple idea brings significant computational savings.

Analysis

How many bases will need to be checked before Algorithm 3.17 terminates? Matoušek [1995] showed that, for nondegenerate LP-type problems, the number of level-k bases $|\mathcal{B}^{(k)}|$ is bounded above by $(k+1)^{\delta-1}$, where δ is the combinatorial dimension of the problem. Thus, the number of iterations required in Algorithm 3.17 is simply $\mathcal{O}((l^*+1)^{\delta-1})$, where $l^* = l(\mathcal{B}^*)$ is the level of the shallowest feasible basis. In other words, l^* is the smallest number of constraints that must be removed from $\mathcal{S}$ to obtain a consensus set. Contrast this to Algorithm 3.16, which simply enumerates all subsets of the data $\mathcal{S}$. However, the search conducted by BFS is still "blind," in that it must enumerate all bases up to level l^*. In Section 3.6.3, an algorithm that conducts a more "guided" search over the tree is presented.

Support Set Updating

Critical to the actual runtime of Algorithm 3.17 is the efficiency in generating child bases by calculating support sets (Step 13). Note that this process is different from the support set updating of Step 7 in Algorithm 2.6—the former is invoked on the subset $\mathcal{C}(\mathcal{B}) \setminus \{c\}$, whose cardinality is generally greater than the combinatorial dimension, whereas the latter is more "primitive" since it is invoked only on subsets of size $(d+1)$. Indeed, Step 13 in Algorithm 3.17 involves solving an LP-type problem on the set $\mathcal{C}(\mathcal{B}) \setminus \{c\}$.

   For problems with linear and quasiconvex residuals, the ℓ_∞ solvers discussed in Sections 2.4 can be applied to conduct support set updating in Step 13. The fact that support set calculations are performed on progressively smaller subsets of $\mathcal{S}$ can be exploited for computational savings. Observe that, except at the initial stage where the LP-type problem needs to be solved from scratch on all $\mathcal{S}$, all other support set computations in Algorithm 3.17 merely require updating a known support set after one constraint is removed. We thus expect $\theta(\mathcal{C}(\mathcal{B}))$ to be close to $\theta(\mathcal{C}(\mathcal{B} \setminus \{c\}))$, and the value of the former can be used to *warm start* the solution of the latter.

3.6.3   A* SEARCH

The A* algorithm is an informed search method used extensively in pathfinding [Hart et al., 1968] and graph search in general [Pearl, 1984]. In the context of tree search for maximum consensus, the A* method employs an *evaluation function e* to prioritize the expansion of the bases in the queue. Specifically, a basis $\mathcal{B}$ in the queue is assigned the value

$$e(\mathcal{B}) = l(\mathcal{B}) + h(\mathcal{B}), \tag{3.63}$$

where $l(\mathcal{B})$ is simply the level of basis $\mathcal{B}$, and $h(\mathcal{B})$ is the *heuristic value* of $\mathcal{B}$. The *heuristic function h* provides an estimate of the number of constraints to remove from $\mathcal{C}(\mathcal{B})$ to make the set of constraints feasible. Bases with low e values are thus shallow and/or close to feasibility. Expanding the queue according to the guidance provided by e (lower e has higher priority) thus accelerates the search; Figure 3.19 illustrates. Algorithm 3.18 summarizes A* search for maximum consensus.

Only a few lines, where the bases are inserted or retrieved from the queue on the basis of evaluation values, differ from Algorithm 3.17.

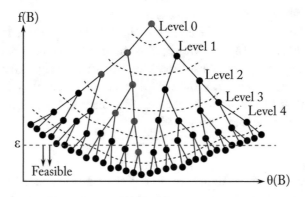

Figure 3.19: A* search to solve maximum consensus. Instead of expanding the bases level by level, the A* algorithm conducts a more informed search using a heuristic function.

An immediate question is whether A* is optimal (i.e., is the first feasible basis found by the algorithm guaranteed to be the shallowest).

Definition 3.15 (Admissibility). A heuristic function h is *admissible* if

$$h(\mathcal{B}) \geq 0 \quad \text{and} \quad h(\mathcal{B}) \leq h^*(\mathcal{B}), \tag{3.64}$$

where $h^*(\mathcal{B})$ is the minimum number of constraints that must be removed from $\mathcal{C}(\mathcal{B})$ to make the set feasible. Implied by the above is that $h(\mathcal{B}) = 0$ if $\mathcal{B}$ is feasible.

Note that calculating $h^*(\mathcal{B})$ amounts to solving the maximum consensus problem on the constraint set $\mathcal{C}(\mathcal{B})$. Also, if $h(\mathcal{B}) = 0$ for all $\mathcal{B}$ (such a heuristic is admissible), then A* reduces to BFS since the queue is prioritized based on only the level of the bases.

Theorem 3.16 *If h is admissible, A* is optimal, i.e., the first feasible basis found by A* has the lowest level among all feasible bases.*

Proof. Let $\mathcal{B}^*$ be the solution to (3.62), i.e., $\mathcal{B}^*$ is a feasible basis with the lowest level. Let $\mathcal{B}^\dagger$ be a suboptimal feasible basis that already exists in the queue. We aim to show that $\mathcal{B}^\dagger$ will not be chosen and tested *before* an optimal basis $\mathcal{B}^*$ exists in the queue. Let $\mathcal{B}$ be another basis in the queue on the path leading to $\mathcal{B}^*$ (such a basis $\mathcal{B}$ always exists in a tree structure; e.g., the root

Algorithm 3.18 A* search for maximum consensus.

Require: LP-type problem (S, f), inlier threshold ϵ.

1: Initialize priority queue q.
2: Initialize hash table T.
3: $\mathcal{B} \leftarrow$ Support set of S.
4: Insert $\mathcal{B}$ with priority $e(\mathcal{B})$ into q.
5: **while** q is not empty **do**
6:    $\mathcal{B} \leftarrow$ Remove from q the item with lowest e value.
7:    **if** $f(\mathcal{B}) \leq \epsilon$ **then**
8:       Return with $\theta(\mathcal{B})$ as the maximum consensus estimate.
9:    **end if**
10:   **for** each $c \in \mathcal{B}$ **do**
11:      **if** indices of $\mathcal{V}(\mathcal{B}) \cup \{c\}$ do not exist in T **then**
12:         Hash indices of $\mathcal{V}(\mathcal{B}) \cup \{c\}$ into T.
13:         $\mathcal{B}' \leftarrow$ Support set of $[\mathcal{C}(\mathcal{B}) \setminus \{c\}]$.
14:         Insert $\mathcal{B}'$ with priority $e(\mathcal{B}')$ into q.
15:      **end if**
16:   **end for**
17: **end while**
18: Return error (no feasible basis).

basis is one). The following can be established:

$$
\begin{aligned}
e(\mathcal{B}^\dagger) &= l(\mathcal{B}^\dagger) && \text{(since } \mathcal{B}^\dagger \text{ is feasible)} \\
&> l(\mathcal{B}^*) && \text{(since } \mathcal{B}^\dagger \text{ is suboptimal)} \\
&= l(\mathcal{B}) + h^*(\mathcal{B}) && \text{(since } \mathcal{B} \text{ leads to } \mathcal{B}^*) \\
&\geq l(\mathcal{B}) + h(\mathcal{B}). && \text{(since } h \text{ is admissible)}
\end{aligned}
\tag{3.65}
$$

The above shows that $\mathcal{B}$, which lies on the path to $\mathcal{B}^*$, will always have a higher priority than $\mathcal{B}^\dagger$ to be tested and expanded. Therefore, A* will always find $\mathcal{B}^*$ before $\mathcal{B}^\dagger$.   □

If the current lowest e value in the queue is given by more than one basis, we choose the $\mathcal{B}$ with the lowest $f(\mathcal{B})$ first. This tie breaking does not affect the optimality of A*.

Heuristic for Consensus Maximization

How should the heuristic function be constructed for maximum consensus? This subsection presents several heuristic functions and investigates their properties. As we shall see, the characteristics of LP-type problems play a big role in the heuristic functions.

Consider applying the outlier removal technique in Algorithm 2.7 on the set of constraints $\mathcal{C}(\mathcal{B})$. Specifically, let

$$\mathcal{O} = \{\mathcal{B}_1, \mathcal{B}_2, \dots, \mathcal{B}_M\}, \quad f(\mathcal{B}_m) > \epsilon \ \forall m \tag{3.66}$$

contain the sequence of support sets that must be recursively removed from $\mathcal{C}(\mathcal{B})$ to make $\mathcal{C}(\mathcal{B})$ feasible, where

$$\mathcal{B}_m = \text{Support set of} \, [\mathcal{C}(\mathcal{B}) \setminus \{\mathcal{B}_1, \dots, \mathcal{B}_{m-1}\}] \ \text{for} \ m > 1$$

and $\mathcal{B}_1 = \mathcal{B}$. For example, Figures 2.13 and 2.24b illustrate such a sequence of support set removal, respectively for the Chebyshev approximation problem and the MEC problem. Given $\mathcal{O}$, a possible heuristic function is

$$h_{rem}(\mathcal{B}) = M, \tag{3.67}$$

i.e., the number of support sets to remove to make $\mathcal{C}(\mathcal{B})$ feasible. For concreteness, Algorithm 3.19 describes the calculation of h_{rem}, which is functionally similar to Algorithm 2.7.

Algorithm 3.19 Calculation of $h_{rem}(\mathcal{B})$, where $\mathcal{B}$ is a basis for LP-type problem $(\mathcal{S}, f)$.

1: If $f(\mathcal{B}) \leq \epsilon$, return 0.
2: $h_{rem} \leftarrow 0$.
3: **while** $f(\mathcal{B}) > \epsilon$ **do**
4:   $h_{rem} \leftarrow h + 1$.
5:   $\mathcal{B} \leftarrow$ Support set of $[\mathcal{C}(\mathcal{B}) \setminus \mathcal{B}]$.
6: **end while**
7: Return h_{rem}.

A more critical question is whether h_{rem} is admissible. Again, the fundamental results presented in Section 2.5 already provide hints to the question. In particular, the following proof of admissibility is basically an extension of Theorem 2.20.

Theorem 3.17 h_{rem} *is admissible.*

Proof. That h_{rem} is nonnegative is obvious. Let $\mathcal{C}(\mathcal{B}) = \mathcal{F}^* \cup \mathcal{O}^*$, where $\mathcal{F}^*$ is the largest feasible subset of $\mathcal{C}(\mathcal{B})$. $\mathcal{O}^*$ is thus the smallest subset that must be removed from $\mathcal{C}(\mathcal{B})$ to achieve feasibility; that is, $h^*(\mathcal{B}) = |\mathcal{O}^*|$.

Let $\mathcal{B}_m$ be a basis in $\mathcal{O}$, where $\mathcal{O}$ is as defined in (3.66). By definition $\mathcal{B}_m$ is not feasible. Then by Property 2.10 (Monotonicity)

$$f(\mathcal{F}^* \cup \mathcal{B}_m) \geq f(\mathcal{B}_m) > \epsilon, \tag{3.68}$$

Algorithm 3.20 Calculation of $h_{ins}(\mathcal{B})$, where $\mathcal{B}$ is a basis for LP-type problem $(\mathcal{S}, f)$.

1: If $f(\mathcal{B}) \leq \epsilon$, return 0.
2: $\mathcal{O} \leftarrow \emptyset$.
3: **while** $f(\mathcal{B}) > \epsilon$ **do**
4:     $\mathcal{O} \leftarrow \mathcal{O} \cup \mathcal{B}$.
5:     $\mathcal{B} \leftarrow$ Support set of $[\mathcal{C}(\mathcal{B}) \setminus \mathcal{B}]$.
6: **end while**
7: $h_{ins} \leftarrow 0, \quad \mathcal{F} \leftarrow \mathcal{C}(\mathcal{B})$.
8: **for** each $\mathcal{B} \in \mathcal{O}$ **do**
9:     **for** each $c \in \mathcal{B}$ **do**
10:         $\mathcal{B}' \leftarrow$ Support set of $[\mathcal{F} \cup \{c\}]$.
11:         **if** $f(\mathcal{B}') \leq \epsilon$ **then**
12:             $\mathcal{F} \leftarrow \mathcal{F} \cup \{c\}$.
13:         **else**
14:             $h_{ins} \leftarrow h_{ins} + 1$.
15:             $\mathcal{F} \leftarrow \mathcal{F} \cup \{c\} \setminus \mathcal{B}'$.
16:         **end if**
17:     **end for**
18: **end for**
19: Return h_{ins}.

i.e., $\mathcal{B}_m$ must contain at least one item from $\mathcal{O}^*$. Consequently, each recursive removal of infeasible support sets from $\mathcal{C}(\mathcal{B})$ removes at least one item of $\mathcal{O}^*$. There are thus at most $|\mathcal{O}^*|$ support set removals before feasibility is achieved. Since each support set removal contributes 1 to $h_{rem}(\mathcal{B})$, its final value cannot be greater $h^*(\mathcal{B})$.

Note also that in general $\mathcal{O}^*$ is not a subset of $\mathcal{O}$ (echoing the notion of a suboptimal consensus set in Section 2.1), and the proof above does not assume that it is. $\qquad\square$

Our second heuristic h_{ins} reverses the computation of $h_{rem}(\mathcal{B})$. First, let $\mathcal{F}$ denote the remaining data after the sequence $\mathcal{O}$ is obtained and removed as in Algorithm 3.19:

$$\mathcal{F} = \mathcal{C}(\mathcal{B}) \setminus \mathcal{O}, \quad \text{where } f(\mathcal{F}) \leq \epsilon. \tag{3.69}$$

(Note that Algorithm 2.7 simply reports $\mathcal{F}$ as an approximate solution to the maximum consensus problem.) To calculate h_{ins}, we attempt to reinsert the data from $\mathcal{O}$ one by one into $\mathcal{F}$. If an insertion makes $\mathcal{F}$ infeasible, the support set of the enlarged $\mathcal{F}$ is removed and the heuristic $h_{ins}(\mathcal{B})$ is incremented by one; if the enlarged $\mathcal{F}$ remains feasible, the insertion is made permanent with no change to the heuristic. Algorithm 3.20 gives a formal description. The following theorem establishes the admissibility of h_{ins}.

Theorem 3.18 h_{ins} *is admissible.*

Proof. That h_{ins} is non-negative is obvious. Let $\mathcal{B}_{ins}$ be the support set of $\mathcal{F} \cup \{\mathbf{x}\}$, where $\mathbf{x}$ is a candidate datum for insertion. If $\mathcal{B}_{ins}$ is infeasible, then from (3.68), $\mathcal{B}_{ins}$ must contain at least an item from $\mathcal{O}^*$. The removal of $\mathcal{B}_{ins}$ from $\mathcal{F} \cup \{\mathbf{x}\}$ thus removes at least one item of $\mathcal{O}^*$ from the enlarged set. There are at most $|\mathcal{O}^*|$ infeasible support set removals. Since each removal adds 1 to $h_{ins}(\mathcal{B})$, its final value cannot be greater than $h^*(\mathcal{B})$. □

Given two different admissible heuristic functions to the same problem, using either in A* will yield the optimal result, as guaranteed by Theorem 3.16. The differences in the heuristics thus affect more on the *performance* of the search, in terms of the number of bases that will need to be checked before finding the optimal basis. The concept of *dominance* allows us to objectively say when a heuristic is "better" than an alternative.

Definition 3.19 (Dominance). Given two admissible heuristics h_1 and h_2, if $h_1(\mathcal{B}) \geq h_2(\mathcal{B})$ for all $\mathcal{B}$, then we say h_1 dominates h_2.

Unsurprisingly, the dominating heuristic will give higher performance in A* search. At one extreme, h^* dominates all other heuristic functions, and using h^* as the heuristic means that A* will never explore suboptimal paths. At the other extreme, using $h(\mathcal{B}) = 0$ for all $\mathcal{B}$ injects no guidance to the search, and A* reduces to BFS. The following establishes a comparison between h_{rem} and h_{ins} in terms of dominance.

Theorem 3.20 h_{ins} *dominates* h_{rem}.

Proof. Recall that all the bases in $\mathcal{O}$ are infeasible, where $\mathcal{O}$ is as defined in (3.66). In Algorithm 3.20, for each $\mathcal{B}_m$ in $\mathcal{O}$, the data in $\mathcal{B}_m$ are inserted into $\mathcal{F}$ one by one. Thus, we are guaranteed that when all of $\mathcal{B}_m$ are inserted into $\mathcal{F}$, the enlarged set will be infeasible. Each basis in $\mathcal{O}$ will contribute at least 1 to h_{ins}, thus h_{ins} is at least equal to h_{rem}.

To see that h_{ins} can be greater than h_{rem}, observe that if $\mathcal{B}_m$ contains more than one item from $\mathcal{O}^*$, then the successive insertion of the data in $\mathcal{B}_m$ into $\mathcal{F}$ may increment h_{ins} by more than 1 because of monotonicity. □

Finally, the fact that the additional cost to the path is increased by exactly one for every descend suggests that it is possible to reuse the heuristic value of a parent basis whenever it is advantageous to do so. Specifically, for two adjacent bases $\mathcal{B}$ and $\mathcal{B}'$ where $\mathcal{B}$ is the parent, define the meta-heuristic

$$h_{met}(\mathcal{B}') = \max\left(h_{ins}(\mathcal{B}'), h_{met}(\mathcal{B}) - 1\right), \tag{3.70}$$

i.e., returns the higher value between h_{ins} and the heuristic value of the parent minus one. The above is an instance of the *pathmax* equation used in the heuristic search literature [Pearl, 1984]. In the initial step, where $\mathcal{B}'$ is the root basis of the search tree, simply take $h_{met}(\mathcal{B}') = h_{ins}(\mathcal{B}')$.

Theorem 3.21 h_{met} *is admissible.*

See Section G in the Appendix for the complete proof of the above theorem. It is also trivial to see that h_{met} dominates h_{ins}. As a final note on heuristics for maximum consensus, note that all the computations here require support set updating after the removal or insertion of a small number of constraints. These can be achieved efficiently by warm starting the optimization, as discussed at the end of Section 3.6.2.

Early Termination

Define $g(\mathcal{B})$ as an upper bound on the number of data that must be removed from $\mathcal{C}(\mathcal{B})$ to make $\mathcal{C}(\mathcal{B})$ feasible. Coupled with the heuristic function, we can thus establish

$$h(\mathcal{B}) \leq h^*(\mathcal{B}) \leq g(\mathcal{B}). \tag{3.71}$$

Given $g(\mathcal{B})$, it is possible to terminate Algorithm 3.18 early. Specifically, if $h(\mathcal{B}) = g(\mathcal{B})$ for the $\mathcal{B}$ currently under test in Line 7 of Algorithm 3.18, we can exit regardless of whether $\mathcal{B}$ is feasible. The maximum consensus estimate should then be taken as $\theta(\mathcal{F})$, where $\mathcal{F}$ is as defined in (3.69).

Theorem 3.22 *A^* is optimal with early termination.*

Proof. The value given by

$$e^*(\mathcal{B}) = \ell(\mathcal{B}) + h^*(\mathcal{B}) \tag{3.72}$$

is the minimum number of constraints that must be removed from $\mathcal{S}$ to achieve feasibility, given that we have removed $\mathcal{V}(\mathcal{B})$. When this is compared with (3.63), it is clear that $e(\mathcal{B}) \leq e^*(\mathcal{B})$.

If the current $\mathcal{B}$ has $h(\mathcal{B}) = g(\mathcal{B})$, then from (3.71), $e(\mathcal{B}) = e^*(\mathcal{B})$. Since we search the tree according to the A* method, $e(\mathcal{B}) \leq e(\mathcal{B}')$ where $\mathcal{B}'$ is any other basis in the queue. Thus $e^*(\mathcal{B}) \leq e(\mathcal{B}') \leq e^*(\mathcal{B}')$, i.e., the path to the optimal basis must pass through $\mathcal{B}$. $\qquad\square$

Any suboptimal maximum consensus estimate can be used to construct an upper bound function. In fact, an upper bound can be obtained as a by-product of Algorithm 3.20:

$$g_{rem}(\mathcal{B}) = |\mathcal{C}(\mathcal{B}) \setminus \mathcal{F}| = |\mathcal{O}|. \tag{3.73}$$

Analysis

Using an admissible heuristic function in Algorithm 3.18 ensures that A* always exits by finding the optimal basis $\mathcal{B}^*$; let $\ell^* = \ell(\mathcal{B}^*)$ be the level at which $\mathcal{B}^*$ is situated. The following result shows that A* will do no worse than BFS.

Theorem 3.23 *Algorithm 3.18 does not generate bases beyond level ℓ^*.*

Proof. Let $\mathcal{B}$ and $\mathcal{B}^\dagger$ be bases currently existing in the queue. Further, let $\mathcal{B}$ be on the path leading to $\mathcal{B}^*$, and $\mathcal{B}^\dagger$ be an infeasible basis of level ℓ^*. Then

$$e(\mathcal{B}^\dagger) = \ell^* + h(\mathcal{B}^\dagger) > \ell^* \tag{3.74}$$
$$\geq \ell(\mathcal{B}) + h(\mathcal{B}) = e(\mathcal{B}) \implies e(\mathcal{B}^\dagger) > e(\mathcal{B}). \tag{3.75}$$

The strict inequality in (3.74) draws from the fact that, for all the heuristic functions discussed above, $h(\mathcal{B}^\dagger) \geq 1$ if $\mathcal{B}^\dagger$ is infeasible. Hence, Algorithm 3.18 will not expand any basis that is already at level ℓ^*.   □

The worst-case performance of A* occurs when all bases up to level ℓ^* are expanded, which is equivalent to the behavior of BFS. As discussed in Section 3.6.2, by invoking a theorem of Matoušek [1995], the number of level-ℓ^* bases is bounded above by $\mathcal{O}((\ell^* + 1)^{\delta-1})$, where δ is the combinatorial dimension of the LP-type problem.

Evaluation

A synthetic data experiment involving the robust fitting of 2D line ($d = 2$) was performed. A data instance was generated by producing $N = 100$ points $\{(p_i, q_i)\}_{i=1}^N$ that lie on a line $q = mp + c$, where $p_i, q_i \in [0, 1]$ and (m, c) are produced randomly. The points were then corrupted with Normal noise with $\sigma = 0.1$. To simulate outliers, a number of points were then randomly chosen and corrupted with a larger noise magnitude ($\sigma = 1$). Based on the residual function (3.1), the inlier threshold was chosen as $\epsilon = 0.3$.

Figure 3.20a shows a typical generated data instance and estimated maximum consensus line by tree search (using the A* method in Algorithm 3.18). Figure 3.20b shows the runtime of several methods as the number of outliers were increased: specifically, RANSAC, ILP (see Section 3.3), tree search with BFS (Algorithm 3.17), and A*. Expectedly, the runtime of BFS increased rapidly with the number of outliers, since it must explore all the levels in the tree before reaching feasibility. However, the runtime of A* increased much more slowly because it takes advantage of the guidance provided by the heuristic. The runtime of ILP also increased quite rapidly as the number of outliers was increased.

Figure 3.21 illustrates the results of applying Algorithm 3.18 on the robust affine image matching and homography estimation problems; refer to Examples 2.3 and 2.4 for the quasi-convex formulation of the residuals. Both problems are of moderate dimensionality, respectively $d = 6$ and $d = 8$. The instances in Figure 3.21 are of size, respectively, $N = 70$ and $N = 58$. With an inlier threshold of $\epsilon = 0.1$ pixels in both cases, the A* algorithm terminated within 10 s. The maximum consensus sets found were of size, respectively, 65 and 54. The maximum depth ℓ^* that A* needed to explore was therefore (just) 5 and 4, respectively. These problem instances can thus be considered easy. In more difficult problem instances where N and ℓ^* can be an order of magnitude higher, one should expect the cost of the algorithm to rise significantly, as predicted by the analysis.

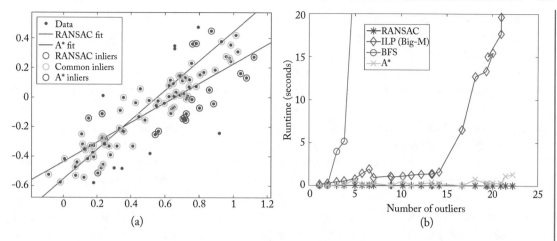

(a)   (b)

Figure 3.20: (a) Sample result of tree search (using the A* method) and RANSAC for robust line fitting on a randomly generated data instance. RANSAC found a suboptimal solution with consensus 76, whereas A* found the globally optimal solution with consensus 87. (b) Runtime of several methods as the number of outliers was increased.

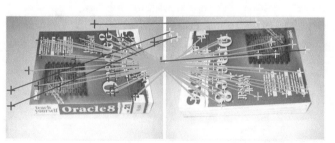

(a) Problem size $N = 70$, maximum tree depth to explore $\ell^* = 5$

(b) Problem size $N = 58$, maximum tree depth to explore $\ell^* = 4$

Figure 3.21: Problem instances for (a) robust affine image matching and (b) robust homography estimation. Green lines indicate true inliers, whereas red lines represent true outliers.

3.7 BIBLIOGRAPHICAL REMARKS

Souvaine and Steele [1987] first proposed the usage of plane sweep for LMedS line fitting in $\mathcal{O}(N^2 \log N)$ time. This was later improved to $\mathcal{O}(N^2)$ by Edelsbrunner and Souvaine [1990] with topological plane sweep. Mount et al. [2000] proposed an approximate algorithm for LMedS line fitting which is also based on the plane sweep/dual transformation technique. The usage of plane sweep for maximum consensus line fitting was first considered by Zrour et al. [2009]. Similar to the algorithm presented in Section 3.2, Zrour et al.'s method runs in $\mathcal{O}(N^2 \log N)$ time, though the underlying theoretical motivations are different.

The connection of maximum consensus to MaxFS was first highlighted by Li [2009a], though a custom-made BnB algorithm instead of ILP was used to solve maximum consensus optimally. Zheng et al. [2011] later directly solved maximum consensus as ILP, but they improved upon the basic version by introducing the unit-norm constraint on the parameter vector to reflect the homogeneous nature of geometric models.

Globally optimal point cloud registration under the maximum consensus framework was first considered by Breuel [1992], whose "adaptive subdivision" algorithm is essentially the BnB method. Chin et al. [2014], Parra Bustos et al. [2014], and Parra Bustos et al. [2016] more recently updated Breuel's approach by designing advanced data structures to speed up the algorithm. Li and Hartley [2007] and Yang et al. [2013] also proposed globally optimal point cloud registration, but under a maximum likelihood framework. Other authors have also considered globally optimal point set registration, for example Olsson et al. [2009], but on application settings where input correspondences are available.

A subset enumeration approach for exactly solving LMedS was proposed by Stromberg [1993]. Erickson et al. [2006] showed that one can unlikely do better than $\mathcal{O}(N^d)$ for LMedS. In computer vision, Olsson et al. [2008] first proposed a subset enumeration technique for maximum consensus, though they focused on the robust Euclidean registration problem. Enqvist et al. [2012] later generalized Olsson et al. results to other robust criteria. More recently, Chin et al. [2015] proposed to search the tree structure of LP-type methods to avoid enumerating all subsets to solve maximum consensus.

CHAPTER 4

Preprocessing for Maximum Consensus

> If you optimize everything, you will always be unhappy.
>
> Donald Knuth

4.1 INTRODUCTION

The fundamental intractability of maximum consensus, as discussed in Section 1.3, forces us to choose between fast approximate algorithms that do not provide optimal solutions or error bounds, and potentially very costly exact algorithms. Realistic operating constraints compel us to be content with approximate solutions. Provided precautions are taken to avoid their pitfalls, approximate methods can be the reliable workhorse for maximum consensus optimization in practical computer vision applications.

In this chapter, a class of approaches that are orthogonal to approximate and exact methods are introduced, specifically, the technique of *preprocessing* for maximum consensus. To begin, the following defines again the general version of maximum consensus:

$$\underset{\omega \in \Omega}{\text{maximize}} \quad \Psi(\omega), \tag{4.1}$$

where Ω is the parameter space of the model of interest, and

$$\Psi(\omega) = \sum_{i=1}^{N} \mathbb{I}\left(r(\omega \mid y_i) \leq \epsilon\right) \tag{4.2}$$

is the consensus of ω w.r.t. the set of input data $\mathcal{D} = \{y_i\}_{i=1}^{N}$. A preprocessing method reduces the input data $\mathcal{D}$ to a smaller subset $\mathcal{D}' \subset \mathcal{D}$, in a manner that *preserves the solution* of the original problem. Specifically, the optimal maximum consensus estimate on $\mathcal{D}$ and $\mathcal{D}'$ are the same. Figure 4.1 illustrates the concept of preprocessing.

Note that $\mathcal{D}'$ may not be a consensus set, i.e., there remain outliers in $\mathcal{D}'$. However, since $\mathcal{D}'$ is smaller than the original data $\mathcal{D}$, it can be expected that solving maximum consensus on $\mathcal{D}'$ will incur a shorter runtime. An example based on ILP optimization (Section 3.3) is already depicted in Figure 4.1. Note that since $\mathcal{D}$ and $\mathcal{D}'$ contain the same optimal solution, the maximum consensus set is also preserved in $\mathcal{D}'$. This implies that the outlier rate in $\mathcal{D}'$ is lower than

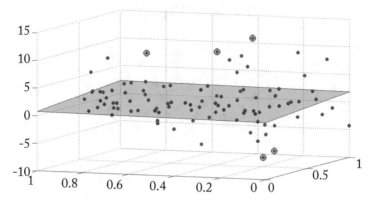

Figure 4.1: Illustrating the concept of preprocessing on maximum consensus plane fitting (this example appeared previously in Figure 3.5). The points in blue indicate the input $\mathcal{D}$ to maximum consensus. The five blue points that are circled in red are the points that are removed from $\mathcal{D}$ to produce the subset $\mathcal{D}'$. The maximum consensus plane on $\mathcal{D}'$ is plotted above, which has the same quality as the global solution on $\mathcal{D}$ (shown in Figure 3.5). However, executing the same ILP solver on $\mathcal{D}'$ yielded a much shorter runtime of 33 s (cf. 420 s in Figure 3.5).

in $\mathcal{D}$. Thus, approximate algorithms such as RANSAC (Section 2.2), whose runtime scales exponentially with the outlier rate, also stand to benefit from such a preprocessing technique. The main issue here is, therefore, how to conduct the preprocessing and whether it can be performed quickly enough to be worthwhile.

Section 4.1.1 formalizes the concept of preprocessing and outlines the underlying theory. The rest of the chapter is devoted to describing specific preprocessing algorithms.

4.1.1   GUARANTEED OUTLIER REMOVAL

Denote by $\mathcal{H} = \{1, \ldots, N\}$ the indices of the data $\mathcal{D} = \{y_i\}_{i=1}^N$. We re-express maximum consensus as

$$\begin{aligned}
\underset{\omega \in \Omega, \mathcal{I} \subseteq \mathcal{H}}{\text{maximize}} \quad & |\mathcal{I}| \\
\text{subject to} \quad & r(\omega \mid y_i) \leq \epsilon \ \ \forall i \in \mathcal{I}.
\end{aligned} \tag{4.3}$$

The solution of the problem is the maximum consensus set $\mathcal{I}^*$. We call the data indexed by $\mathcal{I}^*$ the *true inliers*. Conversely, we call the data indexed by $\mathcal{H} \setminus \mathcal{I}^*$ the *true outliers*.

If $\mathcal{D}' \subset \mathcal{D}$ contains the same maximum consensus set as $\mathcal{D}$, then one can conclude that in the process of reducing $\mathcal{D}$ to $\mathcal{D}'$, only true outliers have been removed. Observe that the removed points in Figure 4.1 are true outliers. For this reason, we also call this preprocessing paradigm *guaranteed outlier removal (GORE)*, since it ensures that any data discarded in the preprocessing does not exist in the maximum consensus set.

The maximum consensus problem can be further re-written as

$$\underset{k \in \mathcal{H}}{\text{maximize}} \quad f_k, \tag{4.4}$$

where f_k is the maximized objective value of the following subproblem:

$$
\begin{aligned}
\underset{\omega \in \Omega, \mathcal{I}_k \subseteq \mathcal{H} \setminus \{k\}}{\text{maximize}} \quad & 1 + |\mathcal{I}_k| \\
\text{subject to} \quad & r(\omega \mid y_i) \le \epsilon \ \ \forall i \in \mathcal{I}_k, \\
& r(\omega \mid y_k) \le \epsilon.
\end{aligned} \tag{P_k}
$$

We dub the above subproblem P_k to facilitate future referencing. Intuitively, P_k seeks the largest consensus set among $\mathcal{D}$, given that datum y_k *must* be in the consensus set. Of course, the re-formulation (4.4) does not make maximum consensus any easier to solve; its utility derives from clarifying how an upper bound on f_k allows identification of true outliers.

Let ℓ be a lower bound to the maximum consensus value: $\ell \le |\mathcal{I}^*|$. Conversely, let $\hat{f}_k$ be an upper bound to the value of P_k, i.e., $\hat{f}_k \ge f_k$. Given the lower and upper bound values, the following result can be established.

Theorem 4.1   *If $\hat{f}_k < \ell$, then y_k is a true outlier—k does not exist in $\mathcal{I}^*$.*

Proof. The proof is by contradiction. If k is in $\mathcal{I}^*$, then we must have that $f_k = |\mathcal{I}^*|$. However, if we are given that $\hat{f}_k < \ell$, then $f_k < \ell \le |\mathcal{I}^*|$, which contradicts the previous condition. Hence, k cannot exist in $\mathcal{I}^*$.   □

Algorithms for GORE apply Theorem 4.1 iteratively for $k = 1, \ldots, N$ to remove true outliers. The key ingredients are the lower bound ℓ and the upper bound $\hat{f}_k$. For the preprocessing to be effective, the bounds should be tight, i.e., ℓ and $\hat{f}_k$ should be as close as possible to their respective target values $|\mathcal{I}^*|$ and f_k. Further, one must be able to compute ℓ and $\hat{f}_k$ efficiently such that the preprocessing step pays off (in Section 4.3.1, we formally define the gain from conducting GORE). The lower bound ℓ can be obtained using any fast approximate algorithms for maximum consensus. The calculation of $\hat{f}_k$ is problem dependent—the rest of this chapter describes the technique for several applications.

4.2   GEOMETRICALLY INSPIRED APPROACHES

Our first group of techniques exploits the underlying geometry of the model of interest to efficiently derive $\hat{f}_k$ and conduct GORE.

4.2.1   2D RIGID TRANSFORMATION

Given a set of noisy correspondences $\mathcal{D} = \{(\mathbf{p}_i, \mathbf{p}'_i)\}_{i=1}^{N}$ in $\mathbb{R}^2$, some of which are erroneous, we wish to robustly estimate the 2D rigid transformation

$$\mathbf{p}' = \mathbf{R}(\theta)\mathbf{p} + \mathbf{t} \tag{4.5}$$

that aligns as many of the corresponding points as possible. A 2D rigid transformation is defined by a 2×2 rotation matrix

$$\mathbf{R}(\theta) = \begin{bmatrix} \cos\theta & -\sin\theta \\ \sin\theta & \cos\theta \end{bmatrix} \tag{4.6}$$

that conducts a rotation of angle θ about the origin in $\mathbb{R}^2$, and a translation vector $\mathbf{t}$. The parameter of interest here is thus $\omega = (\theta, \mathbf{t}) \in [0, 2\pi] \times \mathbb{R}^2$.

Under the framework of maximum consensus, we consider a pair of corresponding points $(\mathbf{p}_i, \mathbf{p}_i')$ aligned if they are brought within distance ϵ; that is, if

$$\left\| \mathbf{R}(\theta)\mathbf{p}_i + \mathbf{t} - \mathbf{p}_i' \right\|_2 \le \epsilon. \tag{4.7}$$

Specializing problem P_k for 2D rigid transformation, we obtain

$$
\begin{aligned}
&\underset{\theta \in [0,2\pi], \mathbf{t} \in \mathbb{R}^2, \mathcal{I}_k \subseteq \mathcal{H}\backslash\{k\}}{\text{maximize}} && 1 + |\mathcal{I}_k| \\
&\text{subject to} && \left\| \mathbf{R}(\theta)\mathbf{p}_i + \mathbf{t} - \mathbf{p}_i' \right\|_2 \le \epsilon \ \forall i \in \mathcal{I}_k, \\
& && \left\| \mathbf{R}(\theta)\mathbf{p}_k + \mathbf{t} - \mathbf{p}_k' \right\|_2 \le \epsilon.
\end{aligned}
\tag{4.8}
$$

To simplify the subproblem, consider the triangle inequality

$$\|\mathbf{x} - \mathbf{y}\|_2 = \|\mathbf{x} + (-\mathbf{y})\|_2 \le \|\mathbf{x}\|_2 + \|\mathbf{y}\|_2. \tag{4.9}$$

Using the triangle inequality, the constraints in the subproblem can be combined into

$$
\begin{aligned}
\left\| \mathbf{R}(\theta)\mathbf{p}_i + \mathbf{t} - \mathbf{p}_i' - \mathbf{R}(\theta)\mathbf{p}_k - \mathbf{t} + \mathbf{p}_k' \right\|_2 &= \left\| \mathbf{R}(\theta)(\mathbf{p}_i - \mathbf{p}_k) - (\mathbf{p}_i' - \mathbf{p}_k') \right\|_2 \\
&\le \left\| \mathbf{R}(\theta)\mathbf{p}_i + \mathbf{t} - \mathbf{p}_i' \right\|_2 + \left\| \mathbf{R}(\theta)\mathbf{p}_k + \mathbf{t} - \mathbf{p}_k' \right\|_2 \\
&\le 2\epsilon.
\end{aligned}
\tag{4.10}
$$

We have thus removed the variable $\mathbf{t}$ from (4.8), leading to the pure rotation problem

$$
\begin{aligned}
&\underset{\theta \in [0,2\pi], \mathcal{I}_k \subseteq \mathcal{H}\backslash\{k\}}{\text{maximize}} && 1 + |\mathcal{I}_k| \\
&\text{subject to} && \left\| \mathbf{R}(\theta)\mathbf{q}_{i,k} - \mathbf{q}_{i,k}' \right\|_2 \le 2\epsilon \ \forall i \in \mathcal{I}_k,
\end{aligned}
\tag{4.11}
$$

where $\mathbf{q}_{i,k} = \mathbf{p}_i - \mathbf{p}_k$ and $\mathbf{q}_{i,k}' = \mathbf{p}_i' - \mathbf{p}_k'$. More intuitively, to convert (4.8) to (4.11), the point set $\{\mathbf{p}_i\}_{i=1}^N$ is translated such that $\mathbf{p}_k$ is at the origin, and similarly for $\{\mathbf{p}_i'\}_{i=1}^N$ with $\mathbf{p}_k'$. Then, the inlier threshold is increased to 2ϵ, to account for the introduced uncertainty.

The increased uncertainty imposed for the conversion also means that the maximum value of (4.11) is an upper bound $\hat{f}_k$ of (4.8). To solve (4.11) to obtain $\hat{f}_k$, define

$$\left[\theta_i^a, \theta_i^b \right] \subseteq [0, 2\pi] \tag{4.12}$$

as the contiguous range of θ that enables $\mathbf{R}(\theta)\mathbf{q}_{i,k}$ to be within 2ϵ from $\mathbf{q}'_{i,k}$. Figure 4.2a illustrates this angular range. Problem (4.11) can then be equivalently expressed as

$$\underset{\theta \in [0,2\pi]}{\text{maximize}} \quad 1 + \sum_{i \neq k} \mathbb{I}\left(\theta \in \left[\theta_i^a, \theta_i^b\right]\right), \tag{4.13}$$

which is simply the classical *interval stabbing* problem; Figure 4.2b illustrates. Note that if an unwrapped angular range exceeds $[0, 2\pi]$, the interval is simply broken up into several sub-intervals without affecting the optimality of (4.13). Interval stabbing can be solved efficiently in $\mathcal{O}(N \log N)$ time. See Section H in the Appendix.

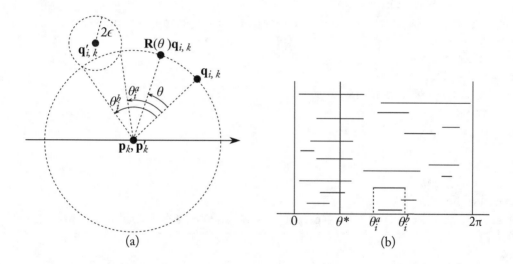

(a) (b)

Figure 4.2: (a) Illustrating problem (4.11), where we wish to rotationally align as many point correspondences as possible. For each i, $\left[\theta_i^a, \theta_i^b\right]$ is the range of θ that enables $\mathbf{R}(\theta)\mathbf{q}_{i,k}$ to align with $\mathbf{q}'_{i,k}$ to within 2ϵ. (b) Unwrapping all the angular ranges into linear intervals, problem (4.11) can be solved by interval stabbing. Here, θ_k^* stabs the most number of intervals.

Let θ^* be the solution to the interval stabbing problem (4.13). The combination $\omega = (\theta^*, -\mathbf{R}(\theta^*)\mathbf{p}_k + \mathbf{p}'_k)$ is also a candidate solution to the original maximum consensus problem, where the quality of the solution can be obtained by evaluating the consensus of ω.

GORE Algorithm

Algorithm 4.21 summarizes the GORE technique for robust estimation of 2D rigid transformation. The procedure is simple: iterate through each correspondence and attempt to reject the correspondence by applying Theorem 4.1 (Step 11 in the algorithm). As soon as a datum is identified as a true outlier, remove it from further consideration. Every time a better incumbent solution is found, the lower bound ℓ is increased to tighten the bound (Step 8). Note that the candidate solution need only be evaluated using the current remaining data indexed by $\mathcal{H}$ (Step 6), since the maximum consensus set is preserved. Accordingly, the size of problem (4.11) also progressively decreases as true outliers are discarded.

Algorithm 4.21 GORE for robust estimation of 2D rigid transformation.

Require: Input point correspondences $\mathcal{D} = \{(\mathbf{p}_i, \mathbf{p}'_i)\}_{i=1}^{N}$, inlier threshold ϵ.
   1: $\mathcal{H} \leftarrow \{1, 2, \ldots, N\}, \mathcal{T} \leftarrow \mathcal{H}$.
   2: $\ell \leftarrow 0$.
   3: **while** $\mathcal{T} \neq \emptyset$ **do**
   4:     $k \leftarrow$ Retrieve an item from $\mathcal{T}$.
   5:     $(\hat{f}_k, \theta^*) \leftarrow$ Optimal value and solution of (4.11) defined on data indexed by $\mathcal{H}$.
   6:     $\mathcal{I}_k \leftarrow \{i \in \mathcal{H} \mid \|\mathbf{R}(\theta^*)(\mathbf{p}_i - \mathbf{p}_k) - (\mathbf{p}'_i - \mathbf{p}'_k)\|_2 \leq \epsilon\}$.
   7:     **if** $|\mathcal{I}_k| > \ell$ **then**
   8:         $\ell \leftarrow |\mathcal{I}_k|$.
   9:         $(\hat{\theta}, \hat{t}) \leftarrow (\theta^*, -\mathbf{R}(\theta^*)\mathbf{p}_k + \mathbf{p}'_k)$.
  10:     **end if**
  11:     **if** $\hat{f}_k < \ell$ **then**
  12:         $\mathcal{H} \leftarrow \mathcal{H} \setminus \{k\}$.
  13:     **end if**
  14:     $\mathcal{T} \leftarrow \mathcal{T} \setminus \{k\}$.
  15: **end while**
  16: **return** Reduced dataset $\mathcal{D}' = \{(\mathbf{p}_i, \mathbf{p}'_i) \mid i \in \mathcal{H}\}$ and best suboptimal solution $(\hat{\theta}, \hat{t})$.

Algorithm 4.21 can be improved by prioritizing the datum k to test (in Step 4, k is chosen in no particular order), such that true outliers are identified earlier to speed up convergence. For example, the data can be sorted according to their residual to the current best solution. See Parra Bustos and Chin [2015] for more details.

Unlike RANSAC, Algorithm 4.21 is a deterministic algorithm. The set of true outliers identified and discarded by GORE depends only on the order in which the removal test is performed. As a whole, Algorithm 4.21 contains only very simple geometric operations. The rejection test for a k consumes $\mathcal{O}(N + N \log N)$ time, which is composed of $\mathcal{O}(N)$ iterations to obtain the N angular intervals (4.12), and $\mathcal{O}(N \log N)$ to solve the stabbing problem. In the worst case, N rejection tests are performed, thus the overall algorithms takes $\mathcal{O}(N^2(\log N + 1))$ time. Note that the worst case runtime of GORE is independent of the outlier rate, which is unlike RANSAC, where runtime scales exponentially with the proportion of outliers.

Figures 4.3 and 4.4 show the results of applying Algorithm 4.21 on a 4DOF point cloud registration problem, which involves estimating a 1DOF in-plane rotation (i.e., the yaw angle) and 3DOF translation. Such a problem occurs, for example, in aerial light detection and ranging

(LIDAR) scanning of terrain, where the attitude of the aircraft is maintained constant throughout the scanning. 3D keypoint detection and matching techniques (specifically, PFH [Rusu et al., 2008], and ISS3D [Zhong, 2009] as implemented on Point Cloud Library[1]) are executed to obtain a set of point correspondences $\mathcal{D} = \{(\mathbf{p}_i, \mathbf{p}'_i)\}_{i=1}^N$ for each input pair of point clouds. To enable Algorithm 4.21, the points are simply projected onto the horizontal plane, which removes 1DOF from the required transformation parameters.

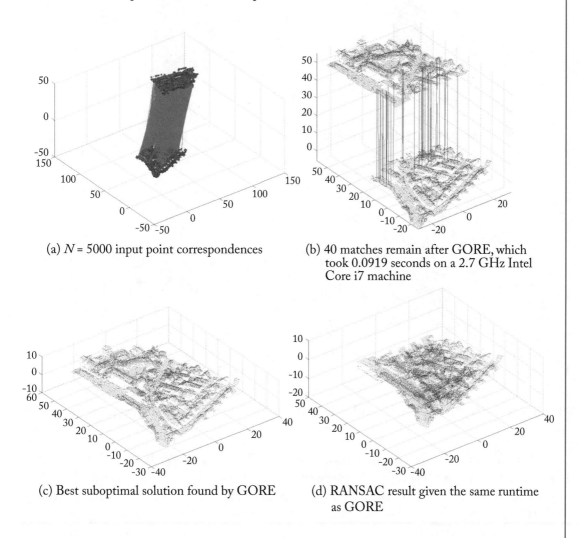

(a) $N = 5000$ input point correspondences

(b) 40 matches remain after GORE, which took 0.0919 seconds on a 2.7 GHz Intel Core i7 machine

(c) Best suboptimal solution found by GORE

(d) RANSAC result given the same runtime as GORE

Figure 4.3: Results of applying Algorithm 4.21 on a 4DOF point cloud registration problem.

---

[1]http://pointclouds.org/

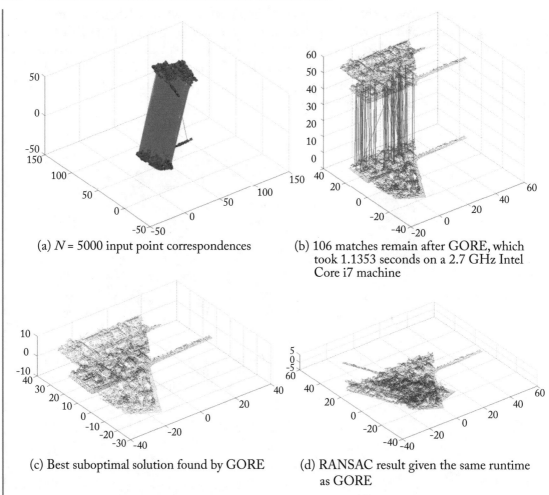

(a) $N = 5000$ input point correspondences

(b) 106 matches remain after GORE, which took 1.1353 seconds on a 2.7 GHz Intel Core i7 machine

(c) Best suboptimal solution found by GORE

(d) RANSAC result given the same runtime as GORE

Figure 4.4: Another result of Algorithm 4.21 on a 4DOF point cloud registration problem.

Unlike their 2D image counterparts such as SIFT [Lowe, 2004], 3D keypoint techniques are much less accurate, which give rise to high outlier rates in the data, e.g., in excess of 99% in Figure 4.3. Nonetheless, Algorithm 4.21 was able to terminate under 1 second in both examples. By visual inspection, most of the remaining correspondences are true inliers, and the best suboptimal solution found by GORE was able to satisfactorily align the point clouds. In contrast, RANSAC was not able to find a decent solution under the same runtime expended by Algorithm 4.21.

We have not invoked a globally optimal maximum consensus algorithm on the resultant reduced data instances $\mathcal{D}'$ in Figures 4.3 and 4.4. Again, by inspection, the small size of $\mathcal{D}'$ and the very low proportion of outliers therein would mean that an exact solution can be found with little effort. In the next section, a higher-dimensional problem is investigated, where there is a bigger need to further optimize on $\mathcal{D}'$.

4.2.2 3D ROTATIONAL ALIGNMENT

Rotational alignment of 3D point sets without *a priori* determined correspondences has been discussed at length in Section 3.4.1. Here, we consider robust 3D rotational alignment with input point correspondences $\mathcal{D} = \{(\mathbf{x}_i, \mathbf{y}_i)\}_{i=1}^N$ [to reduce clutter, a slight departure of notation is applied here, where a pair of matching points are denoted as $(\mathbf{x}_i, \mathbf{y}_i)$ instead of $(\mathbf{p}_i, \mathbf{p}'_i)$]. A 3D rotation acts upon a point by

$$\mathbf{y} = \mathbf{R}\mathbf{x}, \tag{4.14}$$

where $\mathbf{R} \in SO(3)$ is the rotation matrix. Under the maximum consensus framework, we wish to estimate $\mathbf{R}$ that aligns as many of the input correspondences up to distance ϵ; that is,

$$\angle(\mathbf{R}\mathbf{x}_i, \mathbf{y}_i) \leq \epsilon, \tag{4.15}$$

where $\angle(\cdot, \cdot)$ indicates the angular distance. Using the angular distance renders the norm of the points irrelevant. Henceforth, we take all the points to have unit norm.

Specializing subproblem P_k to this case, we have

$$\begin{array}{ll} \underset{\mathbf{R}_k \in SO(3), \mathcal{I}_k \subseteq \mathcal{H} \setminus \{k\}}{\text{maximize}} & 1 + |\mathcal{I}_k| \\ \text{subject to} & \angle(\mathbf{R}_k \mathbf{x}_i, \mathbf{y}_i) \leq \epsilon \ \ \forall i \in \mathcal{I}_k, \\ & \angle(\mathbf{R}_k \mathbf{x}_k, \mathbf{y}_k) \leq \epsilon. \end{array} \tag{4.16}$$

Rotation $\mathbf{R}_k$ can be decomposed into two rotations

$$\mathbf{R}_k = \mathbf{A}\mathbf{B} \tag{4.17}$$

where we define $\mathbf{B}$ as a rotation that honors the condition

$$\angle(\mathbf{B}\mathbf{x}_k, \mathbf{y}_k) \leq \epsilon, \tag{4.18}$$

and $\mathbf{A}$ as a rotation about axis $\mathbf{B}\mathbf{x}_k$. Since $\mathbf{A}$ leaves $\mathbf{B}\mathbf{x}_k$ unchanged, the condition (4.18) and hence the constraint $\angle(\mathbf{R}_k \mathbf{x}_k, \mathbf{y}_k) \leq \epsilon$ in (4.16) are always satisfied. Figure 4.5a illustrates this interpretation of $\mathbf{R}_k$. Solving P_k, as defined in (4.16), thus amounts to finding the combination of the rotation $\mathbf{B}$ (a 2DOF problem, given (4.18)) and the rotation angle of $\mathbf{A}$ (a 1DOF problem, thus giving a total of 3DOF) that maximizes the objective.

The Ideal Case

In the absence of noise and outliers, $\mathbf{x}_i$ can be aligned exactly with $\mathbf{y}_i$ for all i. Based on (4.17), we denote the rotation that solves (4.16) under this ideal case as

$$\hat{\mathbf{R}}_k = \hat{\mathbf{A}}\hat{\mathbf{B}}, \tag{4.19}$$

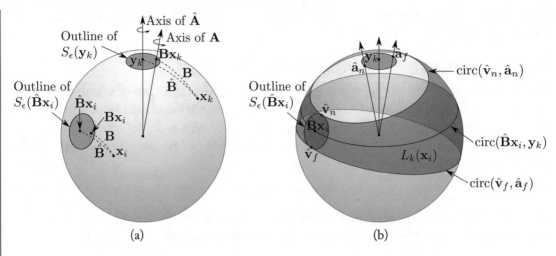

Figure 4.5: (a) Interpreting rotation $\mathbf{R}_k$ according to (4.17). (b) The uncertainty region $L_k(\mathbf{x}_i)$, as defined in (4.28), which bounds the position of $\mathbf{R}_k\mathbf{x}_i$ for all allowable $\mathbf{R}_k$.

which can be solved as follows (refer also to Figure 4.5a). First, find a rotation $\hat{\mathbf{B}}$ that aligns $\mathbf{x}_k$ exactly with $\mathbf{y}_k$; that is,

$$\hat{\mathbf{B}}\mathbf{x}_k = \mathbf{y}_k. \tag{4.20}$$

For example, take $\hat{\mathbf{B}}$ as the rotation that maps $\mathbf{x}_k$ to $\mathbf{y}_k$ with the minimum geodesic motion. To solve for $\hat{\mathbf{A}}$, take any $i \neq k$, then find the angle $\hat{\theta}$ of rotation about axis $\hat{\mathbf{B}}\mathbf{x}_k$ that maps $\hat{\mathbf{B}}\mathbf{x}_i$ to $\mathbf{y}_i$. Then $\hat{\mathbf{A}} = \exp(\hat{\theta}\hat{\mathbf{B}}\mathbf{x}_k)$, where $\exp(\cdot)$ is the exponential map

$$\exp(\theta\hat{\mathbf{v}}) = \mathbf{I} + \sin(\theta)[\hat{\mathbf{v}}]_\times + (1 - \cos(\theta))([\hat{\mathbf{v}}]_\times)^2 \tag{4.21}$$

and $[\hat{\mathbf{v}}]_\times$ indicates the cross product matrix of unit vector $\hat{\mathbf{v}}$. Basically, the exponential map generates a rotation matrix from its axis-angle representation. The above construction of $\hat{\mathbf{R}}_k$ affirms that rotation estimation requires a minimum of two point matches [Horn, 1987].

Uncertainty Bound
In the usual case, we must contend with noise and outliers. Toward the goal of calculating an upper bound of (4.16), we establish a bound on the position of $\mathbf{x}_i$ when acted upon by the set of feasible rotations $\mathbf{R}_k$—that is, those that satisfy $\angle(\mathbf{R}_k\mathbf{x}_k, \mathbf{y}_k) \leq \epsilon$.

The set of $\mathbf{B}$ that maintains (4.18) causes $\mathbf{B}\mathbf{x}_k$ to lie within a spherical region of angular radius ϵ centered at $\mathbf{y}_k$; that is,

$$\mathbf{B}\mathbf{x}_k \in S_\epsilon(\mathbf{y}_k), \tag{4.22}$$

where a spherical region is defined as

$$S_\epsilon(\mathbf{x}) = \{\hat{\mathbf{v}} \mid \angle(\mathbf{x}, \hat{\mathbf{v}}) \leq \epsilon\}. \tag{4.23}$$

Since $\mathbf{B}\mathbf{x}_k$ is the rotation axis of $\mathbf{A}$, the interior of $S_\epsilon(\mathbf{y}_k)$ also represents the set of possible rotation axes for $\mathbf{A}$. Further, for any $i \neq k$, we can establish

$$\angle(\mathbf{B}\mathbf{x}_i, \hat{\mathbf{B}}\mathbf{x}_i) \leq \epsilon; \tag{4.24}$$

see Section I in the Appendix for the proof. Hence, (4.24) also shows that the set of feasible $\mathbf{B}$ cause $\mathbf{B}\mathbf{x}_i$ to lie in a spherical region—that is,

$$\mathbf{B}\mathbf{x}_i \in S_\epsilon(\hat{\mathbf{B}}\mathbf{x}_i). \tag{4.25}$$

Figure 4.5a also shows $S_\epsilon(\mathbf{y}_k)$ and $S_\epsilon(\hat{\mathbf{B}}\mathbf{x}_i)$. The bound on $\mathbf{R}_k\mathbf{x}_i$ can thus be analyzed based on these two regions.

To make explicit the dependence of $\mathbf{A}$ on a rotation axis $\hat{\mathbf{a}}$ and angle θ, we now denote it as $\mathbf{A}_{\theta,\hat{\mathbf{a}}}$, where

$$\mathbf{A}_{\theta,\hat{\mathbf{a}}} = \exp(\theta\hat{\mathbf{a}}). \tag{4.26}$$

For an arbitrary unit-norm point $\hat{\mathbf{v}}$, define

$$\text{circ}(\hat{\mathbf{v}}, \hat{\mathbf{a}}) := \{\mathbf{A}_{\theta,\hat{\mathbf{a}}}\hat{\mathbf{v}} \mid \theta \in [-\pi, \pi]\} \tag{4.27}$$

as the circle traced by $\hat{\mathbf{v}}$ when acted upon by rotation $\mathbf{A}_{\theta,\hat{\mathbf{a}}}$ for all θ at a particular axis $\hat{\mathbf{a}}$.

The set of possible positions of $\mathbf{R}_k\mathbf{x}_i$ is then defined by

$$L_k(\mathbf{x}_i) := \left\{\text{circ}(\hat{\mathbf{v}}, \hat{\mathbf{a}}) \mid \hat{\mathbf{v}} \in S_\epsilon(\hat{\mathbf{B}}\mathbf{x}_i), \hat{\mathbf{a}} \in S_\epsilon(\mathbf{y}_k)\right\}. \tag{4.28}$$

Figure 4.5b illustrates this feasible region, which exists on the unit sphere. The region is bounded within the two circles

$$\text{circ}(\hat{\mathbf{v}}_n, \hat{\mathbf{a}}_n) \quad \text{and} \quad \text{circ}(\hat{\mathbf{v}}_f, \hat{\mathbf{a}}_f), \tag{4.29}$$

which are highlighted in Figure 4.5b. Intuitively, $\hat{\mathbf{v}}_n$ and $\hat{\mathbf{a}}_n$ (respectively, $\hat{\mathbf{v}}_f$ and $\hat{\mathbf{a}}_f$) are the closest (respectively farthest) pair of points from $S_\epsilon(\hat{\mathbf{B}}\mathbf{x}_i)$ and $S_\epsilon(\mathbf{y}_k)$. See Section J in the Appendix for the analytical solution for these four vectors. Note that if $\hat{\mathbf{B}}\mathbf{x}_i$ is antipodal to $\mathbf{y}_k$, the feasible region reduces to the spherical region $S_{3\epsilon}(\hat{\mathbf{B}}\mathbf{x}_i)$.

By the construction method of the region $L_k(\mathbf{x}_i)$, we arrive at the following conclusion.

Theorem 4.2   *For any $i \neq k$, if $S_\epsilon(\mathbf{y}_i)$ does not intersect with $L_k(\mathbf{x}_i)$, then $(\mathbf{x}_i, \mathbf{y}_i)$ cannot be aligned by any rotation $\mathbf{R}_k$ that satisfies $\angle(\mathbf{R}_k\mathbf{x}_k, \mathbf{y}_k) \leq \epsilon$. The correspondence $(\mathbf{x}_i, \mathbf{y}_i)$ can then be safely removed without affecting the result (4.16).*

Theorem 4.2 provides us a simple deterministic technique to calculate an upper bound $\hat{f}_k$ for (4.16): simply count the remaining number of correspondences that survive the pruning by Theorem 4.2, as only these can appear in the solution of (4.16).

Reducing the Uncertainty

For each point match $(\mathbf{x}_i, \mathbf{y}_i)$ that survives the pruning by Theorem 4.2, we reduce its uncertainty bound (4.28) into an *angular interval*. The purpose of this reduction is again to enable the technique of interval stabbing to be used to tighten the upper bound.

Consider rotating an arbitrary unit-norm point $\hat{\mathbf{v}}$ with $\mathbf{A}_{\theta,\hat{\mathbf{u}}}$ for a fixed angle θ and an axis $\hat{\mathbf{u}} \in S_\epsilon(\mathbf{y}_k)$. We wish to bound the possible locations of $\mathbf{A}_{\theta,\hat{\mathbf{u}}}\hat{\mathbf{v}}$ given the uncertainty in $\hat{\mathbf{u}}$. To this end, we establish

$$\max_{\hat{\mathbf{u}} \in S_\epsilon(\mathbf{y}_k)} \angle(\mathbf{A}_{\theta,\hat{\mathbf{u}}}\hat{\mathbf{v}}, \mathbf{A}_{\theta,\mathbf{y}_k}\hat{\mathbf{v}}) \leq \max_{\hat{\mathbf{u}} \in S_\epsilon(\mathbf{y}_k)} \|\theta\hat{\mathbf{u}} - \theta\mathbf{y}_k\|_2$$
$$= 2|\theta| \sin(\epsilon/2), \tag{4.30}$$

where the first line is based on a result of the axis-angle representation (3.22) we have seen in Section 3.4.1, and the second line occurs because $S_\epsilon(\mathbf{y}_k)$ has an angular radius of ϵ.

Now we extend (4.30) to accommodate the uncertainty of $\hat{\mathbf{v}}$ itself as a point from $S_\epsilon(\hat{\mathbf{B}}\mathbf{x}_i)$. We thus establish

$$\max_{\hat{\mathbf{v}} \in S_\epsilon(\hat{\mathbf{B}}\mathbf{x}_i), \hat{\mathbf{u}} \in S_\epsilon(\mathbf{y}_k)} \angle(\mathbf{A}_{\theta,\hat{\mathbf{u}}}\hat{\mathbf{v}}, \mathbf{A}_{\theta,\mathbf{y}_k}\hat{\mathbf{B}}\mathbf{x}_i)$$
$$\leq \max_{\hat{\mathbf{v}} \in S_\epsilon(\hat{\mathbf{B}}\mathbf{x}_i), \hat{\mathbf{u}} \in S_\epsilon(\mathbf{y}_k)} \angle(\mathbf{A}_{\theta,\hat{\mathbf{u}}}\hat{\mathbf{v}}, \mathbf{A}_{\theta,\mathbf{y}_k}\hat{\mathbf{v}}) + \angle(\mathbf{A}_{\theta,\mathbf{y}_k}\hat{\mathbf{v}}, \mathbf{A}_{\theta,\mathbf{y}_k}\hat{\mathbf{B}}\mathbf{x}_i)$$
$$\leq 2|\theta| \sin(\epsilon/2) + \epsilon. \tag{4.31}$$

The second line above results from applying the triangle inequality, whereas the third line invokes (4.30) on the first term of the second line. Define

$$\delta(\theta) = 2|\theta| \sin(\epsilon/2) + \epsilon. \tag{4.32}$$

The inequality (4.31) states that for a fixed θ and for all $\hat{\mathbf{u}} \in S_\epsilon(\mathbf{y}_k)$ and $\mathbf{B}\mathbf{x}_i \in S_\epsilon(\hat{\mathbf{B}}\mathbf{x}_i)$, the point $\mathbf{A}_{\theta,\hat{\mathbf{u}}}\mathbf{B}\mathbf{x}_i$ lies in the spherical region

$$S_{\delta(\theta)}(\mathbf{A}_{\theta,\mathbf{y}_k}\hat{\mathbf{B}}\mathbf{x}_i). \tag{4.33}$$

Figure 4.6 depicts this spherical region. Observe that for all $\theta \in [-\pi, \pi]$, the center of the region lies in $\text{circ}(\hat{\mathbf{B}}\mathbf{x}_i, \mathbf{y}_k)$. Intuitively, this is a circle of a fixed latitude on the globe when $\mathbf{y}_k$ is the North Pole.

The spherical region (4.33) attains the largest angular radius $\delta(\theta)$ at $\theta = \pm\pi$. For a correspondence $(\mathbf{x}_i, \mathbf{y}_i)$, we wish to obtain the angular range

$$\Theta_i = \left[\theta_i^a, \theta_i^b\right] \tag{4.34}$$

for θ that enables $\mathbf{A}_{\theta,\hat{\mathbf{u}}}\mathbf{B}\mathbf{x}_i$ to align with $\mathbf{y}_i$, given the uncertainties $\hat{\mathbf{u}} \in S_\epsilon(\mathbf{y}_k)$ and $\mathbf{B}\mathbf{x}_i \in S_\epsilon(\hat{\mathbf{B}}\mathbf{x}_i)$. This amounts to seeking a bound on the θ that allows $S_{\delta(\theta)}(\mathbf{A}_{\theta,\mathbf{y}_k}\hat{\mathbf{B}}\mathbf{x}_i)$ to touch $S_\epsilon(\mathbf{y}_i)$. In Figure 4.6, an example of θ that give rise to a non-empty intersection is shown.

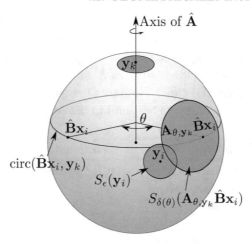

Figure 4.6: Illustrating $S_{\delta(\theta)}(\mathbf{A}_{\theta,\mathbf{y}_k}\hat{\mathbf{B}}\mathbf{x}_i)$ for a particular θ. We wish to find a bounding interval Θ_i of θ that enables $S_{\delta(\theta)}(\mathbf{A}_{\theta,\mathbf{y}_k}\hat{\mathbf{B}}\mathbf{x}_i)$ to intersect with $S_\epsilon(\mathbf{y}_i)$.

Section K in the Appendix gives an analytical solution for Θ_i. By how Θ_i is constructed, we can make the following conclusion.

Theorem 4.3 *For any $i \neq k$, if $S_\epsilon(\mathbf{y}_i)$ intersects with $L_k(\mathbf{x}_i)$, the angle θ such that $\angle(\mathbf{A}_{\theta,\hat{\mathbf{u}}}\mathbf{B}\mathbf{x}_i, \mathbf{y}_i) \leq \epsilon$ for all $\hat{\mathbf{u}} \in S_\epsilon(\mathbf{y}_k)$ and $\mathbf{B}\mathbf{x}_i \in S_\epsilon(\hat{\mathbf{B}}\mathbf{x}_i)$ is bounded in the range Θ_i.*

Interval Stabbing
Let $\mathcal{H}' \subseteq \{1, \ldots, N\} \setminus \{k\}$ be the indices of the correspondences that remain after pruning by Theorem 4.2. Applying Theorem 4.3, we further reduce the remaining correspondences into a set of angular intervals $\{\Theta_i\}_{i \in \mathcal{H}'}$. This enables again the usage of interval stabbing to obtain an upper bound to problem (4.16), i.e.,

$$\underset{\theta \in [-\pi,\pi]}{\text{maximize}} \ 1 + \sum_{i \in \mathcal{H}'} \mathbb{I}\left(\theta \in \left[\theta_i^a, \theta_i^b\right]\right). \tag{4.35}$$

As a by-product of interval stabbing, we derive

$$\mathbf{R}' = \mathbf{A}_{\theta^*,\hat{\mathbf{B}}\mathbf{x}_k}\hat{\mathbf{B}}, \tag{4.36}$$

where θ^* is the angle that solves (4.35). Rotation $\mathbf{R}'$ can be taken as a (suboptimal) candidate maximum consensus solution to rotation estimation. Aligning the input correspondences with $\mathbf{R}'$ thus provides a lower bound ℓ to the maximum consensus value.

GORE Algorithm

The GORE algorithm for 3D rotation is identical to Algorithm 4.21, except for the specific sub-routines to compute the required upper and lower bounds. For completeness, the procedure is listed in Algorithm 4.22. Similar to the analysis of Algorithm 4.21, we can establish that Algorithm 4.22 takes $\mathcal{O}(N^2(\log N + 1))$ effort. Note that the quantities required in the pruning via Theorem 4.2 are obtained analytically (see Section J in the Appendix).

Algorithm 4.22 GORE for robust estimation of 3D rotation.

Require: Input point correspondences $\mathcal{D} = \{(\mathbf{x}_i, \mathbf{y}_i)\}_{i=1}^{N}$, inlier threshold ϵ.

1: $\mathcal{H} \leftarrow \{1, 2, \ldots, N\}$, $\mathcal{T} \leftarrow \mathcal{H}$.
2: $\ell \leftarrow 0$.
3: **while** $\mathcal{T} \neq \emptyset$ **do**
4:    $k \leftarrow$ Retrieve an item from $\mathcal{T}$.
5:    $\mathcal{H}' \leftarrow$ Subset of $\mathcal{H}$ that remains after pruning by Theorem 4.2.
6:    $(\hat{f}_k, \theta^*) \leftarrow$ Optimal value and solution of (4.35).
7:    $\mathbf{R}' \leftarrow \mathbf{A}_{\theta^*, \hat{\mathbf{B}}\mathbf{x}_k} \hat{\mathbf{B}}$ (see (4.20) for the definition of $\hat{\mathbf{B}}$).
8:    $\mathcal{I}_k \leftarrow \{i \in \mathcal{H}' \mid \|\mathbf{R}'\mathbf{x}_i - \mathbf{y}_i\|_2 \leq \epsilon\}$.
9:    **if** $|\mathcal{I}_k| > \ell$ **then**
10:      $\ell \leftarrow |\mathcal{I}_k|$.
11:      $\hat{\mathbf{R}} \leftarrow \mathbf{R}'$.
12:    **end if**
13:    **if** $\hat{f}_k < \ell$ **then**
14:      $\mathcal{H} \leftarrow \mathcal{H} \setminus \{k\}$.
15:    **end if**
16:    $\mathcal{T} \leftarrow \mathcal{T} \setminus \{k\}$.
17: **end while**
18: **return** Reduced dataset $\mathcal{D}' = \{(\mathbf{x}_i, \mathbf{y}_i) \mid i \in \mathcal{H}\}$ and best suboptimal solution $\hat{\mathbf{R}}$.

Figure 4.7 shows a pair of point clouds corresponding to two views of an object that underwent a pure rotational motion on a turntable. A number of N point correspondences were extracted from the point clouds using 3D keypoint detection and matching [Rusu et al., 2008, Zhong, 2009] where $N = 100, 250, 500, 750$ and 1000 (the case of $N = 100$ correspondences are plotted in Figure 4.7). Again, similar to the point clouds from aerial scans used in Figures 4.3 and 4.4, a significant number of the extracted correspondences were erroneous, leading to extremely high outlier rates (more than 90%).

The performance and solution quality of Algorithm 4.22 is shown in Table 4.1. Observe that GORE was able to very quickly (i.e., in less than 1 second) remove a significant proportion of the true outliers, yielding close to outlier-free reduced datasets $\mathcal{D}'$. For comparisons, the runtime and solution quality of RANSAC and BnB rotation search (Algorithm 3.13 can be straightforwardly

Figure 4.7: A problem instance for 3D rotation estimation with $N = 100$ point correspondences. Green lines indicate true inliers, whereas red lines indicate true outliers.

modified to work on point correspondences) are displayed in the table. Observe that, owing to the extremely high outlier rates, RANSAC expended similar computational effort as BnB. However, the solution quality of RANSAC was inferior to BnB. Most importantly, executing BnB on the reduced dataset $\mathcal{D}'$ by GORE yielded the globally optimal solution at a cumulatively much shorter runtime than BnB alone.

Table 4.1: Performance and accuracy of Algorithm 4.22 (GORE) for robust 3D rotation estimation on the data in Figure 4.7. Runtimes were as recorded on a 2.7 GHz Intel Core i7 machine. Legend: N = number of extracted 3D correspondences; ξ = true outlier rate; $|\mathcal{D}'|$ = number of remaining correspondences after GORE; $|\hat{\mathcal{I}}|$ = size of suboptimal solution found by RANSAC; $|\mathcal{I}^*|$ = size of optimal solution found by BnB. Note that GORE+BnB returns the globally optimal solution—same quality as BnB alone.

		GORE		RANSAC		BnB		Gore + BnN
N	ξ	$|\mathcal{D}'|$	Time (s)	$|\hat{\mathcal{I}}|$	Time (s)	$|\mathcal{I}^*|$	Time (s)	Total Time (s)
100	0.90	20	0.003	8	0.125	10	0.095	0.013
250	0.94	21	0.014	12	0.501	14	0.350	0.021
500	0.97	31	0.055	12	1.783	15	1.430	0.066
750	0.98	37	0.146	13	3.270	16	3.435	0.161
1000	0.98	42	0.233	13	6.843	16	7.150	0.264

Figure 4.8 illustrates the application of Algorithm 4.22 on the application of image stitching. In most practical cases of image stitching, the target scene is sufficiently far away such that the effects of parallax can be ignored. Equivalently, we may assume that the camera has undergone a pure rotational motion. The rotation can be estimated from back-projected rays of 2D feature correspondences, which can then be used to construct the 2D homography for image

(a)

(b)

Figure 4.8: (a) Input image pair with $N = 154$ feature matches. Green lines are true inliers, whereas red lines are true outliers. (b) Stitched image using the rotation output by Algorithm 4.22.

alignment; see Szeliski [2004] for details. Using SIFT [Lowe, 2004], $N = 154$ feature matches were extracted for the images in Figure 4.8a. The existence of false correspondences necessitates the use of robust estimation. Figure 4.8b shows stitched images using the rotation output by Algorithm 4.22, which took a mere 10 ms (on a 2.7 GHz Intel Core i7 machine) to execute on this data instance. In addition, GORE has completely removed the true outliers, thus yielding directly the globally optimal result.

4.3   INTEGER LINEAR PROGRAMMING APPROACH

Both of the GORE techniques in Section 4.2 rely heavily on the underlying geometry of the problem to efficiently calculate the upper $\hat{f}_k$ and lower ℓ bounds. At the core of those techniques is the reduction of the subproblem P_k to an interval stabbing problem, which has an efficient and deterministic solution. Such a reduction is not always possible in a broad class of other robust estimation problems in computer vision. In this section, an attempt to extend the idea of GORE by calculating $\hat{f}_k$ using generic optimization is described.

4.3.1   AN INTEGER LINEAR PROGRAM FORMULATION FOR GORE

Our starting point is the ILP formulation of maximum consensus estimation of linear models with data $\mathcal{D} = \{(\mathbf{a}_i, b_i)\}_{i=1}^{N}$ (Section 3.3), which is reproduced below for convenience:

$$
\begin{aligned}
\underset{\mathbf{x}\in\mathbb{R}^d, \mathbf{z}\in\{0,1\}^N}{\text{minimize}} \quad & \sum_{i=1}^{N} z_i \\
\text{subject to} \quad & \left|\mathbf{a}_i^T \mathbf{x} - b_i\right| \leq \epsilon + z_i M, \\
& i = 1, \dots, N.
\end{aligned}
\tag{4.37}
$$

Recasting the derivations in Section 4.1.1 in the context of a minimization problem, maximum consensus can be re-expressed as

$$
\underset{k=1,\dots,N}{\text{minimize}} \quad g^k,
\tag{4.38}
$$

where we define g^k as the optimal objective value of the following subproblem:

$$
\begin{aligned}
\underset{\mathbf{x}\in\mathbb{R}^d, \mathbf{z}\in\{0,1\}^N}{\text{minimize}} \quad & \sum_{i\neq k} z_i \\
\text{subject to} \quad & \left|\mathbf{a}_i^T \mathbf{x} - b_i\right| \leq \epsilon + z_i M, \\
& i = 1, \dots, N, \\
& \left|\mathbf{a}_k^T \mathbf{x} - b_k\right| \leq \epsilon.
\end{aligned}
\tag{4.39}
$$

In words, problem (4.39) seeks to remove as few data as possible to achieve a consistent subset, given that $(\mathbf{a}_k, b_k)$ cannot be removed. Note that (4.39) remains an ILP.

Let $(\hat{\mathbf{x}}, \hat{\mathbf{z}})$ indicate a suboptimal solution to (4.37), and

$$
\hat{u} = \|\hat{\mathbf{z}}\|_1 \geq \|\mathbf{z}^*\|_1
\tag{4.40}
$$

be its value ($\mathbf{z}^*$ are the globally optimal indicator variables for (4.37)). Let $\underline{g}^k$ be a lower bound value to (4.39); that is,

$$\underline{g}^k \leq g^k. \tag{4.41}$$

Given $\hat{u}$ and $\underline{g}^k$, we can perform a test according to the following theorem, which is analogous to Theorem 4.1, to decide whether $(\mathbf{a}_k, b_k)$ is a true outlier.

Theorem 4.4   *If $\underline{g}^k > \hat{u}$, then $(\mathbf{a}_k, b_k)$ is a true outlier.*

Proof. The theorem can again be established via contradiction. The k-th datum $(\mathbf{a}_k, b_k)$ is a true inlier if and only if

$$\beta^k = \|\mathbf{z}^*\|_1 \leq \hat{u}. \tag{4.42}$$

In other words, if $(\mathbf{a}_k, b_k)$ is a true inlier, insisting it to be an inlier in (4.39) does not change the fact that removing $\|\mathbf{z}^*\|_1$ data is sufficient to achieve consensus. However, if we are given that $\underline{g}^k > \hat{u}$, then from (4.41)

$$\hat{u} < \underline{g}^k \leq g^k \tag{4.43}$$

and condition (4.42) cannot hold. Thus $(\mathbf{a}_k, b_k)$ must be a true outlier.   □

The following result shows that there are $(\mathbf{a}_k, b_k)$, where the test above will never give an affirmative answer.

Theorem 4.5   *If $\hat{z}_k = 0$, then $\underline{g}^k \leq \hat{u}$.*

Proof. If $\hat{z}_k = 0$, then, fixing $(\mathbf{a}_k, b_k)$ as an inlier, $(\hat{\mathbf{x}}, \hat{\mathbf{z}})$ is also a suboptimal solution to (4.39). Thus, $\hat{u} \geq g^k \geq \underline{g}^k$, and the condition $\underline{g}^k > \hat{u}$ will never be met.   □

In words, Theorem 4.5 states that if a datum $(\mathbf{a}_k, b_k)$ is identified as an inlier in a suboptimal maximum consensus solution $(\hat{\mathbf{x}}, \hat{\mathbf{z}})$, then using the upper bound $\hat{u} = \|\hat{\mathbf{z}}\|_1$ to perform the test in Theorem 4.4 will not allow us to conclude that $(\mathbf{a}_k, b_k)$ is a true outlier, regardless of the value of the lower bound $\underline{g}^k$.

Calculation of Bounds

The upper bound $\hat{u}$ can be obtained using any approximate maximum consensus algorithm. In general, given a suboptimal maximum consensus set $\tilde{\mathcal{I}}$, we obtain

$$\hat{u} = N - |\tilde{\mathcal{I}}|. \tag{4.44}$$

The main difficulty lies in computing a tight lower bound $\underline{g}^k$. To this end, consider the *LP relaxation* of subproblem (4.39)

$$
\begin{aligned}
\underset{\mathbf{x}\in\mathbb{R}^d,\mathbf{z}\in[0,1]^N}{\text{minimize}} \quad & \sum_{i\neq k} z_i \\
\text{subject to} \quad & \left|\mathbf{a}_i^T\mathbf{x} - b_i\right| \leq \epsilon + z_i M, \\
& i = 1,\ldots,N, \\
& \left|\mathbf{a}_k^T\mathbf{x} - b_k\right| \leq \epsilon,
\end{aligned}
\tag{4.45}
$$

which is exactly the same as the original problem, except that the indicators $\mathbf{z}$ are continuous. By the simple argument that $[0,1]^{N-1}$ is a superset of $\{0,1\}^{N-1}$, the optimal value of (4.45) cannot be greater than g^k, and thus the former can be used as $\underline{g}^k$.

The lower bound obtained solely via (4.45) tends to be loose. Intuitively, observe that since M is very large (see Section 3.3), each continuous z_i in (4.45) need be turned on only slightly to attain sufficient slack, i.e., the optimized $\mathbf{z}$ tends to be small and fractional, leading to a large gap between $\underline{g}^k$ and g^k. To obtain a more useful lower bound, we leverage on existing branch-and-cut (BnC) algorithms for solving ILPs [Conforti et al., 2014] (see also Section 3.3). In the context of solving (4.39), BnC maintains a pair of lower and upper bound values $\underline{g}^k$ and $\overline{g}^k$ over time, where

$$
\underline{g}^k \leq g^k \leq \overline{g}^k.
\tag{4.46}
$$

The lower bound $\underline{g}^k$ is progressively raised by solving (4.45) on recursive subdivisions of the parameter space, as well as by the introduction of *cutting planes* to sharpen the bound.

Effectively, using BnC to obtain $\underline{g}^k$ means that we delegate the bound calculation to a "black box" solver. This is unlike the techniques in Section 4.2, where understanding of the underlying geometry is exploited to develop customized bounding algorithms.

GORE Algorithm

Algorithm 4.23 summarizes an ILP-based GORE method. An approximate maximum consensus algorithm is used to obtain the upper bound $\hat{u}$, and to re-order $\mathcal{D}$ such that the data that are more likely to be true outliers are first tested for removal. Also, as underpinned by Theorem 4.5, testing the data with large residuals first avoids attempting to reject data that will never be removed via Theorem 4.4.

To calculate the bound $\underline{g}^k$ in Step 4, existing implementations of BnC in packages such as IBM ILOG CPLEX and Gurobi Optimizer can be applied. Each instance of BnC in Step 4 is run until either

$$
\underline{g}^k > \hat{u} \ (\text{Condition 1}) \quad \text{or} \quad \overline{g}^k \leq \hat{u} \ (\text{Condition 2}),
\tag{4.47}
$$

or until the time budget of c s (c is a pre-defined input parameter) is exhausted. Satisfying Condition 1 implies that $(\mathbf{a}_k, b_k)$ is a true outlier, while satisfying Condition 2 means that Condition

1 will never be met. Meeting Condition 2 also indicates that a better suboptimal solution $(\hat{\mathbf{x}}, \hat{\mathbf{z}})$ (one that involves identifying $(\mathbf{a}_k, b_k)$ as an inlier) has been discovered, thus $\hat{u}$ should be updated.

Algorithm 4.23 ILP-based GORE.

Require: Data $\mathcal{D} = \{(\mathbf{a}_i, b_i)\}_{i=1}^N$, inlier threshold ϵ, number of rejection tests T, maximum duration per test c.
1: Run approximate maximum consensus algorithm to obtain an upper bound $\hat{u}$.
2: Order $\mathcal{D}$ increasingly based on residuals to approximate solution.
3: **for** $k = N, N - 1, \ldots, N - T + 1$ **do**
4:     Run BnC to solve (4.39) on $\mathcal{D}$ until one of the following is satisfied:

- $\underline{g}^k > \hat{u}$ (Condition 1);

- $\overline{g}^k \leq \hat{u}$ (Condition 2);

- c s have elapsed.

5:     **if** Condition 1 was satisfied **then**
6:         $\mathcal{D} \leftarrow \mathcal{D} \setminus (\mathbf{a}_k, b_k)$
7:     **end if**
8:     **if** Condition 2 was satisfied **then**
9:         $\hat{u} \leftarrow \overline{g}^k$
10:     **end if**
11: **end for**
12: **return** Reduced data $\mathcal{D}' = \mathcal{D}$.

Another point of departure from the GORE techniques in Section 4.2 is that not all the data will be tested for rejection; that is, only T rejection tests are performed in Algorithm 4.23. This is because of the substantially more expensive way to derive the bound $\underline{g}^k$. The upper bound on the runtime of Algorithm 4.23 is therefore $T \cdot c$ (discounting the duration of running the approximate algorithm in Step 1, which tends to be much smaller).

As an example, the true outliers removed in the robust plane fitting ($d = 3$) instance in Figure 4.1 were identified using Algorithm 4.23 (implemented on a 2.7 GHz Intel Core i7 machine) with $T = 5$ and $c = 10$, and by using RANSAC to provide the initial suboptimal solution and upper bound $\hat{u}$. Further optimizing the ILP (4.37) on the remaining data $\mathcal{D}'$ required 33 s to find the global solution.

In general, since at most T true outliers will be removed by Algorithm 4.23, the duration to optimize on $\mathcal{D}'$ must be taken into account to gauge the usefulness of Algorithm 4.23. We measure the computational gain as

$$1 - \frac{\text{time(GORE+EXACT)}}{\text{time(EXACT)}}, \tag{4.48}$$

where time(EXACT) indicates the duration to globally solve the ILP (4.37) on $\mathcal{D}$, and time(GORE+EXACT) indicates the cumulative duration of executing Algorithm 4.23 to pre-process $\mathcal{D}$, then solve to global optimality the ILP (4.37) on $\mathcal{D}'$.

For the problem instance in Figure 4.1, time(EXACT) = 420 s, and time(GORE+EXACT) = $5 \times 10 + 33$ s = 83 s, which amounts to a computational gain of 80%. Here, for simplicity the contribution of RANSAC toward time(GORE+EXACT) was ignored, since the cost of RANSAC is very small relative to the other routines in the GORE pipeline. In the next section, we further empirically investigate the computational gain of ILP-based GORE.

4.3.2   GENERALISED FRACTIONAL MODELS

Section 3.3.2 has explored ILP formulations of maximum consensus with generalized fractional models. For convenience, the formulation is reproduced here,

$$\begin{aligned}
\underset{\mathbf{x}\in\mathbb{R}^d, \mathbf{z}\in\{0,1\}^N}{\text{minimize}} \quad & \sum_{i=1}^{N} z_i \\
\text{subject to} \quad & \|\mathbf{A}_i\mathbf{x} + \mathbf{b}_i\|_p \leq \epsilon\left(\boldsymbol{\alpha}_i^T\mathbf{x} + \beta_i\right) + z_i M \\
& i = 1, \ldots, N,
\end{aligned} \tag{4.49}$$

where p must equal 1 or 2 to produce linear constraints (see Section 3.3.2 for details). The sub-problem analogous to P_k for GORE can be constructed easily by extending (4.39), i.e.,

$$\begin{aligned}
\underset{\mathbf{x}\in\mathbb{R}^d, \mathbf{z}\in\{0,1\}^N}{\text{minimize}} \quad & \sum_{i\neq k} z_i \\
\text{subject to} \quad & \|\mathbf{A}_i\mathbf{x} + \mathbf{b}_i\|_p \leq \epsilon\left(\boldsymbol{\alpha}_i^T\mathbf{x} + \beta_i\right) + z_i M \\
& i = 1, \ldots, N, \\
& \|\mathbf{A}_k\mathbf{x} + \mathbf{b}_k\|_p \leq \epsilon\left(\boldsymbol{\alpha}_k^T\mathbf{x} + \beta_k\right).
\end{aligned} \tag{4.50}$$

Therefore, we can also apply ILP solvers to obtain the upper bound $\bar{g}^k$ for (4.50), and only minimal changes are required to adapt Algorithm 4.23 to conduct GORE.

Applying Algorithm 4.23 to the robust affine image matching problem ($d = 6$) in Figure 3.7 with $T = 10$ and $c = 15$, 10 true outliers were able to be removed in 45.25 s. Note that, in this instance, Algorithm 4.23 was able to achieve Condition 1 for all $T = 10$ tests before the overall time limit of 150 s. Further optimizing the ILP (4.49) on $\mathcal{D}'$ returned the maximum consensus solution in 181.2 s. Therefore, time(GORE+EXACT) = 226.45 s, and with time(EXACT) = 1028.07 s (as reported in Figure 3.7), the computational gain achieved by preprocessing is 78%.

Evaluation

To more thoroughly investigate the potential benefits of ILP-based GORE, a synthetic data experiment was conducted. Measurements of the form $\mathcal{D} = \{(\mathbf{A}_i, \mathbf{b}_i, \boldsymbol{\alpha}_i, \beta_i)\}_{i=1}^{N}$ were produced, where for simplicity, we set $\boldsymbol{\alpha}_i = \mathbf{0}$ and $\beta_i = 1$ for all i. The ground truth $\mathbf{x} \in \mathbb{R}^d$ was generated uniformly in $[-1, 1]^d$. Each $\mathbf{A}_i$ was drawn uniformly randomly from $[-50, 50]^{2 \times d}$, and $\mathbf{b}_i$ was obtained as $\mathbf{b}_i = -\mathbf{A}_i \mathbf{x}$. This justifies the residual

$$\|\mathbf{A}_i \mathbf{x} + \mathbf{b}_i\|_p, \tag{4.51}$$

which is a special case of the generalized fractional model. To simulate outliers, 55% of the "dependent measurements" $\{\mathbf{b}_i\}_{i=1}^N$ were perturbed with i.i.d. uniform noise in the range $[-50, 50]$, and the rest were perturbed with i.i.d. Normal inlier noise with $\sigma = 1$. This produced an outlier rate of 50–60%.

Combinations of (d, N) tested were $(3, 140)$, $(4, 120)$, $(5, 100)$, $(6, 80)$, $(7, 70)$, and $(8, 50)$. We reduced N for higher d to avoid excessively long runtimes; this does not invalidate our assessment of GORE since we are primarily interested in the speed-up ratio. For each (d, N) pair, we created 20 data instances $\mathcal{D}$. On each $\mathcal{D}$, we solved the ILP (4.49) with and without preprocessing by Algorithm 4.23, and with $\epsilon = 2$. For Algorithm 4.23, T was varied from 1 to $\lceil 0.15N \rceil$, and c was fixed to 15. The median gain across the 20 synthetic instances (where gain was measured according to (4.48)) for varying T (expressed as a ratio of N) are shown in Figure 4.9.

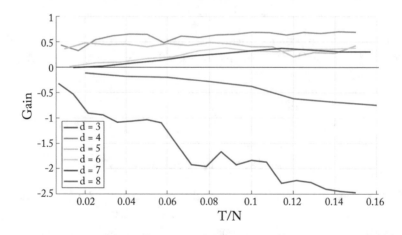

Figure 4.9: Computational gain of GORE on synthetic data for dimensions $d = 3, \ldots, 8$ and increasing number of rejection tests T, where T is expressed as a ratio of problem size N. Time per test c is fixed at 15 s.

The gain was negative for $d = 3$, since optimizing on $\mathcal{D}$ was very fast on such a low dimension, and preprocessing by GORE simply inflated the runtime (although in Figure 4.1, a large positive gain was obtained for a problem with $d = 3$, the type of data and residual function used were different). For $d = 4$ to 7, the gain increased with T, implying that as more true outliers were removed prior to executing ILP, the runtime was reduced quickly. After $T \approx 0.1N$, the gain increased very slowly. For $d = 8$, however, the gain was negative; this was because GORE was unable to reject sufficient true outliers within the limit of $c = 15$ s for the preprocessing to pay off. The result suggests that there exist a lower and upper limit on d for GORE to be useful.

4.4   BIBLIOGRAPHICAL REMARKS

The idea of first quickly removing a portion of the data, before executing a slower exact algorithm on the remaining data of smaller size, is an age-old principle in optimization, including in robust estimation in computer vision. For example, Li [2009a] suggested that the proposed BnB algorithm be used after a RANSAC run where the inlier threshold was set to a sufficiently large value to include (hopefully most of) the inliers, but exclude the most offending outliers. However, such preprocessing does not guarantee that the globally optimal solution is preserved in the reduced data.

The principle of GORE for robust estimation is relatively recent. Svärm et al. [2014] conducted what is effectively GORE for registration from outlier-contaminated 2D-3D point correspondences, though their focus was on the application of camera localization and thus they did not strive to formalize the concept of GORE. The formulation was first done by Parra Bustos and Chin [2015], who established GORE as a bona fide preprocessing technique for robust fitting. Chin et al. [2016] further extended the usability of GORE by proposing the usage of ILP solvers to generate the required lower/upper bounds.

Appendix

A   PROOF OF THEOREM 2.5

Let $\hat{\mathbf{x}}$ be the solution to (2.51), whose input was constructed from the data $\mathcal{D}$ in (2.46) by doubling. Define $\delta(\hat{\mathbf{x}})$ as the value of the problem given by $\hat{\mathbf{x}}$, i.e.,

$$\delta(\hat{\mathbf{x}}) = \max_j \; \boldsymbol{\alpha}_j^T \hat{\mathbf{x}} - \beta_j. \tag{A.1}$$

For any $\hat{\mathbf{x}} + \mathbf{t}$, there exists a k, $1 \le k \le 2N$, such that

$$\boldsymbol{\alpha}_k^T (\hat{\mathbf{x}} + \mathbf{t}) - \beta_k > \delta(\hat{\mathbf{x}}). \tag{A.2}$$

If $1 \le k \le N$, then by construction

$$\left| \mathbf{a}_k^T (\hat{\mathbf{x}} + \mathbf{t}) - b_k \right| > \delta(\hat{\mathbf{x}}). \tag{A.3}$$

If $(N + 1) \le k \le 2N$, then also by construction

$$\left| \mathbf{a}_{(k-N)}^T (\hat{\mathbf{x}} + \mathbf{t}) - b_{(k-N)} \right| > \delta(\hat{\mathbf{x}}). \tag{A.4}$$

Together, the above imply that $\hat{\mathbf{x}}$ is also the solution to (2.46) with value $\delta(\hat{\mathbf{x}})$. The reverse direction of the theorem can be established using similar arguments.

B   PROOF OF THEOREM 2.6

Our proof here is developed based on the derivation in Section 2.3 of Cheney [1966]. First, we quote the following fundamental result from linear algebra.

Theorem B.1   *Let $\mathcal{A}$ be a set of points in $\mathbb{R}^d$. The following system of linear inequalities:*

$$\langle \boldsymbol{\alpha}, \mathbf{x} \rangle > 0, \quad \boldsymbol{\alpha} \in \mathcal{A}, \tag{B.1}$$

is inconsistent (i.e., there does not exist $\mathbf{x}$ such that all inequalities are simultaneously satisfied), if and only if the origin $\mathbf{0}$ lies in the convex hull of $\mathcal{A}$.

The desired proof for Theorem 2.6 is then obtained as follows: if $\hat{\mathbf{x}}$ is not a minimizer of $\delta(\mathbf{x})$, then for some $\mathbf{t}$, $\delta(\hat{\mathbf{x}} - \mathbf{t}) < \delta(\hat{\mathbf{x}})$. Let $\mathcal{K} = \{k \mid r_k(\hat{\mathbf{x}}) = \delta(\hat{\mathbf{x}})\}$. Then for any $k \in \mathcal{K}$,

$$r_k(\hat{\mathbf{x}} - \mathbf{t}) \le \delta(\hat{\mathbf{x}} - \mathbf{t}) < \delta(\hat{\mathbf{x}}) = r_k(\hat{\mathbf{x}}), \tag{B.2}$$

meaning that

$$\alpha_k^T(\hat{\mathbf{x}} - \mathbf{t}) - \beta_k < \alpha_k^T \hat{\mathbf{x}} - \beta_k \implies \langle \alpha_k, \mathbf{t} \rangle > 0 \quad \forall k \in \mathcal{K}. \tag{B.3}$$

By Theorem B.1, the origin does not lie in the convex hull of $\{\alpha_k \mid k \in \mathcal{K}\}$.

To establish the converse, suppose that the origin does not lie in the convex hull of $\{\alpha_k \mid k \in \mathcal{K}\}$. By Theorem B.1 again, the system of inequalities $\langle \alpha_k, \mathbf{x} \rangle > 0$ for $k \in \mathcal{K}$ must be consistent. Then, there exists $\mathbf{t}$ such that the value

$$a = \min_{k \in \mathcal{K}} \langle \alpha_k, \mathbf{t} \rangle \tag{B.4}$$

is positive. For $\lambda > 0$ and $k \in \mathcal{K}$,

$$r_k(\hat{\mathbf{x}} - \lambda \mathbf{t}) = r_k(\hat{\mathbf{x}}) - \lambda \langle \alpha_k, \mathbf{t} \rangle \le \delta(\hat{\mathbf{x}}) - \lambda \langle \alpha_k, \mathbf{t} \rangle \le \delta(\hat{\mathbf{x}}) - \lambda a. \tag{B.5}$$

The above implies that the residuals $r_k(\hat{\mathbf{x}})$ for $k \in \mathcal{K}$ will decrease in the direction $-\mathbf{t}$. By construction, the residuals $r_j(\hat{\mathbf{x}})$ for $j \notin \mathcal{K}$ are less than $\delta(\hat{\mathbf{x}})$, and by argument of continuity these residuals will still be less than $\delta(\hat{\mathbf{x}})$ in a neighborhood around $\hat{\mathbf{x}}$. Thus, there are points near $\hat{\mathbf{x}}$ that yield lower costs than $\hat{\mathbf{x}}$; that is, $\hat{\mathbf{x}}$ is not the minimizer of $\delta(\mathbf{x})$.

C   PROOF THAT (2.88) HAS A VERTEX SOLUTION

To begin, the KKT conditions [Nocedal and Wright, 2006, Chapter 12] of problem (2.96) are as follows:

$$\begin{aligned}
&\mathbf{u}^T(-\lambda \mathbf{C}\mathbf{v} + \lambda \boldsymbol{\beta} + \mathbf{1} + \boldsymbol{\delta}^{\mathcal{G}}) = 0, \\
&\mathbf{s}^T(\lambda \mathbf{1} - \boldsymbol{\delta}^{\mathcal{H}}) = 0, \\
&\mathbf{v}^T(-\lambda \mathbf{C}^T \mathbf{u} + \mathbf{C}^T \boldsymbol{\delta}^{\mathcal{H}}) = 0, \\
&(\boldsymbol{\delta}^{\mathcal{H}})^T(\mathbf{s} - \mathbf{C}\mathbf{v} + \boldsymbol{\beta}) = 0, \\
&(\boldsymbol{\delta}^{\mathcal{G}})^T(\mathbf{1} - \mathbf{u}) = 0, \\
&\mathbf{s} - \mathbf{C}\mathbf{v} + \boldsymbol{\beta} \ge \mathbf{0}, \\
&\mathbf{1} - \mathbf{u} \ge \mathbf{0}, \\
&\boldsymbol{\delta}^{\mathcal{H}}, \boldsymbol{\delta}^{\mathcal{G}}, \mathbf{u}, \mathbf{v}, \mathbf{s} \ge \mathbf{0},
\end{aligned} \tag{C.1}$$

where $\boldsymbol{\delta}^{\mathcal{H}} = [\delta_1^{\mathcal{H}}, \dots, \delta_M^{\mathcal{H}}]^T$ and $\boldsymbol{\delta}^{\mathcal{G}} = [\delta_1^{\mathcal{G}}, \dots, \delta_M^{\mathcal{G}}]^T$ are the Lagrange multipliers for the first two types of constraints in (2.88). By rearranging, the KKT conditions can be summarized by the following relations:

$$\mathbf{M}'\mathbf{z}' + \mathbf{q}' \ge \mathbf{0}, \quad \mathbf{z}' \ge \mathbf{0}, \quad (\mathbf{z}')^T(\mathbf{M}'\mathbf{z}' + \mathbf{q}') = 0, \tag{C.2}$$

where

$$\mathbf{z}' = \begin{bmatrix} \mathbf{z}^T & (\boldsymbol{\delta}^{\mathcal{H}})^T & (\boldsymbol{\delta}^{\mathcal{G}})^T \end{bmatrix}^T,$$

$$\mathbf{M}' = \begin{bmatrix} \mathbf{0} & \mathbf{0} & -\lambda\mathbf{C} & \mathbf{0} & \mathbf{I} \\ \mathbf{0} & \mathbf{0} & \mathbf{0} & -\mathbf{I} & \mathbf{0} \\ -\lambda\mathbf{C}^T & \mathbf{0} & \mathbf{0} & \mathbf{C}^T & \mathbf{0} \\ \mathbf{0} & \mathbf{I} & -\mathbf{C} & \mathbf{0} & \mathbf{0} \\ -\mathbf{I} & \mathbf{0} & \mathbf{0} & \mathbf{0} & \mathbf{0} \end{bmatrix}, \tag{C.3}$$

$$\mathbf{q}' = \begin{bmatrix} (\lambda\boldsymbol{\beta} + \mathbf{1})^T & \lambda\mathbf{1}^T & \mathbf{0}^T & \boldsymbol{\beta}^T & \mathbf{1}^T \end{bmatrix}^T.$$

Finding a feasible $\mathbf{z}'$ for (C.2) is an instance of a *linear complementarity problem (LCP)* [Mangasarian, 1978]. Define the convex set

$$\mathcal{P}' = \left\{ \mathbf{z}' \in \mathbb{R}^{4M+d+1} \mid \mathbf{M}'\mathbf{z}' + \mathbf{q}' \geq 0, \ \mathbf{z}' \geq 0 \right\}. \tag{C.4}$$

We invoke the following result from [Mangasarian, 1978, Lemma 2].

Theorem C.1   *If the LCP defined by the constraints* (C.2) *has a solution, then it has a solution at a vertex of* $\mathcal{P}'$.

Theorem C.1 implies that the KKT points of (2.96) (including the solutions of the problem) occur at the vertices of $\mathcal{P}'$. This also implies that (2.96) has a vertex solution.

Theorem C.2   *For any vertex*

$$\mathbf{z}'_v = \begin{bmatrix} \mathbf{z}_v^T, & (\boldsymbol{\delta}_v^{\mathcal{H}})^T, & (\boldsymbol{\delta}_v^{\mathcal{G}})^T) \end{bmatrix}^T \tag{C.5}$$

of $\mathcal{P}'$, $\mathbf{z}_v$ *is a vertex of* $\mathcal{P}$.

Proof. If $\mathbf{z}'_v$ is a vertex of $\mathcal{P}'$, then, there is a diagonal matrix $\mathbf{E}$ such that

$$\mathbf{M}'\mathbf{E}\mathbf{z}'_v + \mathbf{q}' - \boldsymbol{\gamma}' = 0, \tag{C.6}$$

where $\mathbf{E}_{i,i} = 1$ if the i-th column of $\mathbf{M}'$ appears in the basic solution corresponding to vertex $\mathbf{z}'_v$, and $\mathbf{E}_{i,i} = 0$ otherwise (the nonnegative vector $\boldsymbol{\gamma}'$ contains the values of additional slack variables to convert the constraints in $\mathcal{P}'$ into standard form). Let $\mathbf{M}'_J$ be the last-$2M$ rows of $\mathbf{M}'$. Then,

$$\mathbf{M}'_J\mathbf{E}\mathbf{z}'_v + \begin{bmatrix} \boldsymbol{\beta}^T & \mathbf{1}^T \end{bmatrix}^T - \boldsymbol{\gamma}'_J = 0, \tag{C.7}$$

where $\boldsymbol{\gamma}'_J$ is the last-$2M$ elements of $\boldsymbol{\gamma}'$. Note that, since the right-most $2M \times 2M$ submatrix of $\mathbf{M}'_J$ is a zero matrix (see (C.3)), then

$$\mathbf{M}'_J\mathbf{E}_K\mathbf{z}_v + \begin{bmatrix} \boldsymbol{\beta}^T & \mathbf{1}^T \end{bmatrix}^T - \boldsymbol{\gamma}'_J = 0, \tag{C.8}$$

where $\mathbf{E}_K$ is the first-$(2M + d + 1)$ columns of $\mathbf{E}$. Since $\mathbf{M}'_J\mathbf{E}_K = \mathbf{M}$, then (C.8) implies that $\mathbf{z}_v$ is a vertex of $\mathcal{P}$.   □

D   PROOF OF THEOREM 3.5

To establish (3.27), it is sufficient to show that, if there is an $\mathbf{r} \in \mathbb{B}$ that can match $\mathbf{p}_i$ and $\mathbf{p}'_j$, then $\mathbf{p}_i$ and $\mathbf{p}'_j$ must contribute 1 to the function $\hat{\Psi}_{\text{ball}}(\mathbb{B})$.

If $\mathbf{p}_i$ and $\mathbf{p}'_j$ are matched by applying $\mathbf{R_r}$ on $\mathbf{p}_i$, then

$$\left\| \mathbf{R_r} \mathbf{p}_i - \mathbf{p}'_j \right\|_2 \le \epsilon. \tag{D.1}$$

By the triangle inequality,

$$
\begin{aligned}
\left\| \mathbf{R_r} \mathbf{p}_i - \mathbf{p}'_j + \mathbf{R_c} \mathbf{p}_i - \mathbf{R_r} \mathbf{p}_i \right\|_2 = \left\| \mathbf{R_c} \mathbf{p}_i - \mathbf{p}'_j \right\|_2 \\
\le \left\| \mathbf{R_r} \mathbf{p}_i - \mathbf{p}'_j \right\|_2 + \left\| \mathbf{R_c} \mathbf{p}_i - \mathbf{R_r} \mathbf{p}_i \right\|_2 \\
\le \epsilon + \delta_{\mathbf{p}_i}.
\end{aligned}
\tag{D.2}
$$

Hence, $\mathbf{p}_i$ and $\mathbf{p}'_j$ must contribute 1 to $\hat{\Psi}_{\text{ball}}(\mathbb{B})$.

To prove the convergence of $\hat{\Psi}_{\text{ball}}(\mathbb{B})$ to $\Psi(\mathbf{R_r})$, observe that if $\mathbb{B} = \mathbf{r}$, then $\mathbf{c} = \mathbf{r}$ and $\alpha_{\mathbb{B}} = \delta_{\mathbf{p}_i} = 0$ for all i.

E   PROOF OF THEOREM 3.6

To establish (3.33), it is sufficient to show that, if there is an $\mathbf{r} \in \mathbb{B}$ that can match $\mathbf{p}_i$ and $\mathbf{p}'_j$, then $\mathbf{p}_i$ and $\mathbf{p}'_j$ must contribute 1 to the function $\hat{\Psi}_{\text{patch}}(\mathbb{B})$.

Let $\mathbf{p}_i$ and $\mathbf{p}'_j$ be a pair that are matched under $\mathbf{r} \in \mathbb{B}$. Then, $\|\mathbf{R_r} \mathbf{p}_i - \mathbf{p}'_j\|_2 \le \epsilon$ or $\mathbf{R_r} \mathbf{p}_i \in l_\epsilon(\mathbf{p}'_j)$. Since $\mathbf{r} \in \mathbb{B}$, then $\mathbf{R_r} \mathbf{p}_i \in S_{\alpha_{\mathbb{B}}}(\mathbf{R_c} \mathbf{p}_i)$. This establishes that $S_{\alpha_{\mathbb{B}}}(\mathbf{R_c} \mathbf{p}_i) \cap l_\epsilon(\mathbf{p}'_j)$ contains at least the item $\mathbf{R_r} \mathbf{p}_i$ and is thus non-empty.

To prove the convergence of $\hat{\Psi}_{\text{patch}}(\mathbb{B})$ to $\Psi(\mathbf{R_r})$, observe that if $\mathbb{B} = \mathbf{r}$, then $\mathbf{c} = \mathbf{r}$, $\alpha_{\mathbb{B}} = 0$ and $S_{\alpha_{\mathbb{B}}}(\mathbf{R_c} \mathbf{p}_i) = \mathbf{R_r} \mathbf{p}_i$ for all i.

F   PROOF OF THEOREM 3.14

It is sufficient to show that any basis $\mathcal{B}' \in \mathcal{B}^{(k+1)}$ has a predecessor in $\mathcal{B}^{(k)}$.

Let $\mathcal{P} \subseteq \mathcal{S}$ be the coverage set $\mathcal{C}(\mathcal{B}')$ of $\mathcal{B}'$. Let $s \in \mathcal{V}(\mathcal{B}')$ indicate items in the violation set of $\mathcal{B}'$, and let s_0 be an item in $\mathcal{V}(\mathcal{B}')$ that gives the smallest value of $f(\mathcal{P} \cup \{s\})$. The choice of s_0 among all $s \in \mathcal{V}(\mathcal{B}')$ is unique; since if $f(\mathcal{P} \cup \{s_0\}) = f(\mathcal{P} \cup \{s\})$ for $s \ne s_0$, then the support set of $\mathcal{P} \cup \{s_0\}$ equals the support set of $\mathcal{P} \cup \{s\}$ owing to the assumption of nondegeneracy, which in turn implies that $f(\mathcal{P} \cup \{s_0\}) = f(\mathcal{P})$, which is a contradiction.

Let $\mathcal{B}$ be the support set of $\mathcal{P} \cup \{s_0\}$. By design, therefore, $\mathcal{B}$ is adjacent to $\mathcal{B}'$; to prove the theorem, we must additionally show that $\mathcal{B}$ lies in $\mathcal{B}^{(k)}$. This is equivalent to establishing that $\mathcal{V}(\mathcal{B}) \cup \{s_0\} = \mathcal{V}(\mathcal{B}')$, which implies that $l(\mathcal{B}') = l(\mathcal{B}) + 1$. By adjacency, we have that $\mathcal{V}(\mathcal{B}) \cup \{s_0\} \subseteq \mathcal{V}(\mathcal{B}')$. Suppose that the inclusion is proper, i.e., $\mathcal{V}(\mathcal{B}) \cup \{s_0\} \subset \mathcal{V}(\mathcal{B}')$, then there is some $s \in \mathcal{V}(\mathcal{B}'), s \ne s_0$, that does not violate $\mathcal{B}$. By Property 2.11 (Locality), s does not violate $\mathcal{P} \cup \{s_0\}$

either, thus $f(\mathcal{P} \cup \{s_0\}) = f(\mathcal{P} \cup \{s_0, s\})$. However, this is a contradiction since we already have $f(\mathcal{P} \cup \{s\}) > f(\mathcal{P} \cup \{s_0\})$.

G   PROOF OF THEOREM 3.21

If $\mathcal{B}'$ is the root basis of the search tree, then $h_{met}(\mathcal{B}') = h_{ins}(\mathcal{B}') \leq h^*(\mathcal{B}')$ from Theorem 3.18. We thus aim to establish by induction that, given $h_{met}(\mathcal{B}) \leq h^*(\mathcal{B})$ for a basis $\mathcal{B}$, the condition $h_{met}(\mathcal{B}') \leq h^*(\mathcal{B}')$ is always true for a child basis $\mathcal{B}'$ of $\mathcal{B}$.

Let $\mathcal{C}(\mathcal{B}) = \mathcal{O}^* \cup \mathcal{F}^*$, where $\mathcal{F}^*$ is the maximum consensus set of $\mathcal{C}(\mathcal{B})$, and $h^*(\mathcal{B}) = |\mathcal{O}^*|$. Since $\mathcal{B}'$ is a child basis of $\mathcal{B}$, the former is obtained by removing a constraint s from $\mathcal{B}$ and obtaining the support set of $[\mathcal{C}(\mathcal{B}) \setminus \{s\}]$; see Step 13 in Algorithm 3.18. Recursively, we define $\mathcal{C}(\mathcal{B}') = \mathcal{O}'^* \cup \mathcal{F}'^*$, where $\mathcal{F}'^*$ is the maximum consensus set of $\mathcal{C}(\mathcal{B}')$, and $h^*(\mathcal{B}') = |\mathcal{O}'^*|$. Clearly, since $\mathcal{C}(\mathcal{B}') = \mathcal{C}(\mathcal{B}) \setminus \{s\}$, then

$$|\mathcal{C}(\mathcal{B}')| = |\mathcal{C}(\mathcal{B})| - 1 \quad \text{and} \quad |\mathcal{F}'^*| \leq |\mathcal{F}^*|. \tag{G.1}$$

Subtracting the latter from the former yields

$$h^*(\mathcal{B}') \geq h^*(\mathcal{B}) - 1. \tag{G.2}$$

Since given $h_{met}(\mathcal{B}) \leq h^*(\mathcal{B})$, (G.2) can be extended to yield

$$h^*(\mathcal{B}') \geq h^*(\mathcal{B}) - 1 \geq h_{met}(\mathcal{B}) - 1. \tag{G.3}$$

Invoking the admissibility of h_{ins},

$$h^*(\mathcal{B}') \geq h_{ins}(\mathcal{B}'), \tag{G.4}$$

and reconciling (G.4) and (G.3) yields

$$h^*(\mathcal{B}') \geq \max\left(h_{ins}(\mathcal{B}'), h_{met}(\mathcal{B}) - 1\right), \tag{G.5}$$

which implies that $h^*(\mathcal{B}') \geq h_{met}(\mathcal{B}')$.

H   INTERVAL STABBING

Several algorithms in Chapter 4 require the solution of interval stabbing: given a set of intervals $\mathcal{D} = \{[a_i, b_i]\}_{i=1}^N$, where each $[a_i, b_i]$ is a subset of the real line, find $x \in \mathbb{R}$ that lies in as many of the intervals as possible. Mathematically, interval stabbing is defined as

$$\underset{x \in \mathbb{R}}{\text{maximize}} \sum_{i=1}^N \mathbb{I}\left(x \in [a_i, b_i]\right). \tag{H.1}$$

An example problem instance is illustrated in Figure H.1.

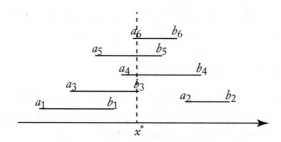

Figure H.1: An instance of an interval stabbing problem with 6 input intervals. Here, the intervals are stacked vertically for better presentation; be reminded that the vertical positions of the intervals do not matter. In this instance, we can stab at most 4 intervals.

Algorithm 4.24 Interval stabbing.

Require: Intervals $\mathcal{D} = \{[a_i, b_i]\}_{i=1}^{N}$.
1: Initialize array of $2N$ tuples $T = [(a_1, 1), (b_1, -1), (a_2, 1), (b_2, -1), \ldots, (a_N, 1), (b_N, -1)]$.
2: Sort T according to the first element in the tuples.
3: $acc \leftarrow 0$.
4: $acc^* \leftarrow 0, x^* \leftarrow NULL$.
5: **for** $i = 1, \ldots, N$ **do**
6:      $(w, k) \leftarrow i$-th tuple in T.
7:      $acc \leftarrow acc + k$.
8:      **if** $acc > acc^*$ **then**
9:          $acc^* \leftarrow acc$.
10:         $x^* \leftarrow w$.
11:     **end if**
12: **end for**
13: **return** x^*, acc^*.

Chapter 10 of de Berg et al. [2008] contains a comprehensive exposition of data structures for intervals, in particular the *interval tree*, that facilitates fast geometric operations on intervals including stabbing. For our purposes, it is sufficient to consider the much simpler technique summarized in Algorithm 4.24.

The principle of the algorithm is simple, and is best illustrated by an example. Using the data in Figure H.1, the sorted array of tuples T and the value of the accumulator as the algorithm steps through T is illustrated in Figure H.2. Note that the largest value attained by the accumulator is 4, coinciding with the inclusion of the 6th interval. The costliest process in the algorithm is in sorting T, thus the runtime of the algorithm is $\mathcal{O}(N \log N)$.

T	acc
$(a_1,1)$	1
$(a_3,1)$	2
$(a_5,1)$	3
$(b_1,-1)$	2
$(a_4,1)$	3
$(a_6,1)$	4
$(b_3,-1)$	3
$(b_5,-1)$	2
$(b_6,-1)$	1
$(a_2,1)$	2
$(b_4,-1)$	1
$(b_2,-1)$	0

Figure H.2: Invoking Algorithm 4.24 on the intervals in Figure H.1.

I   PROOF OF ANGULAR BOUND

From Section 4.2.2 in Chapter 4, given a point pair $(\mathbf{x}_k, \mathbf{y}_k)$, let $\hat{\mathbf{B}}$ and $\mathbf{B}$ be two rotations that act independently on $\mathbf{x}_k$, such that

$$\hat{\mathbf{B}}\mathbf{x}_k = \mathbf{y}_k \quad \text{and} \quad \angle(\mathbf{B}\mathbf{x}_k, \mathbf{y}_k) = \angle(\mathbf{B}\mathbf{x}_k, \hat{\mathbf{B}}\mathbf{x}_k) \leq \epsilon. \tag{I.1}$$

We aim to show that, given the above inputs and conditions, the bound

$$\angle(\mathbf{B}\mathbf{x}_i, \hat{\mathbf{B}}\mathbf{x}_i) \leq \epsilon \tag{I.2}$$

is satisfied for an arbitrary point $\mathbf{x}_i$.

Without loss of generality, we define $\hat{\mathbf{B}}$ as the rotation that brings $\mathbf{x}_k$ to $\mathbf{y}_k$ along the shortest geodesic. Also, we decompose $\mathbf{B}$ as

$$\mathbf{B} = \tilde{\mathbf{B}}\hat{\mathbf{B}}, \tag{I.3}$$

which, when acting upon $\mathbf{x}_k$, has the interpretation of first rotating $\mathbf{x}_k$ with $\hat{\mathbf{B}}$ to coincide with $\mathbf{y}_k$, then rotating $\mathbf{y}_k$ with $\tilde{\mathbf{B}}$ to a point that makes at most angle ϵ with $\mathbf{y}_k$.

We then invoke Lemma 1 in Hartley and Kahl [2009] to yield

$$\angle(\mathbf{B}\mathbf{x}_i, \hat{\mathbf{B}}\mathbf{x}_i) \leq \theta(\hat{\mathbf{B}}\mathbf{B}^T) = \theta(\tilde{\mathbf{B}}^T) \leq \epsilon, \tag{I.4}$$

where $\theta(\mathbf{R})$ gives the angle of the rotation $\mathbf{R}$.

J   DETERMINING REGION $L_k(\mathbf{x}_i)$

A core operation in the GORE preprocessing technique in Section 4.2.2 is determining the uncertainty region

$$L_k(\mathbf{x}_i) := \left\{ \mathrm{circ}(\hat{\mathbf{v}}, \hat{\mathbf{a}}) \mid \hat{\mathbf{v}} \in S_\epsilon(\hat{\mathbf{B}}\mathbf{x}_i), \hat{\mathbf{a}} \in S_\epsilon(\mathbf{y}_k) \right\}, \tag{J.1}$$

where $S_\epsilon(\hat{\mathbf{B}}\mathbf{x}_i)$ and $S_\epsilon(\mathbf{y}_k)$ are spherical regions of angular radius ϵ, centerd at unit vectors $\hat{\mathbf{B}}\mathbf{x}_i$ and $\mathbf{y}_k$ respectively; see Figure J.1.

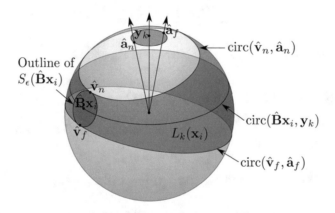

Figure J.1: The uncertainty region $L_k(\mathbf{x}_i)$, as defined in (J.1).

To this end, we seek the two circles, $\mathrm{circ}(\hat{\mathbf{v}}_n, \hat{\mathbf{a}}_n)$ and $\mathrm{circ}(\hat{\mathbf{v}}_f, \hat{\mathbf{a}}_f)$, that bound $L_k(\mathbf{x}_i)$, in particular, the four unit vectors $\hat{\mathbf{v}}_n, \hat{\mathbf{a}}_n, \hat{\mathbf{v}}_f$, and $\hat{\mathbf{a}}_f$ that define the boundary circles. Observe that the four vectors lie on the same plane as $\hat{\mathbf{B}}\mathbf{x}_i$ and $\mathbf{y}_k$, and thus the vectors of interest can be obtained by rotating $\hat{\mathbf{B}}\mathbf{x}_i$ or $\mathbf{y}_k$ by angle ϵ. The axis of rotation can be obtained by taking the cross product of $\hat{\mathbf{B}}\mathbf{x}_i$ or $\mathbf{y}_k$. Using the axis-angle representation of rotations and the exponential map to generate rotation matrices, the four unit vectors are

$$\hat{\mathbf{v}}_n = \exp\left(\epsilon(\hat{\mathbf{B}}\mathbf{x}_i \times \mathbf{y}_k)/\|\hat{\mathbf{B}}\mathbf{x}_i \times \mathbf{y}_k\|\right) \hat{\mathbf{B}}\mathbf{x}_i; \tag{J.2}$$

$$\hat{\mathbf{a}}_n = \exp\left(\epsilon(\mathbf{y}_k \times \hat{\mathbf{B}}\mathbf{x}_i)/\|\mathbf{y}_k \times \hat{\mathbf{B}}\mathbf{x}_i\|\right) \mathbf{y}_k; \tag{J.3}$$

$$\hat{\mathbf{v}}_f = \exp\left(\epsilon(\mathbf{y}_k \times \hat{\mathbf{B}}\mathbf{x}_i)/\|\mathbf{y}_k \times \hat{\mathbf{B}}\mathbf{x}_i\|\right) \hat{\mathbf{B}}\mathbf{x}_i; \text{ and} \tag{J.4}$$

$$\hat{\mathbf{a}}_f = \exp\left(\epsilon(\hat{\mathbf{B}}\mathbf{x}_i \times \mathbf{y}_k)/\|\hat{\mathbf{B}}\mathbf{x}_i \times \mathbf{y}_k\|\right) \mathbf{y}_k. \tag{J.5}$$

K   DETERMINING INTERVAL Θ_i

In Section 4.2.2, we have established that the position of vector $\mathbf{x}_i$ under rotation $\mathbf{A}_{\theta,\hat{\mathbf{u}}}\mathbf{B}$ with θ fixed, $\hat{\mathbf{u}} \in S_\epsilon(\mathbf{y}_k)$ and $\mathbf{B}\mathbf{x}_i \in S_\epsilon(\hat{\mathbf{B}}\mathbf{x}_i)$, is bounded within the spherical region

$$S_{\delta(\theta)}\left(\mathbf{A}_{\theta,\mathbf{y}_k}\hat{\mathbf{B}}\mathbf{x}_i\right), \tag{K.1}$$

where

$$\delta(\theta) = 2|\theta|\sin(\epsilon/2) + \epsilon. \tag{K.2}$$

See Figure K.1 for an illustration of this region. We wish to find the range Θ_i of angle θ that will enable $S_{\delta(\theta)}(\mathbf{A}_{\theta,\mathbf{y}_k}\hat{\mathbf{B}}\mathbf{x}_i)$ to intersect with the target spherical region $S_\epsilon(\mathbf{y}_i)$.

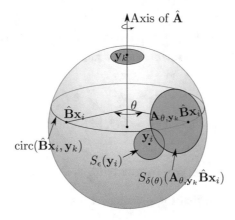

Figure K.1: Illustrating $S_{\delta(\theta)}(\mathbf{A}_{\theta,\mathbf{y}_k}\hat{\mathbf{B}}\mathbf{x}_i)$ for a particular θ. We wish to find a bounding interval Θ_i of θ that enables $S_{\delta(\theta)}(\mathbf{A}_{\theta,\mathbf{y}_k}\hat{\mathbf{B}}\mathbf{x}_i)$ to intersect with $S_\epsilon(\mathbf{y}_i)$.

In the rest of this section, concepts from the spherical coordinate system (e.g., azimuth, inclination, and meridian) are used with reference to $\mathbf{y}_k$ as the North Pole.

K.1   DEGENERATE CASES

If $\hat{\mathbf{B}}\mathbf{x}_i$ is close to $\mathbf{y}_k$, the North Pole may lie in $L_k(\mathbf{x}_i)$. If this occurs, we take $\Theta_i = [-\pi, \pi]$.

K.2   NON-DEGENERATE CASES

Define $\phi(\mathbf{y}_i)$ and $\psi(\mathbf{y}_i)$ respectively as the azimuth and inclination of $\mathbf{y}_i$. The spherical region $S_\epsilon(\mathbf{y}_i)$ is contained between the meridians $\phi(\mathbf{y}_i) - \gamma_i$ and $\phi(\mathbf{y}_i) + \gamma_i$, where

$$\gamma_i = \arcsin\left(\frac{\sin(\epsilon)}{\sin(\psi(\mathbf{y}_i))}\right) \tag{K.3}$$

following the geometric considerations in Figure K.2. Let $\theta_i \in [-\pi, \pi]$ be the rotation angle such that the point $\mathbf{A}_{\theta_i,\mathbf{y}_k} \hat{\mathbf{B}} \mathbf{x}_i$ is on the meridian $\phi(\mathbf{y}_i)$. Refer to Figure K.3.

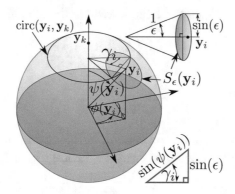

Figure K.2: Solving for γ_i in the red triangle. The cathetus of the triangle is half of the longest segment connecting points in $S_\epsilon(\mathbf{y}_i)$, and its hypotenuse is the radius of $\text{circ}(\mathbf{y}_i, \mathbf{y}_k)$.

Case 1: $\theta_i \in [0, \pi]$

This case is shown in Figure K.3. Define $\Theta_i = [\theta_i^a, \theta_i^b]$. The desired bounding interval Θ_i can be obtained by taking

$$\theta_i^a = \theta_i - \gamma_i - \alpha_i \quad \text{and} \quad \theta_i^b = \theta_i + \gamma_i + \beta_i, \tag{K.4}$$

where α_i is the largest value such that the spherical region

$$S_{\delta(\theta_i^a)}\left(\mathbf{A}_{\theta_i^a,\mathbf{y}_k} \hat{\mathbf{B}} \mathbf{x}_i\right) \tag{K.5}$$

still touches the meridian $\phi(\mathbf{y}_i) - \gamma_i$, and β_i is the largest value such that the spherical region

$$S_{\delta(\theta_i^b)}\left(\mathbf{A}_{\theta_i^b,\mathbf{y}_k} \hat{\mathbf{B}} \mathbf{x}_i\right) \tag{K.6}$$

still touches the meridian $\phi(\mathbf{y}_i) + \gamma_i$. Refer to Figure K.3. To determine Θ_i, we must find α_i and β_i. From (K.2),

$$\delta(\theta_i^a) = 2|\theta_i - \gamma_i - \alpha_i| \sin(\epsilon/2) + \epsilon \quad \text{and} \tag{K.7}$$
$$\delta(\theta_i^b) = 2|\theta_i + \gamma_i + \beta_i| \sin(\epsilon/2) + \epsilon. \tag{K.8}$$

Applying the same geometric considerations in Figure K.2 on the spherical regions (K.5) and (K.6), we have

$$\sin(\alpha_i) = \frac{\sin(\delta(\theta_i^a))}{\sin(\psi(\mathbf{x}_i))}, \quad \sin(\beta_i) = \frac{\sin(\delta(\theta_i^b))}{\sin(\psi(\mathbf{x}_i))}. \tag{K.9}$$

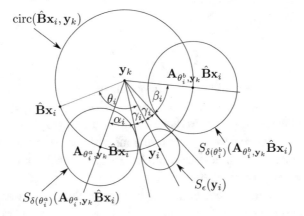

Figure K.3: To simplify the diagram and to aid intuition, the sphere in Figure K.1 is stereographically projected to the 2D plane using the North Pole ($\mathbf{y}_k$) as the projection pole. Recall that the stereographic projection preserves circles [Needham, 1997], thus the shapes of all the circles and spherical regions on the sphere are preserved. Note that stereographic projection is for presentation only and is not required in practice.

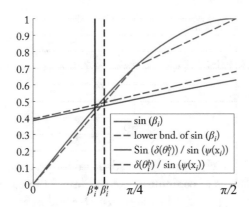

Figure K.4: Solving for β_i in (K.9) using the proposed linear approximations. Note that the obtained solution β_i' is always greater than the exact solution β_i^*, thus guaranteeing that the upper limit θ_i^b of Θ_i is a valid bound.

Note that the functions on both sides of each equation have the unknowns α_i and β_i respectively.

Figure K.4 plots the two sine functions $\sin(\beta_i)$ and $\sin(\delta(\theta_i^b))/\sin(\psi(\mathbf{x}_i))$. We consider only $\beta_i \in [0, \pi/2]$, since the condition where the two functions do not intersect before $\beta_i \leq \pi/2$ corresponds to the degeneracies in Section K.1. Further, since usually $\epsilon \ll \pi$, the period of the second sine function

$$\frac{2\pi}{2\sin(\epsilon/2)} \gg 2\pi \tag{K.10}$$

is much greater than 2π, thus explaining the almost linear trend of the second sine function for $\beta_i \in [0, \pi/2]$. A largely identical plot occurs for the functions involving α_i.

Analytically solving the equations in (K.9) is nontrivial. However, since all that we require is a bounding interval Θ_i, we can replace the sine functions with more amenable approximations that yield a valid bounding interval. An identical technique is used to solve for α_i and β_i, respectively, thus we describe our solution only for β_i.

We replace $\sin(\beta_i)$ with a lower-bounding two-piece linear function; see Figure K.4. To obtain an upper-bounding line to $\sin(\delta(\theta_i^b))/\sin(\psi(\mathbf{x}_i))$, we use Jordan's inequality

$$\sin(t) \le t \quad \text{for} \quad t \le \frac{\pi}{2}, \tag{K.11}$$

which enables us to replace the second sine function with

$$\frac{\delta(\theta_i^b)}{\sin(\psi(\mathbf{x}_i))} = \frac{2|\theta_i + \gamma_i + \beta_i|\sin(\epsilon/2) + \epsilon}{\sin(\psi(\mathbf{x}_i))}. \tag{K.12}$$

This upper-bounding line is legitimate for

$$2|\theta_i + \gamma_i + \beta_i|\sin(\epsilon/2) + \epsilon \le \frac{\pi}{2}, \tag{K.13}$$

where in the worst case requires

$$2\pi \sin(\epsilon/2) + \epsilon \le \frac{\pi}{2} \tag{K.14}$$

or $\epsilon \le \pi/(2\pi + 2) \equiv 21.7°$, which is more than adequate for practical applications. Solving for β_i in the manner above allows us to compute the upper limit θ_i^b in constant time.

Note that the resulting upper limit θ_i^b may extend beyond π; to "wrap around" the interval, we break $\Theta_i = [\theta_i^a, \theta_i^b]$ into two connected intervals $[\theta_i^a, \pi]$ and $[\theta_i^b - 2\pi, -\pi]$.

Case 2: $\theta_i \in [-\pi, 0]$
Case 2 is simply a mirror of Case 1 and the same steps apply with the directions reversed.

Bibliography

K. Aftab and R. I. Hartley. Convergence of iteratively reweighted least squares to robust M-estimators. In *Winter Conference on Applications in Computer Vision (WACV)*, 2015. DOI: 10.1109/wacv.2015.70. 13

S. Agarwal, N. Snavely, and S. M. Seitz. Fast algorithms for l_∞ problems in multiview geometry. In *IEEE Computer Society Conference on Computer Vision and Pattern Recognition (CVPR)*, 2008. DOI: 10.1109/cvpr.2008.4587713. 44, 47, 79

E. Amaldi, P. Belotti, and R. Hauser. Randomized relaxation methods for the maximum feasible subsystem problem. In *Integer Proramming and Combinatorial Optimization Conference (IPCO)*, 2005. DOI: 10.1007/11496915_19. 92

E. Amaldi, M. Bruglieri, and G. Casale. A two-phase relaxation-based heuristic for the maximum feasible subsystem problem. *Computers and Operations Research*, 35 (5): 1465–1482, 2008. DOI: 10.1016/j.cor.2007.04.001. 91

N. Amenta, M. Bern, and D. Eppstein. Optimal point placement for mesh smoothing. *Journal of Algorithms*, 30 (2): 302–322, 1999. DOI: 10.1006/jagm.1998.0984. 53, 54

B. Aronov and S. Har-Peled. On approximating the depth and related problems. *SIAM Journal on Computing*, 38 (3): 899–921, 2008. DOI: 10.1137/060669474. 18

K. S. Arun, T. S. Huang, and S. D. Blostein. Least-squares fitting of two 3-D point sets. *IEEE Transactions on Pattern Analysis and Machine Intelligence*, 9 (5): 698–700, 1987. DOI: 10.1109/tpami.1987.4767965. 26

A. Bab-Hadiashar and D. Suter. Robust optic flow estimation using least median of squares. In *IEEE International Conference on Image Processing (ICIP)*, 1996. DOI: 10.1109/icip.1996.559546. 3

D. H. Ballard. Generalizing the Hough transform to detect arbitrary shapes. *Pattern Recognition*, 13 (2): 111–122, 1981. DOI: 10.1016/0031-3203(81)90009-1. 11

S. Ben-David, N. Eiron, and H. Simon. The computational complexity of densest region detection. *Journal of Computer and System Sciences*, 64 (1): 22–47, 2002. DOI: 10.1006/jcss.2001.1797. 18

T. Bernholt. Robust estimators are hard to compute. *Technical Report*, Universität Dortmund, 2006. DOI: 10.17877/DE290R-14253. 18

A. Björck. *Numerical methods for least squares problems.* *SIAM*, 1996. DOI: 10.1137/1.9781611971484. 12, 22

P. Bloomfield and W. Steiger. Least absolute deviations curve-fitting. *SIAM Journal on Scientific Computing*, 1 (2): 290–301, 1980. DOI: 10.1137/0901019. 33

S. Boyd and L. Vandenberghe. *Convex Optimization.* Cambridge University Press, 2004. DOI: 10.1017/cbo9780511804441. 31, 37, 48

T. M. Breuel. Fast recognition using adaptive subdivisions of transformation space. In *IEEE Computer Society Conference on Computer Vision and Pattern Recognition (CVPR)*, 1992. DOI: 10.1109/cvpr.1992.223152. 126

T. M. Breuel. Implementation techniques for geometric branch-and-bound matching methods. *CVIU*, 90 (3): 258–294, 2003. DOI: 10.1016/s1077-3142(03)00026-2. 95

B. Chazelle, L. J. Guibas, and D. T. Lee. The power of geometric duality. In *IEEE Foundation of Computer Science*, pages 217–225, 1983. DOI: 10.1109/sfcs.1983.75. 85

G. Chen and G. Lerman. Spectral curvature clustering (SCC). *International Journal of Computer Vision*, 81 (3): 317–330, 2009. DOI: 10.1007/s11263-008-0178-9. 27

H. Chen and P. Meer. Robust regression with projection based M-estimators. In *IEEE International Conference on Computer Vision (ICCV)*, 2003. DOI: 10.1109/iccv.2003.1238441. 8

E. W. Cheney. *Introduction to Approximation Theory.* McGraw-Hill, 1966. 43, 108, 109, 151

T.-J. Chin, H. Wang, and D. Suter. Robust fitting of multiple structures: The statistical learning approach. In *International Conference on Computer Vision (ICCV)*, 2009. DOI: 10.1109/iccv.2009.5459150. 8

T.-J. Chin, J. Yu, and D. Suter. Accelerated hypothesis generation for multi-structure data via preference analysis. *IEEE Transactions on Pattern Analysis and Machine Intelligence*, 34 (4): 625–638, 2012. DOI: 10.1109/tpami.2011.169. 27

T.-J. Chin, A. Parra Bustos, M. S. Brown, and D. Suter. Fast rotation search for real-time interactive point cloud registration. In *ACM SIGGRAPH Symposium on Interactive 3D Graphics and Games (I3DG)*, 2014. DOI: 10.1145/2556700.2556712. 126

T.-J. Chin, P. Purkait, A. Eriksson, and D. Suter. Efficient globally optimal consensus maximisation with tree search. In *IEEE Computer Society Conference on Computer Vision and Pattern Recognition (CVPR)*, 2015. DOI: 10.1109/cvpr.2015.7298855. 126

T.-J. Chin, Y. H. Kee, A. Eriksson, and F. Neumann. Guaranteed outlier removal with mixed integer linear programs. In *IEEE Conference on Computer Vision and Pattern Recognition*, 2016. DOI: 10.1109/cvpr.2016.631. 149

J. Chinneck. *Feasibility and Infeasibility in Optimization: Algorithms and Computational Methods.* Springer, 2007. DOI: 10.1007/978-0-387-74932-7. 88

S. Choi, T. Kim, and W. Yu. Performance evaluation of RANSAC family. In *British Machine Vision Conference (BMVC)*, 2009. DOI: 10.5244/c.23.81. 9, 19, 28

O. Chum and J. Matas. Matching with PROSAC—progressive sample consensus. In *IEEE Computer Society Conference on Computer Vision and Pattern Recognition (CVPR)*, 2005. DOI: 10.1109/cvpr.2005.221. 27, 74

O. Chum and J. Matas. Optimal randomized RANSAC. *IEEE Transactions on Pattern Analysis and Machine Intelligence*, 30 (8): 1472–1482, 2008. DOI: 10.1109/tpami.2007.70787. 28

O. Chum, J. Matas, and J. Kittler. Locally optimized RANSAC. In *DAGM-Symposium*, pages 236–243, 2003. DOI: 10.1007/978-3-540-45243-0_31. 26, 65, 73

O. Chum, T. Werner, and J. Matas. Two-view geometry estimation unaffected by a dominant plane. In *IEEE Computer Society Conference on Computer Vision and Pattern Recognition (CVPR)*, 2005. DOI: 10.1109/cvpr.2005.354. 29

M. Conforti, G. Cornuéjols, and G. Zambelli. *Integer Programming.* Springer, 2014. DOI: 10.1007/978-3-319-11008-0. 90, 145

J.-P. Crouzeix and J. A. Ferland. Algorithms for generalized fractional programming. *Mathematical Programming*, 52: 191–207, 1991. DOI: 10.1007/bf01582887. 44

M. de Berg, O. Cheong, M. van Kreveld, and M. Overmars. *Computational Geometry: Algorithms and Applications.* Springer-Verlag, 2008. DOI: 10.1007/978-3-540-77974-2. 57, 102, 156

R. Deriche, Z. Zhang, Q.-T. Luong, and O. D. Faugeras. Robust recovery of the epipolar geometry for an uncalibrated stereo rig. In *European Conference on Computer Vision (ECCV)*, 1994. DOI: 10.1007/3-540-57956-7_64. 3

R. O. Duda and P. E. Hart. Use of the Hough transformation to detect lines and curves in pictures. *Communications of the ACM*, 15: 11–15, 1972. DOI: 10.1145/361237.361242. 3, 10

H. Edelsbrunner and D. L. Souvaine. Computing least median of squares regression lines and guided topological sweep. *Journal of the American Statistical Association*, 85 (409): 115–119, 1990. DOI: 10.2307/2289532. 13, 14, 88, 125

H. Edelsbrunner, J. O'Rourke, and R. Seidel. Constructing arrangements of lines and hyperplanes with applications. *SIAM Journal on Computing*, 15: 341–363, 1986. DOI: 10.1137/0215024. 111

D. W. Eggert, A. Lorusso, and R. B. Fisher. Estimating 3-D rigid body transformations: A comparison of four major algorithms. *Machine Vision and Applications*, 9: 272–290, 1997. DOI: 10.1007/s001380050048. 26

O. Enqvist, E. Ask, F. Kahl, and K. Åström. Robust fitting for multiple view geometry. In *European Conference on Computer Vision (ECCV)*, 2012. DOI: 10.1007/978-3-642-33718-5_53. 126

D. Eppstein. Quasiconvex programming. *Combinatorial and Computational Geometry*, 25, 2005. 53

J. Erickson. New lower bounds for convex hull problems in odd dimensions. *SIAM Journal on Computing*, 28 (4): 1198–1214, 1999. DOI: 10.1137/s0097539797315410. 13, 18

J. Erickson, S. Har-Peled, and D. M. Mount. On the least median square problem. *Discrete and Computational Geometry*, 36 (4): 595–607, 2006. DOI: 10.1007/s00454-006-1267-6. 18, 126

M. A. Fischler and R. C. Bolles. Random sample consensus: A paradigm for model fitting with applications to image analysis and automated cartography. *Communications of the ACM*, 24 (6): 381–395, 1981. DOI: 10.1145/358669.358692. 3, 9, 19, 22

J.-M. Frahm and M. Pollefeys. RANSAC for (quasi-)degenerate data (QDEGSAC). In *IEEE Computer Society Conference on Computer Vision and Pattern Recognition (CVPR)*, 2006. DOI: 10.1109/cvpr.2006.235. 29

M. Frank and P. Wolfe. An algorithm for quadratic programming. *Naval Research Logistics Quaterly*, 3 (95), 1956. DOI: 10.1002/nav.3800030109. 70

J. H. Friedman, J. L. Bentley, and R. A. Finkel. An algorithm for finding best matches in logarithmic expected time. *ACM Transactions on Mathematical Software*, 3 (3), 1977. DOI: 10.1145/355744.355745. 102

W. Gander, G. H. Golub, and R. Strebel. Least-squares fitting of circles and ellipses. *BIT Numerical Mathematics*, 34 (4): 558–578, 1994. DOI: 10.1007/bf01934268. 24·

M. R. Garey and D. S. Johnson. *Computers and Intractability: A Guide to the Theory of NP-completeness*. A series of books in the mathematical sciences. W. H. Freeman and Co., San Francisco, CA, 1979. 17

B. Gärtner. A subexponential algorithm for abstract optimization problems. In *Proc. 33rd IEEE Symposium on Foundations of Computer Science*, pages 464–472, 1992. DOI: 10.1109/sfcs.1992.267805. 57

P. E. Hart, N. J. Nilsson, and B. Raphael. A formal basis for the heuristic determination of minimum cost paths. *IEEE Transactions on Systems Science and Cybernetics*, 4 (2): 100–107, 1968. DOI: 10.1109/tssc.1968.300136. 117

R. Hartley and A. Zisserman. *Multiple View Geometry in Computer Vision*. Cambridge University Press, 2nd ed., 2004. DOI: 10.1017/cbo9780511811685. 19, 23, 26

R. Hartley, J. Trumpf, Y. Dai, and H. Li. Rotation averaging. *International Journal of Computer Vision*, 103 (3): 267–305, 2013. DOI: 10.1007/s11263-012-0601-0. 96

R. I. Hartley and F. Kahl. Global optimization through rotation space search. *International Journal of Computer Vision*, 82: 64–79, 2009. DOI: 10.1007/s11263-008-0186-9. 98, 157

R. I. Hartley and F. Schaffalitzky. l_∞ minimization in geometric reconstruction problems. In *IEEE Conference on Computer Vision and Pattern Recognition (CVPR)*, 2004. DOI: 10.1109/cvpr.2004.1315073. 53, 79

D. M. Hawkins. The feasible set algorithm for least median of squares regression. *Computational Statistics and Data Analysis*, 16: 81–101, 1993. DOI: 10.1016/0167-9473(93)90246-p. 57

B. K. P. Horn. Closed-form solution of absolute orientation using unit quaternion. *Journal of the Optical Society of America*, A4: 629–642, 1987. DOI: 10.1364/josaa.4.000629. 26, 136

R. Horst and H. Tuy. *Global Optimization: Deterministic Approaches*. Springer, 2003. DOI: 10.1007/978-3-662-03199-5. 90

P. V. C. Hough. Method and means for recognizing complex patterns. U.S. Patent 3 069 654, Dec 1962. 10

P. J. Huber. *Robust Statistics*. Wiley, 1981. DOI: 10.1002/0471725250. 3

C. G. J. Jacobi. De formatione et proprietatibus determinantium. *J. Reine Angew. Math.*, 9: 315–317, 1841. DOI: 10.1017/cbo9781139567978.014. 29

D. S. Johnson and F. P. Preparata. The densest hemisphere problem. *Theoretical Computer Science*, 6: 93–107, 1978. DOI: 10.1016/0304-3975(78)90006-3. 18

F. Kahl. Multiple view geometry and the l_∞-norm. In *ICCV*, 2005. 79

F. Kahl and R. I. Hartley. Multiple-view geometry under the l_∞-norm. *IEEE Transactions on Pattern Analysis and Machine Intelligence*, 30 (9): 1603–1617, 2008. DOI: 10.1109/tpami.2007.70824. 35, 36

K. Kanatani. *Statistical Optimization for Geometric Computation: Theory and Practice*. Elsevier Science, Amsterdam, The Netherlands, April 1996. DOI: 10.1109/icpr.2014.11. 3

Y. Kanazawa and H. Kawakami. Detection of planar reginos with uncalibrated stereo using distributions of feature points. In *British Machine Vision Conference (BMVC)*, 2004. DOI: 10.5244/c.18.27. 27

Q. Ke and T. Kanade. Quasiconvex optimization for robust geometric reconstruction. In *International Conference on Computer Vision (ICCV)*, 2005. DOI: 10.1109/iccv.2005.197. 79

Z. Kukelova, M. Bujnak, and T. Pajdla. Automatic generator of minimal problem solvers. In *European Conference on Computer Vision (ECCV)*, 2008. DOI: 10.1007/978-3-540-88690-7_23. 26

Z. Kukelova, M. Bujnak, and T. Pajdla. Polynomial eigenvalue solutions to minimal problems in computer vision. *IEEE Transactions on Pattern Analysis and Machine Intelligence*, 34 (7): 1381–1393, 2012. DOI: 10.1109/tpami.2011.230. 26

H. Le, T.-J. Chin, and D. Suter. An exact penalty method for locally convergent maximum consensus. In *IEEE Conference on Computer Vision and Pattern Recognition (CVPR)*, 2017. 73, 79

K. Lebeda, J. Matas, and O. Chum. Fixing the locally optimized RANSAC. In *British Machine Vision Conference (BMVC)*, 2012. DOI: 10.5244/c.26.95. 26, 65, 74

K.-M. Lee, P. Meer, and R.-H. Park. Robust adaptive segmentation of range images. *IEEE Transactions on Pattern Analysis and Machine Intelligence*, 20: 200–205, 1998. DOI: 10.1109/34.659940. 14

H. Li. A practical algorithm for l_∞ triangulation with outliers. In *IEEE Conference on Computer Vision and Pattern Recognition (CVPR)*, 2007. DOI: 10.1109/cvpr.2007.383068. 79

H. Li. Consensus set maximization with guaranteed global optimality for robust geometry estimation. In *IEEE International Conference on Computer Vision (ICCV)*, 2009a. DOI: 10.1109/iccv.2009.5459398. 126, 149

H. Li. Efficient reduction of l-infinity geometry problems. In *IEEE Conference on Computer Vision and Pattern Recognition (CVPR)*, 2009b. DOI: 10.1109/cvprw.2009.5206653. 57

H. Li and R. Hartley. The 3d-3d registration problem revisited. In *IEEE International Conference on Computer Vision (ICCV)*, 2007. DOI: 10.1109/iccv.2007.4409077. 126

D. G. Lowe. Distinctive image features from scale-invariant key points. *IJCV*, 60 (2): 91–110, 2004. DOI: 10.1023/b:visi.0000029664.99615.94. 76, 94, 95, 134, 142

O. L. Mangasarian. Charaterization of linear complementarity problems as linear programs. In *Complementarity and Fixed Point Problems*, pages 74–87. Springer, 1978. DOI: 10.1007/bfb0120783. 153

O. L. Mangasarian. Misclassification minimization. *Journal of Global Optimization*, 5 (4): 309–323, 1994. DOI: 10.1007/bf01096681. 70

J. Matas. State-of-the-art RANSAC. In *IEEE Computer Society Conference on Computer Vision and Pattern Recognition (CVPR), Tutorial on Tools and Methods for Image Registration*, 2011. 9, 19, 28

J. Matoušek. On geometric optimization with few violated constraints. *Discrete Comput. Geom.*, 14 (1): 365–384, 1995. DOI: 10.1007/bf02570713. 14, 113, 117, 124

J. Matoušek, M. Sharir, and E. Welzl. A subexponential bound for linear programming. *Algorithmica*, 16: 498–516, 1996. DOI: 10.1007/s004539900062. 49, 55, 56, 57, 58

P. Meer. Robust techniques for computer vision. In G. Medioni and S. B. Kang, Eds., *Emerging Topics in Computer Vision*. Prentice Hall, 2004. 1, 28, 29

K. Mikolajczyk, T. Tuytelaars, C. Schmid, A. Zisserman, J. Matas, F. Schaffalitzky, T. Kadir, and L. van Gool. A comparison of affine region detectors. *International Journal of Computer Vision (IJCV)*, 65 (1): 43–72, 2005. DOI: 10.1007/s11263-005-3848-x. 2, 8

K. Mikolajczyk and C. Schmid. A performance evaluation of local descriptors. *IEEE Trans. Pattern Anal. Mach. Intell.*, 27(10): 1615–1630, 2005. 2

D. M. Mount, N. S. Netanyahu, C. D. Piatko, R. Silverman, and A. Y. Wu. Quantile approximation for robust statistical estimation and k-enclosing problems. *International Journal of Computational Geometry and Applications*, 10: 593–608, 2000. DOI: 10.1142/s0218195900000334. 14, 125

D. R. Myatt, P. H. S. Torr, S. J. Nasuto, J. M. Bishop, and R. Craddock. NAPSAC: High noise, high dimensional robust estimation—it's in the bag. In *British Machine Vision Conference (BMVC)*, 2002. DOI: 10.5244/c.16.44. 27

T. Needham. *Visual Complex Analysis*. Clarendon Press, 1997. 161

D. Nister. Preemptive RANSAC for live structure and motion estimation. In *IEEE International Conference on Computer Vision (ICCV)*, 2003. DOI: 10.1109/iccv.2003.1238341. 28

D. Nister. An efficient solution to the five-point relative pose problem. *IEEE Transactions on Pattern Analysis and Machine Intelligence*, 26 (6): 756–770, 2004. DOI: 10.1109/tpami.2004.17. 26

J. Nocedal and S. Wright. *Numerical Optimization*. Springer Science and Business Media, 2006. DOI: 10.1007/b98874. 17, 66, 69, 70, 152

C. F. Olson. An approximation algorithm for least median of squares regression. *Information Processing Letters*, 63 (5): 237–241, 1997. DOI: 10.1016/s0020-0190(97)00132-4. 14

C. Olsson, A. Eriksson, and F. Kahl. Efficient optimization for l_∞-problems using pseudoconvexity. In *IEEE International Conference on Computer Vision (ICCV)*, 2007. DOI: 10.1109/iccv.2007.4409087. 35, 44, 47, 79

C. Olsson, O. Enqvist, and F. Kahl. A polynomial-time bound for matching and registration with outliers. In *IEEE Computer Society Conference on Computer Vision and Pattern Recognition (CVPR)*, 2008. DOI: 10.1109/cvpr.2008.4587757. 126

C. Olsson, F. Kahl, and M. Oskarsson. Branch-and-bound methods for Euclidean registration problems. *IEEE Transactions on Pattern Analysis and Machine Intelligence*, 31 (5): 783–794, 2009. DOI: 10.1109/tpami.2008.131. 126

C. Olsson, A. Eriksson, and R. Hartley. Outlier removal using duality. In *IEEE Computer Society Conference on Computer Vision and Pattern Recognition (CVPR)*, 2010. DOI: 10.1109/cvpr.2010.5539800. 79

M. Padberg. *Linear Optimization and Extensions*. Springer, 1999. DOI: 10.1007/978-3-662-12273-0. 91

A. Parra Bustos and T.-J. Chin. Guaranteed outlier removal for rotation search. In *IEEE International Conference on Computer Vision (ICCV)*, 2015. DOI: 10.1109/iccv.2015.250. 132, 149

A. Parra Bustos, T.-J. Chin, and D. Suter. Fast rotation search with stereographic projections for 3D registration. *IEEE Computer Society Conference on Computer Vision and Pattern Recognition (CVPR)*, 2014. DOI: 10.1109/cvpr.2014.502. 126

A. Parra Bustos, T.-J. Chin, A. Eriksson, H. Li, and D. Suter. Fast rotation search with stereographic projections for 3D registration. *IEEE Transactions on Pattern Analysis and Machine Intelligence*, DOI: 10.1109/TPAMI.2016.2517636, 2016. DOI: 10.1109/cvpr.2014.502. 102, 126

J. Pearl. *Heuristics: Intelligent Search Strategies for Computer Problem Solving*. Addison-Wesley, 1984. 117, 122

R. Raguram, O. Chum, M. Pollefeys, J. Matas, and J.-M. Frahm. USAC: A universal framework for random sample consensus. *IEEE Transactions on Pattern Analysis and Machine Intelligence*, 35 (8): 2022–2038, 2013. DOI: 10.1109/tpami.2012.257. 9, 19, 28

M. V. Ramakrishna and J. Zobel. Performance in practice of string hashing functions. In *International Conference on Database Systems for Advanced Applications*, 1997. DOI: 10.1142/9789812819536_0023. 115

A. Rosenfeld. *Picture Processing by Computer*. New York, Academic, 1969. DOI: 10.1145/356551.356554. 3

P. J. Rousseeuw. Least median of squares regression. *Journal of the American Statistical Association*, 79: 871–880, 1984. DOI: 10.2307/2288718. 3, 13, 19

P. J. Rousseeuw and A. M. Leroy. *Robust Regression and Outlier Detection.* Wiley, 1987. DOI: 10.1002/0471725382. 13, 19

R. B. Rusu, N. Blodow, Z. C. Marton, and M. Beetz. Aligning point cloud views using persistent feature histograms. In *International Conference on Intelligent Robots and Systems (IROS)*, 2008. DOI: 10.1109/iros.2008.4650967. 102, 133, 140

N. Scherer-Negenborn and R. Schaefer. Model fitting with sufficient random sample coverage. *Int. J. Comput. Vision*, 89: 120–128, 2010. DOI: 10.1007/s11263-010-0329-7. 29

C. Schmid, R. Mohr, and C. Bauckhage. Evaluation of interest point detectors. *International Journal of Computer Vision (IJCV)*, 37 (2): 151–172, 2000. DOI: 10.1023/A:1008199403446. 8

Y. Seo, H. Lee, and S. W. Lee. Outlier removal by convex optimization for l-infinity approaches. In *Pacific Rim Symposium on Advances in Image and Video Technology (PSIVT)*, 2009. DOI: 10.1007/978-3-540-92957-4_18. 79

M. I. Shamos and D. Hoey. Geometric intersection problems. In *EEE Symposium on Foundations of Computer Science (FOCS)*, 1976. DOI: 10.1109/sfcs.1976.16. 86

K. Sim and R. Hartley. Removing outliers using the l_∞ norm. In *IEEE Computer Society Conference on Computer Vision and Pattern Recognition (CVPR)*, 2006. DOI: 10.1109/cvpr.2006.253. 54, 79

D. L. Souvaine and J. M. Steele. Time- and space-efficient algorithms for least median of squares regression. *Journal of the American Statistical Association*, 82 (399): 794–801, 1987. DOI: 10.2307/2288788. 14, 85, 88, 125

J. M. Steele and W. L. Steiger. Algorithms and complexity for least median of squares regression. *Discrete Applied Mathematics*, 14: 93–100, 1986. DOI: 10.1016/0166-218x(86)90009-0. 15

C. V. Stewart. MINPRAN: A new robust estimator for computer vision. *IEEE Transactions on Pattern Analysis and Machine Intelligence*, 17 (10): 925–938, 1995. DOI: 10.1109/34.464558. 8

C. V. Stewart. Robust parameter estimation in computer vision. *SIAM Review*, 41 (3): 513–537, 1999. DOI: 10.1137/s0036144598345802. 1, 3

A. J. Stromberg. Computing the exact least median of squares estimate and stability diagnostics in multiple linear regression. *SIAM Journal on Scientific Computing*, 14 (6): 1289–1299, 1993. DOI: 10.1137/0914076. 15, 126

R. Subbarao and P. Meer. Beyond RANSAC: User independent robust regression. In *Workshop on 25 Years of RANSAC*, 2006. DOI: 10.1109/cvprw.2006.43. 8

L. Svärm, O. Enqvist, M. Oskarsson, and F. Kahl. Accurate localization and pose estimation for large 3d models. In *IEEE Conference on Computer Vision and Pattern Recognition (CVPR)*, 2014. DOI: 10.1109/cvpr.2014.75. 149

R. Szeliski. Image alignment and stitching: A tutorial. *TechReport MSR-TR-2004-92*, Microsoft Research, 2004. DOI: 10.1561/0600000009. 142

B. J. Tordoff and D. W. Murray. Guided-MLESAC: Faster image transform estimation by using matching priors. *IEEE Transactions on Pattern Analysis and Machine Intelligence*, 27 (10): 1523–1535, 2005. DOI: 10.1109/tpami.2005.199. 27, 74

P. H. S. Torr. The development and comparison of robust methods for estimating the fundamental matrix. *International Journal of Computer Vision*, 24 (3), 1997. DOI: 10.1023/A:1007927408552. 3

P. H. S. Torr and D. W. Murray. Outlier detection and motion segmentation. In *Proc. SPIE Sensor Fusion VI*, pages 432–443, 1993. DOI: 10.1117/12.150246. 19

Q.-H. Tran, T.-J. Chin, W. Chojnacki, and D. Suter. Sampling minimal subsets with large spans for robust estimation. *International Journal of Computer Vision*, 106 (1): 93–112, 2014. DOI: 10.1007/s11263-013-0643-y. 28, 29, 31

A. Vedaldi and B. Fulkerson. VLFeat: An open and portable library of computer vision algorithms. In *Proc. of the 18th ACM International Conference on Multimedia*, 2010. DOI: 10.1145/1873951.1874249. 76

H. M. Wagner. Linear programming techniques for regression analysis. *Journal of the American Statistical Association*, 54: 206–212, 1959. DOI: 10.2307/2282146. 33

H. Wang and D. Suter. Robust adaptive-scale parametric model estimation for computer vision. *IEEE Transactions on Pattern Analysis and Machine Intelligence*, 26 (11): 1459–1474, 2004. DOI: 10.1109/tpami.2004.109. 8

L. Xu, E. Oja, and P. Kultanan. A new curve detection method: Randomized Hough transform (RHT). *Pattern Recognition Letters*, 11: 331–338, 1990. DOI: 10.1016/0167-8655(90)90042-z. 11

J. Yang, H. Li, and Y. Jia. Go-ICP: Solving 3d registration efficiently and globally optimally. In *IEEE International Conference on Computer Vision (ICCV)*, 2013. DOI: 10.1109/iccv.2013.184. 126

J. Yu, A. Eriksson, T.-J. Chin, and D. Suter. An adversarial optimization approach to efficient outlier removal. In *IEEE International Conference on Computer Vision (ICCV)*, 2011. DOI: 10.1109/iccv.2011.6126268. 79

Z. Zhang. Parameter estimation techniques: A tutorial with application to conic fitting. *Image and Vision Computing*, 15 (1): 59–76, 1997. DOI: 10.1016/s0262-8856(96)01112-2. 1, 24

Z. Zhang, R. Deriche, O. D. Faugeras, and Q. Luong. A robust technique for matching two uncalibrated images through the recovery of the unknown epipolar geometry. *Artificial Intelligence*, 78: 87–119, 1995. DOI: 10.1016/0004-3702(95)00022-4. 19

Y. Zheng, S. Sugimoto, and M. Okutomi. Deterministically maximizing feasible subsystems for robust model fitting with unit norm constraints. In *IEEE Computer Society Conference on Computer Vision and Pattern Recognition (CVPR)*, 2011. DOI: 10.1109/cvpr.2011.5995640. 126

Y. Zhong. A shape descriptor for 3d object recognition. In *Workshop on 3D Representation and Recognition (3DRR), in Association with International Conference on Computer Vision (ICCV)*, 2009. 102, 133, 140

R. Zrour, Y. Kenmochi, H. Talbot, L. Buzer, Y. Hamam, I. Shimizu, and A. Sugimoto. Optimal consensus set for digital line and plane fitting. In *Proc. of the 13th International Workshop on Combinatorial Image Analysis (IWCIA)*, 2009. DOI: 10.1109/iccvw.2009.5457503. 126

Authors' Biographies

TAT-JUN CHIN

Tat-Jun Chin was born and raised in Nibong Tebal, Penang. He received his B.Eng. in Electrical Engineering (Mechatronics) from Universiti Teknologi Malaysia (UTM) in 2003, and his Ph.D. in Computer Systems Engineering from Monash University in 2007 with a thesis titled "Kernel Subspace Methods in Computer Vision". His undergraduate studies were partly supported by an Agilent Technologies Scholarship, and his Ph.D. studies were mainly supported by an Endeavour Australia-Asia Award. He was a Research Fellow at the Institute for Infocomm Research (I2R) in Singapore from 2007–2008. Since 2008 he has been a Senior Research Associate (2008–2010), Lecturer (2010–2013), and Senior Lecturer (2014-2016) at The University of Adelaide. Since 2017 he was an Associate Professor at the same university. His research interests include robust estimation and geometric optimization. He won a CVPR award and DSTO award (both in 2015) for his research work.

DAVID SUTER

David Suter was born in Leeds, UK. He holds the following degrees: BSc (Applied Maths and Physics, The Flinders University of SA, 1977); Grad. Dip. Ed. (Secondary Teaching, The Flinders University of SA, 1978); Grad. Dip. Comp. (Royal Melbourne Institute of Technology, 1984); Ph.D. (Computer Vision, La Trobe University, 1991). He has held the following appointments: Lecturer at La Trobe University 1988-1992); Senior Lecturer, Associate Professor and Professor at Monash University (1992–2008), Professor at The University of Adelaide (2008–). He has served on the Australian Research Council College of Experts (2008–10) and the editorial boards of several journals: International Journal of Computer Vision (2004–2013), Journal of Mathematical Imaging and Vision (200—2010), Machine Vision and Applications (2006–2008). He was general co-chair of two major conferences: ACCV2002 and ICIP2013 (both hosted in Melbourne Australia).

Index